ROSEMARY EVANS was born in Yorkshire, but her Welsh father soon took the family to Wiltshire where she grew up.

After studying English at Cambridge she pursued a career in publishing and journalism. She has travelled widely in Europe, Asia, Africa and the Americas, including work assignments in spots as diverse as Zimbabwe, Siberia, Tipperary and the Gaza Strip.

In 1979 she moved from southern England to live in Northern Ireland and currently enjoys the challenging job of publishing manager with the Northern Ireland Tourist Board.

D1500884

NORTHERN IRELAND

0   30km

0   20 miles

Rathlin Island

PORTRUSH   BALLYCASTLE

COLERAINE

LIMAVADY   **CHAPTER 7**

Lough Foyle

LONDONDERRY

BALLYMENA   LARNE

STRABANE

CHAPTER 6   ANTRIM   CARRICKFERGUS

COOKSTOWN   BANGOR

Lough Neagh   **CHAPTER 1**

OMAGH   BELFAST   NEWTOWNARDS

DUNGANNON   LISBURN

Lower Lough Erne   **CHAPTER 2**

CHAPTER 5   BALLYNAHINCH   DOWNPATRICK

ENNISKILLEN   PORTADOWN   BANBRIDGE

ARMAGH

Upper Lough Erne   **CHAPTER 4**   **CHAPTER 3**

NEWRY   NEWCASTLE

THE VISITOR'S GUIDE TO
NORTHERN IRELAND

ROSEMARY EVANS

THE
BLACKSTAFF PRESS
BELFAST

KEY TO SYMBOLS USED ON MAPS

※	Garden	⌂	Church/Ecclesiastical site
ᴴ	Castle/Fortification	⊞	Building of interest
✳	Other Place of Interest	Ⴕ	Archaeological site
⚘	Nature reserve/Animal interest	⌂	Museum/Art gallery
♣	Parkland	▲	Mountain
✈	Airport	ᴕ	Steam railway
ᴵ	View/Natural feature	➘	Birdlife
		⅄	Recommended walk

KEY TO MAPS

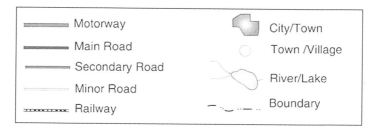

═══	Motorway	⬠	City/Town
━━━	Main Road	○	Town /Village
───	Secondary Road		River/Lake
⋯⋯	Minor Road		
▫▫▫	Railway	─·─···	Boundary

GETTING TO NORTHERN IRELAND

Direct air services: some 30 scheduled flights every weekday from London's airports to Belfast. Over 50 flights per week each from Manchester and Birmingham, with most other major cities in Britain having good connections seven days a week. Regular flights to City of Derry airport from Glasgow and Manchester.

Regular flights from Boston and New York to Belfast via Shannon. Direct charter flights to Belfast from Toronto. Direct Amsterdam–Belfast service.The bus service from Belfast International airport to the city centre is regular and reliable. From Belfast City airport take a taxi into the centre (about £4 to City Hall). Similarly, you'll need a taxi to get from City of Derry airport.

Car ferries: quickest crossings to Northern Ireland from Britain are the high speed ferries from Scotland to Belfast and Larne. The crossing from Cairnryan to Larne, for example, takes only one hour. There is also an overnight Liverpool–Belfast crossing and sailings from Wales to the Republic of Ireland.

TRAVELLING AROUND NORTHERN IRELAND

'Drive on the left and overtake on the right' is the rule of the road throughout Britain and Ireland. Speed limits, seat belt wearing, drink/drive laws, petrol prices etc, are the same in Northern Ireland as in Great Britain, though the volume of traffic is markedly lower. Speed limits: 30 mph in towns unless signs show otherwise; 60 mph on single carriageways; 70 mph on dual carriageways and motorways. Seat belts are mandatory for drivers and all passengers, and motorcyclists must wear helmets.

Main international car rental firms have airport desks. There are also many local firms. Insurance and VAT may be added to the quoted price, so check what the total cost will be when you book. Most cars have manual gearshift, so ask in advance if you need automatic transmission. If you plan to cross into the Irish Republic, check that the rental insurance covers you. Similarly, if you are coming north from the Republic, check the insurance position. If you want to drop the car off in the South, find out what the surcharge will be. It is usually cheaper to do a round trip and return the car to the pick-up point.

24-hour breakdown service: ☎ 0800 887766 (AA)
☎ 0800 828282 (RAC).

BUS AND RAIL SERVICES

There's a good bus network with regular services to towns not served by a rail link. The four main rail routes from Belfast Central station go north to Londonderry via Ballymena and Coleraine, north-east to Larne (for the shortest ferry crossing to Scotland), east to Bangor, and south to Dublin.

Express coaches run from Belfast to all main towns and the Dublin-Belfast express coach service runs seven times a day, three times on Sunday, and takes three hours. Set-down points include Newry, Banbridge, Dromore and Hillsborough. The coach also stops at Dublin airport and will pick up Belfast-bound passengers.

Belfast has two bus stations, one behind the Europa Hotel, the other on Laganside. It is easy to go to the wrong one. Phone to check if you are in doubt.

There are eight trains each day, five on Sunday, from Connolly station, Dublin, to Belfast Central. The Dublin–Belfast express train takes about two hours. Stops for ordinary trains include Newry, Portadown and Lisburn. Note for backpackers: there are no left luggage facilities at Belfast Central.

Bus information: ☎ (01232) 333000.
Rail information: ☎ (01232) 899411.

FOREWORD

Much has changed in Northern Ireland since this book's first edition appeared ten years ago. For visitors, the news is almost all good. First, there is a hugely improved choice of places to stay, plus an expanded cultural and entertainment scene, easier access to outdoor activities like cruising, fishing and golf, better signposting too, and more and quicker ways to get here. And visitors are better fed. *Good Food Guide* sleuths and Michelin inspectors testify to that. These developments in the tourism environment have been a response and a stimulus to a remarkable growth in visitor numbers, as this hospitable and pretty country steadily becomes a normal holiday destination.

But if much has changed, more has remained the same. The natural beauty and variety of the countryside, the historic landscape and the friendly people are still what holidaymakers remember best. There have been, it's true, remorseless increases in road traffic and equally inevitable, false dawns on the political front, but the Ulster driving style remains non-combative and even false dawns can leave a warm afterglow. Equally, it is still the case that *the North is different*. The cliché contains a truth that resonates at every level among people who understand or think about or visit Ireland. It expresses a fact about the history of the island and reflects the attitudes of many of its inhabitants.

The main focus of this book is on things to see and do. It aims to give visitors a modest insight into what they will encounter while travelling around. Historical events are mentioned when relevant which, it must be said, is fairly often. A few saints get a mention and one or two giants, but no leprechauns.

Don't be watching the clock, now. Slow down, tune in. The pleasures of discovering the real Northern Ireland are all ahead of you.

ROSEMARY EVANS
CARRYDUFF, MAY 1998

INTRODUCTION

The six counties of Ulster which form part of the United Kingdom of Great Britain and Northern Ireland are Antrim, Armagh, Down, Fermanagh, Londonderry and Tyrone. The province is 5,500 square miles in area, barely 85 miles from north to south and about 110 miles wide. Right in the middle is Lough Neagh, the largest lake in the British Isles. This huge expanse of water is impressive seen from an aircraft coming in to land at the international airport but is almost invisible at ground level because the surrounding land is so flat.

To the north-west are the wild Sperrin moors, good walking country frequented by golden plover and red grouse, with the lava-capped Antrim plateau in the north-east reaching the coast in magnificent cliffs. Most of the small lakes and rivers of the forested south-west drain into Lough Erne, a 50-mile-long waterway which is popular for fishing and boating holidays. The lowlands of south Down and Armagh are liberally sprinkled with small whale-backed hillocks called 'drumlins' which stick up through the peaty bogland in a wide belt right over to the Atlantic west coast, in reckless disregard of the 250-mile border with the Republic of Ireland to the south.

The shapely Mourne mountains tucked away in Ulster's south-east corner dominate the south Down landscape and Strangford Lough. Highest of the twelve peaks over 2,000ft is Slieve Donard (2,796ft). From the top you can see the Isle of Man, the Belfast hills and the pale line of Lough Neagh. On a lucky day, you can also see the Scottish coast, Snowdon in Wales and also the Cumbrian hills in England. The Irish Sea is quite wide here but drive up the coast to Torr Head and you are hardly 13 miles from the Mull of Kintyre in Scotland.

Weather

Visitors are instantly struck by the greenness of the countryside and the big cloudy skies that seem to press down over the fields even in a comparatively dry summer. Ulster's weather is often abused, and certainly it rains a lot. Ferns and plants like sedges and reeds grow luxuriantly in ditches and the grass is an emerald green. What makes it palpably different from, for example, England, is the combination of water vapour in the atmosphere and slow natural drainage.

Clouds drift in from the Atlantic over Ireland all year round, an island only a third the size of Britain. Much of the moisture discharged has nowhere to go. A lot hangs in the air and casts a soft misty light over the landscape, giving it a curious dreamlike quality, especially in the mountains and across in the west. But the north of Ireland is also breezy. When the south-westerly winds drive the clouds out to sea, the scene can change dramatically. The sky turns blue and the air is suddenly clear and sharp. 'The blue skies of Ulster' is a favourite phrase with some graffiti artists and can sometimes be seen scrawled on walls and in public telephone boxes.

Agriculture plays an important role in Ulster —
modern arable farming near Limavady, County Londonderry,
with Binevenagh in the background

Touring by Car

Travelling by car is the most efficient and agreeable way of getting to see the country. The road network is outstanding, with 70 miles of motorway for those in a hurry, about 1,500 miles of dual carriageway and 'A' roads, and very low traffic density. The only route that could be called remotely busy starts at Larne which is a major port for container traffic to all parts of the island. It runs south via the Belfast Westlink dual carriageway, where more container lorries, from Belfast port, join the road, along the M1 to Lisburn and down the A1 to Newry and the border with the Republic.

The two main motorways striking out from Belfast skirt Lough

Dramatic scenery and sandy beaches at White Rocks on the Antrim coast

Neagh to the south and north. The M1 goes deep into County Tyrone, to the edge of the Clogher Valley and points west to the Fermanagh Lakeland. The shorter M2 ends in the middle of nowhere just beyond Antrim town, but by then you are well on the way to the north Antrim coast and the Giant's Causeway. Minor roads are smooth, well signposted and remarkably free of traffic. If you miss a turn it is reasonable to assume that the next turn will take you to the same place since even a hamlet can have half a dozen ways in and out. With nearly 15,000 miles of road to fit into such a small country, they all have to go somewhere. Apart from Belfast in the rush hour, when traffic jams can compete with Europe's worst, it is hard to mention Northern Ireland's roads without hyperbole. They are excellent.

Compared with the rest of Ireland, the province gives a general impression of neatness. If the County Down farmer tends to trim his hedges too severely, at least there is no wholesale uprooting for prairie-style agriculture. In Down and Antrim especially, the country roads are tidy looking, with pavements and stone kerbs, cut verges, and marking the high ground beyond the tonsured hedgerows, the towers and steeples of parish churches. In leafy inland parts like Armagh, unruly thorn bushes laden with blossom in summer run round the edges of tiny sloping fields, sometimes containing a pony, or a cow with her calf, munching buttercups. Fuchsia hedges are common and purple rhododendrons grow wild on the Antrim plateau and in the Mournes. Golden whin (gorse) grows everywhere in great profusion, in fields, gardens and banked in bright masses on stony ridges. The blossoms smell like sweet coconut. Boiling eggs in whin to dye them yellow is an Easter custom, and some farmers pound the prickles to feed to horses. It is said to keep their coats glossy.

Ulster at Work

With just over 1½ million people, Northern Ireland's population density is 286 per square mile, about 2½ times greater than that of the Republic. For more than 150 years there has been a steady shift into industrial east Ulster and now most people live on the eastern side of the province. Apart from Derry City, only a handful of towns west of the Bann river have over 10,000 inhabitants.

AGRICULTURE

Outside the industrialised area around Belfast the country has stayed rural. Agriculture remains the most important industry, with 60,000 people working on the land, and another 20,000 in food processing.

Nearly all farmers own their farms though many are too small to provide a living. The average size of the 30,000 commercial farms is 87 acres, half the UK average. Cattle, sheep and dairying account for at least 70 per cent of farming, with pigs and poultry (like the famous north Antrim turkey) making up most of the rest. The beef goes mostly to Britain, lamb to France, and a quarter of all UK bacon is Ulster bacon. Though pig rearing is now nearly all in indoor production units, the occasional (accompanied) porker can be seen snuffling along the road verge. Farm animals in the province have an excellent health record, with Ulster cattle being fed almost exclusively on grass. Land quality and the weather do not favour large-scale crop production. Distinctive field patterns give the countryside an attractive patchwork appearance. The main crops are grass, barley and wheat for animal feed, and potatoes. Seed potatoes in bulk go to Mediterranean countries. The apple orchards of Armagh are a glorious sight in spring, though nowadays there is more money in mushrooms. Almost half the province's horticultural production comes out of mushroom tunnels.

In addition to the bigger farms, there are thousands of tiny units — 20,000 at the last count — some no more than a couple of fields with a few heifers, a pet donkey, hens and perhaps some geese being fattened for Christmas. 'Conacre', the custom of seasonally letting some or all of your land to someone else, is widespread. The field adjoining the farmhouse may be let for grazing while the farmer, and his wife too, work in the nearby town. Many of these smallholders have full-time jobs in every kind of business, from telephone engineers and shipyard workers to policemen and bus drivers. Ask them what their main occupation is and the answer is often 'farmer', for the Ulsterman has a strong attachment to his land, however little it may be. With employment insecurity and general uncertainty about the future, official efforts to curb 'double jobbing' make little impact. On the other hand, official encouragement of 'farm tourism' is beginning to have its effect. Visitors can spend a day down on the farm learning about sheep shearing and the mechanics of milking a modern cow.

The biggest social event of the farmer's year is the Royal Ulster Agricultural Society Show in May, with sheep shearing and horse-shoeing contests, goat and foxhound parades and other diversions going on late into the long, light evenings. Heavy horse shows and horse ploughing matches at Fair Head, Ballycastle, are held every year. There is also an established autumn competition when, if they can find a field large enough, fifty ploughmen on fifty tractors plough a hundred acres in unison. The Ulster Folk & Transport Museum near

Belfast has regular demonstrations of vanished or vanishing rural skills but, despite the fact that farming generally is highly mechanised, you can sometimes see ploughing with horses, turf cutting, scything and, occasionally, thatching being done beside the road.

LINEN

The reverse of the Northern Ireland £1 coin shows a flax plant, the fibrous fibre of the industry that made Belfast the linen centre of the world. A hundred years ago 240,000 acres were given over to flax growing and as early as 1787 the province had nearly 400 bleach greens, where the woven cloth was spread on the grass to bleach in the sun. When the agriculturist Arthur Young visited in the 1770s, he

Kilkeel in County Down has an important fishing fleet

Painting the past: Inch Abbey, County Down

was dismayed by the size and extent of the industry. He thought it had destroyed the country's agriculture: 'A whole province peopled by weavers!' Tours of linen factories and mills are popular with visitors, and the industrial archaeology of linen, the province's most important single industry during the eighteenth, nineteenth and early twentieth centuries, is preserved in country parks and museums and found on river banks everywhere, most noticeably along the Bann, the Lagan and the rivers flowing into Lough Neagh.

Flax flowers last for just a week, usually in early July depending on the weather. The attractive seed heads linger a while longer. A field of flax in full bloom is a glorious sight, though now rather rare. Small acreages of new white-flowering strains, not the traditional blue variety, are grown experimentally from time to time, but for the last 40 years textile companies have imported their flax. Linen manufacture is on the increase, with exports of linen cloth going mostly to Japan and Italy for high fashion garments. The fabric is an important element in the collections of Irish fashion houses.

FISHING
Pleasure angling — game, sea and coarse — has a strong attraction for visitors but fishing is also a sizeable industry. Ulster people seem to prefer a good beefsteak, a pity in a country where all the rivers are full of fish. The Foyle and Bann are big salmon rivers and there have long been rich salmon fisheries along the north coast. On one extraordinary day in 1635, sacred in the annals of Ulster fishing,

62 tons of salmon was taken from the Bann at Coleraine. Trout, freshwater herring and especially eels are caught commercially in Lough Neagh. William Laud, the archbishop of Canterbury who was executed by the Puritans in 1645, rated Lough Neagh eels 'the fairest and the fattest'. Salmon and trout are widely available in restaurants but eels are hardly ever on the menu. You can buy them at some fishmongers but they mostly end up, smoked, on Dutch dinner tables.

The principal fishing ports, Kilkeel, Portavogie and Ardglass, are on the east coast. Apart from cod, herring, mackerel and whiting, some 5,000 tons of shellfish are trawled each year from the Irish Sea, including lobsters and the large 'Dublin Bay' prawns. As the boats come in, small knots of residents and caravanners with plastic bags gather at the harbour ready to strike a quick bargain before the main catch is landed. Restaurateurs have regular orders, some have their own lobster pots and nets. There are a dozen or so trout farms and oyster farming in Strangford Lough is big business. The UK's largest producer of Pacific oysters is based here, harvesting over a million of these tasty molluscs from the Strangford beds each year.

Historic Monuments

More than most, the Northern Irish are intensely interested in and knowledgeable about their historical heritage. Anyone living near a ruined castle, for instance, will be able to tell you how it came to be that way. From Stone Age tombs to seventeenth-century castles, there is a pleasant informality in the way Ulster's historic monuments sit in the corner of a field, at the end of the high street or in someone's front garden. The early Christian farmsteads called 'raths' — interesting if unspectacular circular earthen banks with ditches — are so common in Ireland that archaeologists can do little more than count them and mark them on maps. There are 1,300 in County Down alone. Much rarer are 'cashels', stone-built defended homesteads of the same period, and their watery equivalent, the 'crannog', an artificial island in a shallow lake.

Monuments with immediate eye appeal are the Neolithic tombs, 'dolmens', where one huge flat stone is balanced on three or more unhewn upright ones. The capstone is usually slightly tilted, sometimes with one end resting on a pair of tall stones and a shorter stone supporting the other end, like a shaky three-legged stool. Though not so big nor so thick on the ground as in Brittany, the dolmens of Ulster have a special charm because they occur in some delightful places.

Many of these, and later monuments too, from early churches to 'plantation' castles, are in state care. From the tenth to the thirteenth century the monks built round towers — the one on Devenish Island is especially fine. From the seventh to the twelfth century, crosses and high crosses went up all over Christian Ireland — the crosses at Ardboe and Donaghmore, both in County Tyrone, are good examples of this peculiarly Irish religious art. Early monasteries and primitive churches, Anglo-Norman mottes and castles, Elizabethan tower houses and plantation 'bawns' (fortified enclosures round castles and manor houses) are also part of the cultural past.

The twelfth-century castle at Carrickfergus was in continuous military use from its foundation until 1928 and is a complete roofed building — most unusual in Ireland. Almost all the medieval buildings that survive are in ruins, having been destroyed in fighting or abandoned, and then robbed for stone. These often splendid remains are being conserved, unspoiled by 'restoration', and where interpretive centres have been built for visitors most of them are reasonably unobtrusive. About a dozen properties have year-round custodians, and there are guides on a number of other sites in summer. Some seventeenth-century castles, much altered, are in use as private homes, one is a hotel, another does bed and breakfast, and the pretty William and Mary house at Springhill near Moneymore is a National Trust property open to the public. Like the ruined castles round Lough Erne and on the Tyrone–Armagh border, they were built by the Scottish and English 'planters' who settled in the north of Ireland following the submission of the Gaelic chieftains to Elizabeth I in 1603.

After simmering and fuming for a few years, the defeated chieftains fled to Europe in 1607 to rally support against England, and never came back. Their abrupt departure, known as the Flight of the Earls, was the final blow to the old clan social system, and the Roman Catholic interest in Ireland submerged for several hundred years. The Gaelic lands in Fermanagh, Tyrone, Coleraine and elsewhere were seized and granted to Protestant settlers in return for a commitment to invest capital and labour, plus, of course, allegiance to the Crown.

The companies of the City of London were much involved, not always enthusiastically, in providing men and money to build whole towns. Several junior branches of the departed O'Neills and Magennises survived as large landlords, though not as chiefs. Fortresses like Monea, Balfour and Castlecaulfield, built by the farmer-colonists right in the middle of the forfeited estates, inevitably came under attack. In the 1641 rising they were sacked, some were patched up and changed hands several times before being finally abandoned.

Bellaghy Bawn, County Londonderry

Few had as brief a heyday as Tully Castle, built in 1613 by a Berwickshire knight on the shores of Lough Erne and burnt on Christmas Day 1641. An on-site information board gives the melancholy details. Once symbols of both reassurance and oppression, the province's atmospheric castles are now among Northern Ireland's finest architectural treasures.

Towns & Architecture

The towns planned and built by the London companies, including Coleraine and Londonderry, shared most of the following features: a ditch and earthen rampart, or a fortified town wall, a grid street pattern with two main streets intersecting in the middle to form a square or diamond, a market house, a church, a mill by the river, and the planter's residence, often with a bawn round it. These towns differ from others in Northern Ireland which typically have a single, straight, wide street (Cookstown's is 1¼ miles long and 130ft wide), and also from the nineteenth-century mill villages, like Bessbrook and Sion Mills, which were planned round greens.

Bawns or sections of bawns are quite common, particularly in isolated parts outside towns. They were built to protect the family and livestock of the planter. His poorer neighbours could find shelter inside in the event of an attack, and the bawns doubled as a base for a small garrison. Look out for the massive flanker towers built at the

Shipquay Street with the Guildhall at Londonderry, which stands
just outside the fortified city walls

corners of the walls. An unusually well-preserved one is at Bellaghy,
west of Lough Beg, off the A6. Built by the Vintners' Company in 1619,
it has been restored and is the repository of a permanent exhibition on
the poet Seamus Heaney, born near Bellaghy in 1939. Nearer to
Belfast and viewed only from the road, Dalway's Bawn (1609) is on
the B90 3 miles north-east of Carrickfergus.

   Hardly an original building in the little plantation towns has
survived but the street pattern is still apparent, and is particularly

noticeable in Moneymore because everything is on such a small scale. The 1817 reconstruction of this village by its seventeenth-century founders, the Drapers' Company of London, has given Moneymore some delightful buildings.

Minor Georgian houses, and farmhouses of the same period, are dotted here and there around the countryside. Some have lost their sash windows, sprouted modern extensions and gained ugly if practical front porches. Armagh has groups of Georgian townhouses and public buildings and so has Hillsborough. The visitor with an interest in how the privileged few lived will want to see the big country houses that escaped the depredations of weather, war and time and are now looked after by the National Trust. Grandest of all the demesnes dating from the Age of Enlightenment (often, in Ireland, called the age of the Anglo-Irish ascendancy) is Castle Coole built for the Earl of Belmore by the English architect James Wyatt. The Trust's only other truly 'stately' stately homes in Northern Ireland are Florence Court (1764), seat of the Earls of Enniskillen, and Castle Ward, built by Lord Bangor in 1765. Other Trust houses in the province have an appeal for visitors who like the intimacy of the smaller scale, for example, a thatched seventeenth-century rectory, an early-nineteenth-century gentleman's house and a manor house with an eighteenth-century cobbled working farmyard. Unfortunately, several Trust houses cannot be visited midweek except in high summer.

People & Places

Differences in accent are intriguing for newcomers. It takes time to tune in. The systematic settlement of a Gaelic-speaking country where there were few roads and fewer bridges, and when the English-speaking colonisers were from all over Britain, was bound to affect the way people spoke, and still speak. The vigorous dialect and accents of the Presbyterians and other dissenters from the Scottish lowlands, who settled along the valley of the Lower Bann river, can be heard in Ballymena, principal town of Antrim county. These dissenters built a large number of plain 'barn' churches. East of the Bann valley, the Glens of Antrim accent is soft and well modulated. The Glens people are descendants of the native Irish and of their Scottish Hebridean cousins from across the narrow Sea of Moyle. The long isolation of the Glens, cut off by rivers and without a proper road until after 1834, helped preserve the language — this is one of the last places in Northern Ireland where Gaelic was spoken. The small English-style parish churches in the Lagan Valley, and the Vale of

Evesham-style apple orchards of Armagh, indicate settlers originating from the English west country, and the voices are different.

Nowadays everyone living in say, Ballymoney, seems to speak with that robust mid-Antrim accent, and a soft-voiced farmer from Fermanagh is as likely to have settler as native antecedents. In the larger villages and towns, churches of all denominations cluster single spire or tower of the Church of Ireland, and the French-Gothic towers (often twin) of Catholicism. As is often the case in Northern Ireland, however, generalisations can mislead. For instance, the tall three-tiered Lombard-Gothic tower opposite Queen's University, Belfast, is a Presbyterian church of 1862, now used for concerts and students' exams, and Newry has one of similar Italianate inspiration.

PLACE-NAMES

Ulster may be the most British part of Ireland but it has more Gaelic place-names than any other region. The explanation for the paradox is that while other parts of the island came under English influence in the Middle Ages, the 'woodie and boggie' province of Ulster remained thoroughly Gaelic, with powerful chieftains and without agriculture or internal trade, right up to the seventeenth century. The planters who took over the land also took over the place-names and anglicised them. A glance at the index of this book shows that a common one is Bally (from *baile* — town) as in Ballynahinch, Ballywalter and so on, Drum or Drom (*droim* — ridge) as in Dromore, Ard (*ard* — height) as in Ards Peninsula, Ardboe, Ardress and also Armagh (*Ard Macha*). Dun (*dún* — fort) as in Dungannon and Dungiven, appears in literally hundreds of town, village and townland names. A townland is the smallest of Irish land divisions, no bigger than 300 acres, and there are 60,462 in Ireland as a whole. We know that because the Ordnance Survey recorded them all on the famous series of 6 inch:1 mile maps made in 1846. People are much attached to their particular district and, so far, townland names have survived the Post Office's introduction of postcodes and dreary postal areas.

THE AMERICAN CONNECTION

Curiosity about their ancestry brings many people to the province. The North American connection is especially strong. However you look at it, the Ulster contribution to the foundation and development of early America seems to have been disproportionately great for such a small country. About 250,000 Ulstermen, mostly dissenters, took a one-way ticket to America in the eighteenth century. Five of them signed the Declaration of Independence, which was printed by

John Dunlap from Strabane in County Londonderry. The printer's shop where he learned his trade is open to the public. Another Ulsterman, Charles Thomson, who was born at Upperlands, north-west of Lough Neagh, was secretary to the first Congress. At least a dozen US presidents had Ulster ancestry. They include Andrew Jackson, hero of the Battle of New Orleans, Ulysses S. Grant, commander of the Union army, and Woodrow Wilson. Wilson's grandfather left County Tyrone in 1807, at the beginning of a century in which 4 million Irish people emigrated. The founder of the American Presbyterian Church, Francis Makemie, sailed for Virginia in 1682, and John Hughes, first archbishop of New York (Roman Catholic) went in 1817.

Americans with Ulster roots, as recorded at the Ulster-American Folk Park near Omagh, include Davy Crockett, Sam Houston who avenged the Alamo, Mark Twain, and Neil Armstrong, the first man on the moon. The first American potato patch was planted in New Hampshire in 1720 by a Gaelic-speaking Presbyterian minister from Limavady, and Catherine O'Hare, mother of the first white child born west of the Rockies (delivered by Indian midwives in 1862), was a native of Rathfriland in the Mournes. The Northern Ireland Tourist Board has developed a heritage trail which includes four US presidential ancestral homes that have been restored. Genealogy is a significant part of Northern Ireland's tourism industry, and although most people's ancestors were neither famous nor especially brave, visitors who have come to trace their own roots in libraries, or to hunt through dusty parish records, are glad of a few hours off to visit places on the trail.

World War II provides more recent links with the US. Londonderry was the largest UK escort base for transatlantic convoys, and there are remains of many American training airfields. Outside the city hall in Belfast an obelisk commemorates the arrival of the first US troops in Europe — in Northern Ireland in January 1942.

DOWN UNDER: LINKS & LEGACY

Ulster's ancestral connections with Australia and New Zealand are less well known. Emigration to Australia was on a smaller scale — some 300,000 people from Ireland as a whole in the nineteenth century — and most left from the south and south-west of Ireland. However, among those who went from Ulster were doctors, teachers, explorers, administrators, a handful of future mayors and state governors, and a sprinkling of entrepreneurial farmers like 'butter king' Samuel Charles of Ballyronan, County Londonderry, and 'wool king' Samuel McCaughey of Ballymena. There were also a few

Colourful characters in Belfast city centre

bushrangers with Ulster antecedents, like Andrew 'Captain Moon-lite' Scott, son of a Rathfriland clergyman, and John Tennant, sentenced at Carrickfergus courthouse to transportation. Tennant was an even worse nuisance Down Under. He became known as the Terror of Argyle and his name was given to Mount Tennant, the mountain near Canberra where he lurked in the 1820s. Ulster's legacy to New Zealand includes at least three prime ministers. At Glenavy in County Antrim, the birthplace of 'Rainmaker' John Ballance, pioneer of the welfare state in New Zealand and prime minister 1891–93, is open to the public.

Arts & Culture

FAIRS AND FESTIVALS
Being so far west and north, the country has long winters with short daylight hours. The compensation is long summer days and

everyone makes the most of them. There is always a *feis* (pronounced 'fesh') or a *fleadh* ('flah') — traditional Irish music and dancing — or a horse fair, agricultural show, regatta or folk festival going on somewhere. If you miss a fête in one place, you are likely to catch one at the next village. Sheepdog trials, terrier races and gun dog scurries are popular, and there are medieval pageants in the grounds of castles such as Carrickfergus, Hillsborough Fort and Gosford.

An annual fixture for at least the last 200 years has been a curious pageant at Scarva on the Upper Bann river. On 13 July thousands of Blackmen (cousins to the Orangemen — members of the Orange Order, a Protestant society that has a high profile in Northern Ireland) converge on this picturesque village (population 300) for a parade and symbolic re-enactment of the Battle of the Boyne in 1690, the outcome of which established the Protestant succession in Britain. Highlight of the day is a joust (the Sham Fight) between two horsemen in period costume representing James II and William III. 'James' always obliges by falling off his horse. The previous day, 12 July, or 'The Twelfth', is a general holiday in the province when Orangemen celebrate William's victory by marching with bands and banners to a central meeting place, usually an open field, to listen to religious and political speeches. These colourful parades take place simultaneously in about twenty towns. The marchers wear an orange sash, good walking shoes and, if they own them, a bowler hat and white gloves. Some of the country parades have a few 'lambegs', giant drums with vividly painted goatskins and hoops, weighing over 30lb, and their 'blattering' can be heard for miles across the countryside. The lambeg drummers do their loudest drumming at Sandy Row, the main assembly point in Belfast, before the parade moves off to the field 7 miles away. After the speeches or, often, during them, the marchers flop out on the grass for a picnic. Then they change their socks for the long walk back.

There are about 2,000 parades every year, mostly small ones, and many of them are a kind of practice run for mega-parades like 12 July and another big one at the end of August. The Feast of the Assumption (15 August) sees the Hibernians donning their finery to walk in similar though smaller processions with bands and painted banners. The Hibernians are also in evidence in parades on St Patrick's Day, 17 March. Their sashes are green, the banners bear different images, but some of the tunes are the same and the style closely resembles the Orangemen's. The bands are very important. Occasionally, if there is a shortage, it is not unheard of for a band that has played in an Orange parade one week to turn out for a Hibernian one the next. An uninitiated onlooker can find it all rather confusing.

The number of parades and, in particular, the traditional routes taken by some Orange parades, have been the subject of protests in recent years. It remains to be seen what the multicultural future will hold.

The province is well provided with bands of all sorts — pipe, flute, silver, brass and accordion. Popular music of all kinds, folk, authentic country, traditional Irish, punk, rock, jazz and gospel, has an avid following. Rock star Van Morrison, flautist James Galway and pianist Barry Douglas, as well as various punk bands that made the big time, are homegrown talent. Folk and gospel concerts draw especially big crowds. You can still buy an Irish harp made locally but you have to go to a concert to hear one. However, the *uilleann* pipes (Irish bagpipes), fiddle and *bodhrán* (small single-skin drum) can be heard for the price of a pint of Guinness in pubs offering traditional music sessions once or twice weekly (check which days), and certainly at a Saturday night *céilí* ('kaylee' — dance) in nationalist areas.

Apart from star names at the international arts festival in November in Belfast, autumn festivals in Armagh, Derry, Omagh, Enniskillen, Newry and other towns have chamber music and theatre, with ballad singers coming up from the Republic to reinforce local talent. The province has a good-sized orchestra, the Ulster Orchestra, based in Belfast. The city is well off for theatres and has a swanky new concert hall on the Lagan and an opera house (1894) by Frank Matcham who also designed the London Coliseum. Bear in mind that after the 'proms' in June, the orchestra takes a long summer break. Some Belfast theatres also close in July and August but there is light comedy at Portrush, Newcastle has theatre midweek and Irish nights at weekends, and the waterside theatre in Enniskillen has a summer programme.

LITERARY ASSOCIATIONS

Northern Ireland's literary associations are interesting and, although some of its writers do not 'travel' well, the modern poets Louis MacNeice and Seamus Heaney, and playwright Brian Friel have international reputations. Oscar Wilde and Samuel Beckett were educated at Portora School, Enniskillen; William Congreve, master of Restoration comedy, and Jonathan Swift are associated with Carrickfergus; Anthony Trollope wrote the first of his 'Barsetshire' novels in Belfast, where he worked for the Post Office; the novelist Joyce Cary and dramatist George Farquhar (who wrote *The Beaux' Stratagem* in 1707) were born in Londonderry. Boswell, Samuel Johnson's biographer, came on a visit from Scotland in 1769 — but was not able to persuade the portly doctor to accompany him on what was then a difficult journey. Thackeray enjoyed himself travelling around in Ulster in 1842 and wrote memorably about the Giant's Causeway; and Walter Scott, Wordsworth and John Keats also visited long before the days of one-hour air hops to Belfast International. The best-known religious writer born in the province is C. S. Lewis, who 'made righteousness readable', but there are others, especially hymn writers, like the Rev. H. F. Lyte ('Abide with me'), Joseph Scriven ('What a friend we have in Jesus') and the prolific Mrs Frances Alexander, wife of a bishop of Derry. Mrs Alexander wrote scores of children's hymns. The best known are 'Once in royal David's city', 'There is a green hill far away', and 'All things bright and beautiful'.

Hospitality for the Holidaymaker

ACCOMMODATION

There is a good choice of reasonably priced bed-and-breakfast farm-houses, guesthouses and private homes scattered across the country, though visitors are less able to tour around without accommodation reservations than in the past, and you are advised to book a couple of nights ahead in the main holiday season. Breakfasts are large, and an evening meal in one of these comfortable houses is good value. Unlike England, Scotland and Wales, which have no similar legisla-tion, Northern Ireland has a statutory classification and grading system for hotels and guesthouses. All tourist accommodation, down to the smallest B&B cottage, is registered with the tourist board and inspected annually, so you can be sure of acceptable physical stand-ards, cleanliness and so on. Rather few guesthouses have a licensed restaurant but many (but not all) will serve your own wine at table. Tourist information centres listed in the Fact File will make overnight reservations.

Backpackers will find hostels in picturesque settings along the coast and in the mountains. The large modern city centre youth hostels in Belfast and Londonderry fill up quickly with budget travellers who come from all over the world, eager to explore these interesting cities, very different from each other. Both cities were neglected by tourists in the 1970s and early 1980s and although hotels are now springing up again, the limited accommodation, a legacy of the earlier neglect, comes under pressure at holiday time.

Self-catering accommodation is still rather scarce though what there is is good. New chalet and apartment complexes are available in the main holiday areas, there are hunting lodges on private estates, anglers' chalets on islands, and traditional agricultural workers' houses and cottages which have been carefully renovated and all

Salmon harvesting at Glenarm, County Antrim

mod cons added. The book *Where to Stay in Northern Ireland*, published annually by the Northern Ireland Tourist Board, gives full details and prices of all visitor accommodation in Northern Ireland, including self-catering and touring caravan parks.

Cruising on the Fermanagh lakes has always been a popular kind of self-catering holiday. The old Victorian canal linking the Shannon to the Erne system reopened in 1994 and there is now a continuous waterway all the way from Limerick to Belleek at the west end of Lower Lough Erne. The Fermanagh cruisers are well equipped and you can stock up at handy provision shops around the lough shores. Self-caterers should resist the ubiquitous prepacked hamburger, since local beef, lamb, ham and home-made sausages are all good.

FOOD & DRINK

Bread-making is something the Northern Irish excel at. Every little town has its home bakery with laden shelves of 'farls' — soda farls, wheaten farls, treacle farls and potato farls. This rather odd word is from 'fardel', fourth part or quarter. Shaped like triangles with one rounded side, farls are baked on a griddle. Soda and buttermilk, instead of yeast, provide the leavening, and wheaten flour is often used. Potato bread is eaten cold or fried in bacon fat for breakfast. Other bread specialities are soft and crusty baps, wholemeal cobs, bannocks and brown barmbracks with fruit and spices. As in northern parts of Britain, high tea is an institution, and moderately priced. Served from about 5.30pm to 7pm it consists typically of cakes and scones with, say, a lamb cutlet, roast chicken, ham or fried fish with chips and several varieties of bread. Fully fledged dinner in the evening is still not universally available in hotels, and in some restaurants the meal can be expensive and undistinguished though helpings will be hefty. In some country areas cafés serving afternoon tea are hard to find but a pot of tea with biscuits or fresh scones is available in many pubs at any time during the day, sometimes at amazingly low cost. Pubs are open all day, Monday to Saturday. On Sunday most open at lunchtime and from seven in the evenings, though a few publicans still observe the traditional Sabbath and remain closed.

Going out for Sunday lunch (usually after church) is another institution and always good value. Book if you can. Sunday is the one day when you need to think ahead about meals. Some licensed restaurants are shut and others open for lunch only. *Where to Eat in Northern Ireland*, an annual pocketbook detailing about 1,800 eating places, gives opening times and also lists restaurants and pubs offering the real 'Taste of Ulster' by using the best local produce in season. Local dishes to look out for include baked Ulster ham, Irish stew, and champ, a wonderful combination of potatoes mashed with milk and chopped spring onions.

Ireland's most famous drink is Guinness. Its particular taste and texture depend on how it is stored, and poured, so do not try to hurry the barman. Caffrey's is a genuine local beer, brewed in Belfast, and real ale has made some headway in Northern Ireland in the last few years. The distillery at Bushmills on the north Antrim coast has been making whiskey since 1608 and is billed as the world's oldest (licit) distillery. Irish whiskey is often drunk with a bottle of Guinness. The order 'a bottle and a half 'un' is frequently heard in country pubs.

A precondition of good whiskey distilling is of course good water.

It is worth knowing that Ulster's ordinary drinking water straight from the tap is very good, cold and sweet. Survivors from Spanish Armada ships wrecked off the coast in 1588 remarked on the sweetness of the local water and could not understand why the Irish should want to drink anything else.

Outdoor Activities

Weekends and holidays find people pottering around the loughs and coast, boating, fishing or out on the golf links. Others go on family expeditions to the mountains and forest parks. Nine of the province's sixty-odd forests are established forest parks. Most were once part of great patrician estates and retain features of historical interest such as big houses, outbuildings and planned gardens. Usual amenities are an information/interpretive centre, shop, café, camping and caravan sites, signposted walks and nature trails, fishing, and sometimes provision for boating, pony-trekking and orienteering. A few country parks have similar amenities.

Large areas of the countryside are designated AONBs (areas of outstanding natural beauty). They include almost all the coast, the Antrim glens, the Mournes and the Sperrin mountains, and the Lagan riverside parkland which extends into south Belfast and is much used and appreciated by the people of a city that has very little in the way of green areas in the middle. The AONBs embrace National Trust-owned coastal stretches, whole fishing villages, beaches and sand dunes — to all of which there is year-round access. The Ulster Way, one of Europe's great long-distance footpaths, is waymarked for a large part of its 500-mile circular route, reaching all the scenic corners of the province. It has other trails coming in to join it, from Donegal and Cavan, as well as loops and extensions of its own, such as the Moyle Way, which runs across the wild Antrim plateau.

Northern Ireland's position on the western fringe of Europe makes birdwatching a specially rewarding activity in autumn and early winter. Huge flocks of ducks, waders and geese from higher latitudes come to pass mild winters on the Ulster wetlands. Waterfowl number up to 100,000 on Lough Neagh. Strangford Lough, another internationally important wetland, supports enormous rafts of geese, mainly pale-bellied brent, and up to 50,000 waders.

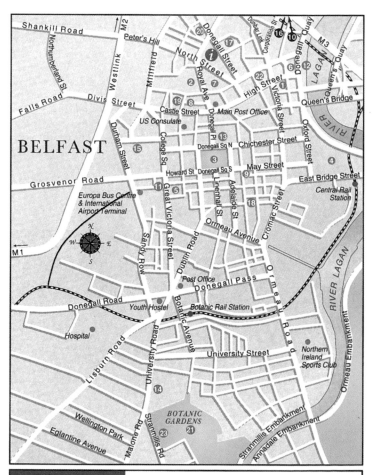

KEY TO MAP

Places of Interest

1 Albert Memorial Clock Tower
2 Castlecourt Shopping Centre
3 City Hall
4 Waterfront Hall
5 Crown Liquor Saloon
6 Custom House
7 First Presbyterian Church
8 Kelly's Cellars
9 May St Presbyterian Church
10 Harbour Office
11 Opera House
12 Lagan Weir Lookout
13 Linen Warehouse (M&S)
14 Queen's University
15 Royal Belfast Academical
Institution
16 Sinclair Seamen's Church
17 St Anne's Cathedral
18 St Malachy's
19 St Mary's
20 'The Front Page' Pub
21 Palm House
22 Ulster Bank
23 Ulster Museum

1

IN AND AROUND BELFAST

In a country where cities are the size of small English towns and many towns are hardly larger than an English village, Belfast stands out as a true metropolis.

Half a million people — a third of the province's population — live within 10 miles of Belfast city hall. The city, when you walk round it, has the air of being distinctly more prosperous than economic and political commentators suggest it ought to be. The centre has been redeveloped, with restaurants, cinemas, theatres, art galleries, and shopping arcades that echo to the music of buskers with fiddles and *bodhráns* (single-skin drums), or a lone tin whistle. A large statue of Queen Victoria in front of the city hall gazes regally down Donegall Place into the main shopping area. With chainstore names like Boots, Debenhams, Tesco and Marks & Spencer you might at first glance believe yourself in Manchester or Liverpool. Like those breezy cities across the Irish Sea, Belfast was a phenomenon of the Industrial Revolution.

In a century when the population of Ireland was cut by half through emigration and famine, the town mushroomed from 20,000 in 1800 to a linen boom city of 387,000 by 1911, almost the size of Dublin and soon to overtake it. By the beginning of World War II the population had swollen to 438,000 but its traditional industries — shipbuilding, rope-making, tobacco and linen too — were already in decline. Even so, the giant cranes of **Harland & Wolff** looming up behind the Albert Memorial clock tower preside over what is still the UK's largest shipyard, with a repair dock taking ships up to 200,000 tons and an innovatory engineering yard.

Like other industrial cities built on rivers Belfast has recently rediscovered its waterfront. A new weir, futuristically illuminated at night, has raised the level of the water, allowing navigation on the

Lagan again. At the west end of the weir there is a strategic view of activities on the river from a small conical building, the **Lagan Lookout**. A new bridge, Belfast's seventh, carries traffic and trains across the Lagan estuary above the sea ferry terminals. Waterborne travellers passing through Belfast port each year are edging towards the two million mark, and Belfast handles a greater tonnage of goods than any other Irish port. Old maritime buildings have been conserved and, a little upstream, the **Waterfront Hall**, a 2,500-seat concert/conference centre has been built, with a Hilton hotel beside it. Round the next bend upstream the old **Gasworks**, closed in 1978, is being put to new uses. (Natural gas is at last coming to Belfast. Some customers, including high profile users like the Waterfront Hall, were connected in 1997.) Visitors interested in Belfast's seafaring history — only London and Liverpool were larger in the nineteenth century — may be able to see inside the handsome **Harbour Office**, completed in 1895 and now the most historic feature of the regenerated waterfront. Across the river is Shorts' aircraft works, adjoining Belfast City Airport.

If you fly into this small city-centre airport (not to be confused with Belfast International which is 20 miles west) you may well be sitting in a Shorts 360 aircraft, on a domestic flight from Gatwick, Birmingham, Manchester or Glasgow. The airport is based on the airstrip where Short Brothers have tested their aircraft for the past 50 years. The Sunderland flying boat was developed here, and so was the SC1, the first vertical take-off jet. The SC1 prototype is in the Ulster Folk & Transport Museum at Cultra a few miles away. Today the company is best known for its commuter aircraft and weapons systems. These two large employers, and engineering firms making textile machinery, micro-electronics and electrical goods, continue to draw people away from the country to the eastern seaboard, a region that has especially close historical links with Great Britain.

The City Centre

A walk round the city centre and a visit to the university and museum area provide a good introduction to Belfast for first-time visitors who are touring by car and have only limited time available. First find a carpark. There are plenty on the perimeter of the central shopping area which is pedestrianised except for buses and the cars of disabled drivers. On-street parking is the pay-and-display kind and is most easily found behind the city hall and around St Anne's cathedral.

The rather splendid **City Hall** dominates Donegall Square and was meant to. Built of white Portland stone, the main façade is 300ft long with a copper dome rising 173ft above the traffic. After Belfast was declared a city in 1888 the city fathers set about demolishing the White Linen Hall of 1784 to build a city hall worthy of the new civic status. The architect, Brumwell Thomas, was knighted on its completion in 1906 but he had to sue the corporation to get his fees. George V opened the first Northern Ireland parliament here at city hall in a grand ceremony in 1921. Behind the railings is a statue of Sir Edward Harland, who came to Belfast from Yorkshire as a young marine engineer in the 1850s. Just behind him — rather uncomfortably close! — a marble figure commemorates the loss of the *Titanic* in 1912. *Titanic* was only one of many huge ships built here, including the P & O liner *Canberra* (1960) and the oil tanker *Myrina*, the largest vessel ever built in Europe when she was launched in 1967.

The dashing nobleman with handlebar moustaches and cocked hat in the little temple on the west side is the first Marquis of Dufferin who, among other things, was governor of Canada, ambassador to Moscow and viceroy of India. The statue was unveiled in 1906.

The city hall interior features colourful Italian marble, an oak-panelled banqueting hall, a large industrial mural and, in the great hall, a magnificent red carpet from Oughterard, Galway. This room, 120ft long, was destroyed by a German bomb in spring 1941 when nearly 1,000 Belfast citizens were killed in the blitz. It was rebuilt in time for Queen Elizabeth II's visit in coronation year (1953).

On Donegall Square North is the **Linen Hall Library**, established in 1788, to 'improve the mind and excite a spirit of general enquiry'. It is still maintained by public subscription and houses an important Irish collection and a large archive of press coverage of the 'troubles' since 1969. An early librarian, Thomas Russell, was executed in 1803 for his revolutionary activities.

Most of Donegall Square West is occupied by the massive **Scottish Provident building**, interesting for its voluminous stone decoration. There are dozens of lions' heads, queens, dolphins and sphinxes. Other sculptures, of ropes, spinning wheel, loom and ship, represent the industries that made Belfast prosperous. The city's street architecture includes many ornamental Victorian and Edwardian sculptures over doors and windows. Indians and Chinamen, gods and goddesses perch on the high ledges of shops and banks. Sculptured heads of famous men, Shakespeare, Homer, Michelangelo and George Washington, keep a beady eye on the back of the city hall from the façade of a pretty warehouse (No 10 Donegall Square South). The front of the Venetian-style linen warehouse on Donegall Square North offers no clues to its present occupants, Marks & Spencer,

The Waterfront Hall

Belfast City Hall

behind the pink stone of this attractive building designed by
W. H. Lynn in 1869.

The **Grand Opera House**, Great Victoria Street, designed by the
celebrated theatre-architect Frank Matcham (1854–1920), was
restored in 1980. It has a particularly gorgeous interior and comfortable seats. The reopening signalled a revival of evening entertainment in the city after the 'troubles' of the 1970s. At about that time the
arts scene in Belfast, particularly theatre and music, began to emerge
as a life-enhancing force in this resilient city. Next door is the 200-
room **Europa Hotel**, the biggest, indeed for a time the only, city centre
hotel. Now much altered, with a nightclub on the top floor, it is still
recognisable as the hotel that managed to stay open during all the
years when high profile commercial enterprises in Belfast were
targets of criminal elements. This whole area is lively from early in the

morning when commuters and shoppers pour out of the railway station adjacent. Just opposite is a pub much admired by John Betjeman, the **Crown Liquor Saloon**, formerly part of a Victorian railway hotel. Its stained and painted glass and panelled snugs lit by the original gas lamps have been restored by the National Trust. Cosy atmospheric pubs are to be found in the narrow passageways called 'entries' in the High Street area. **White's Tavern** in three-cornered Wine Cellar Entry is the city's oldest pub. Off Castle Street an even narrower entry, which has now disappeared, was called Squeeze-Gut Entry. Before **St Mary's** (1784) opened in Chapel Street, Catholics gathered there to celebrate mass. **Kelly's Cellars**, Bank Street, a haunt of the United Irishmen who rebelled in 1798, has traditional music sessions at night. There are a number of other session pubs, including the **Rotterdam**, **Liverpool** and **Pat's Bar**, all in the docks area. **McHugh's Bar** in Queen's Square (Nos 31–33) opposite the Custom House occupies the oldest surviving building in Belfast — a house built in 1715.

Some of the city's best buildings are banks. The old National Bank with copper pinnacles in High Street is near the **Albert Memorial clock tower**, a kind of mini Big Ben which subsidence has made lean more than a yard from the vertical. One of two fine **Waring Street banks** is No 2 on the corner with North Street, Belfast's earliest public building now surviving. Built in 1769 as a market house, it was the venue in 1792 for a famous assembly of Irish harpers.

You could probably visit a different church in Belfast every day of the year, though not more than a handful are architecturally distinguished. The oldest church (1737) is, strictly speaking, a bit outside, on the A24 driving south, just before the ring road. **Knockbreda parish church**, dark and bawn-like, is clearly visible on a hill (right). Its architect, Richard Cassels, designed Leinster House in Dublin, where the Irish parliament has met since 1923, and many other notable Dublin houses. The chancel has a starry blue ceiling. The Duke of Wellington's mother, Lady Anne Hill, worshipped here and it was a fashionable place in which to be buried. The churchyard contains some superb late-eighteenth-century tombs, big enough to live in.

Churches in the city centre to note include: **St Malachy's** (Roman Catholic, opened 1844), Alfred Street, with a fine fan-vaulted ceiling and romantic turrets overlooking the neat Housing Executive terraces of the Upper Markets area. The nearby **May Street Presbyterian church** (1829) was built for the Rev. Henry Cooke, a formidable Victorian who campaigned against the theological errors of the time. Cooke's statue stands at the top of Wellington Place in front of the well-proportioned façade of 'Inst', the **Royal Belfast Academical Institution** where Lord Kelvin's father taught mathematics. Kelvin (1824–1907) introduced the absolute scale of temperature (the Kelvin Scale). He also made a fortune from his submarine cable patents. His birthplace in College Square East has been demolished but a statue stands inside the gates of the Botanic Gardens, appropriately placed midway between Queen's University and the Ulster Museum. 'Inst' opened in 1814 as an ecumenical school. The poet–physician William Drennan (1754–1820) saw the school as a place 'where the youth of Ireland might sit together on these benches and learn to love and esteem one another'. Son of a Presbyterian minister, Drennan helped found the United Irishmen Society and was inspired by the spirit of free thought sweeping through Europe. He was the first to call Ireland the 'emerald isle'.

The **First Presbyterian church**, Rosemary Street, completed 1783 and praised for its admirable elliptical interior by John Wesley, occasionally has lunchtime concerts. **Sinclair Seamen's church** (1857), Corporation Square, is like a maritime museum inside. The organ has port and starboard lights and the pulpit is a ship's prow. The church, though not the interior, was designed by Charles Lanyon who was also architect of the handsome E-shaped **Custom House**, opened the same year. The twentieth-century Anglican cathedral, **St Anne's**, is in Donegall Street. Nearby are the offices of two of the province's three main newspapers: the evening *Belfast Telegraph* and, opposite the **Front Page** pub, the nationalist *Irish News*, a morning newspaper. Production of the other morning paper, the venerable *News Letter*, founded in 1737 and unionist in outlook, has moved to a larger site but the richly decorated façade of its old buildings (Nos 49–67) lends character to this part of Donegall Street. Northern Ireland also has two Sunday tabloids, about forty weeklies, a handful of *Tatler*-ish monthlies and some government-funded glossy multicultural periodicals. The number of shops selling religious books in Belfast, a city with rather few general bookshops, is striking — everything from evangelism to catechetics. No other readership is so well catered for.

The area around **Queen's University** is good for moderately priced restaurants, art galleries and theatre. The main college building, revived Tudor-style in mellow brick, with cloisters and an entrance tower paraphrased from Magdalen, Oxford, was designed by Lanyon in 1849 and stands at the centre of charming little mid-Victorian terraces with magnolia trees in their front gardens. The university's arts and law schools occupy most of the houses. About 8,000 students with some 10,000 others on short courses carry on the

The Crown Liquor Saloon, preserved by the National Trust

traditions of learning and science for which Queen's has an international reputation. The film theatre attached to Queen's shows art films.

Next door in the **Botanic Gardens**, the **Palm House** is one of the finest and earliest surviving examples of curvilinear glass and cast-iron work in Europe. It was built between 1839 and 1852 by the Dublin iron founder Richard Turner. In the **tropical ravine** opposite there is a view from the balcony down into a steamy sunken glen of exotic plants. The **Ulster Museum** faces into the gardens. Among its antiquities is the Spanish treasure from the Armada galleass *Girona* which sank in 1588 off the Giant's Causeway. Gold and silver jewellery and much else was salvaged in 1967–69 by Belgian divers.

Queen's University,
Belfast

The Palm House,
Botanic Gardens

Among items in the permanent Made in Belfast exhibition is John Boyd Dunlop's bicycle, for which he made the first practical pneumatic tyre in 1889.

Irish paintings in the art department include works by Belfast-born artists Sir John Lavery, Andrew Nicholl and William Conor, and pictures by Paul Henry, Jack Yeats and George Russell (Æ). Continental painters of the seventeenth and early eighteenth centuries are well represented and there is good silver, glass and Irish furniture. The museum's numismatics cabinet with 40,000 specimens is a major collection.

On the lower slopes of **Cave Hill** to the north is **Belfast Castle**, a Scottish baronial pile presented to the city by the Earl of Shaftesbury in 1934. It has a square six-storey tower and a baroque staircase snaking up from flowerbeds and lawns. A heritage centre on the top floor is open long hours, including Sunday. Cave Hill itself is popular for walks and picnics in summer. The five caves near the top are man-made, carved out by Neolithic men and used as shelter by hundreds of later generations. At **McArt's Fort** on the summit, Wolfe Tone, Henry Joy McCracken and other United Irishmen in 1795 plotted rebellion for two heady days and nights and pledged themselves to the cause of Irish independence.

Here, you are at 1,200ft and it is a good spot from which to appreciate Belfast's fine setting, ringed by hills rising to nearly 1,600ft (Divis mountain), a deep sea lough and the valley of the Lagan river. Golf courses and parks on the city's outskirts are now visible, including the rolling parklands around the former parliament building at **Stormont** 4 miles east of Belfast. The green sward even at this distance is clearly divided by an impressive avenue, nearly a mile long, running up to the white portico. It is a splendid hilltop site. Opened in 1932, the building is not generally open to the public though visitors can stroll in the immaculate grounds and take photographs. An expressive statue of Sir Edward Carson (1854–1935), the Dublin lawyer who led the opposition to Irish home rule in 1912, thus keeping Northern Ireland in the United Kingdom, stands in the middle of the avenue. Stormont, and the city centre Royal Courts of Justice completed the following year, are unmistakable architectural symbols of the Northern Ireland state. Also on Cave Hill, **Belfast Zoo** faces over the city. It is a real mountain zoo, getting steeper and steeper as you penetrate further. Once past the flamingoes on the lake, with a crannog (early Christian artificial island) in the middle, and heading for the polar bears, you are literally moving up the side of the mountain.

The **murals** of west Belfast — gable-end wall paintings — are the main attraction of this so-called 'seismic' part of the city, immediately west of the centre. It takes only 10 minutes or so to drive along nationalist (Catholic) Falls Road and loyalist (Protestant) Shankill Road. The two roads are linked by a small cross-street, Northumberland Street, which has a yellow barrier at one end, normally open. On the Falls popular ports of call for visitors are the café–bookshop at the **Cultúrlann Arts Centre** where the menu is in Irish Gaelic, and the republican shrines of **Milltown Cemetery**. The most distinguished building on the Shankill is the Anglican **Shamrock Church** of St Matthew (1872). The social history of the Shankill district during the home rule crisis of 1912 and the 1914–18 and 1939–45 world wars is well told at **Fernhill House Museum**, Glencairn Road, a mile west of St Matthew's Church. The **Belfast Living History Tour** with expert commentary, leaving from the central post office, provides an efficient way to inspect Belfast's murals, with their vivid colours and dire messages.

Fans of the rock star **Van Morrison** will happily plunge into the heavy traffic of east Belfast to visit his Hyndford Street birthplace (1945). He started his career as the taciturn lead singer of a Belfast rhythm-and-blues group.

Around Belfast

Try to visit the parks on the south side of the city along the **Lagan Valley**. International rose trials are held in **Dixon Park** — Rose Week is the third week in July. There are at least 20,000 rose bushes and trees, and copses and shrubberies on different levels. A Japanese garden possessing at least some of the six essentials of the perfect garden — spaciousness, seclusion, artifice, antiquity, abundant water and broad views — has been developed in the park, not far from the entrance.

Focal point of **Barnett Park** is an attractive late Georgian mansion, Malone House, with views over the Lagan. Previously the National Trust's headquarters, gutted by fire in 1976, and now restored, the house is used for trade shows and other functions. It has a restaurant and tea room, a greenhouse, old paintings and watercolours and a permanent exhibition on Belfast parks. Beyond the demesne is the Mary Peters athletics track established in honour of the province's gold medal winner in the pentathlon at the Munich Olympics (1972).

The steep slope from Malone House down to **Shaw's Bridge** carpark is favoured by tobogannists after snow. This is a convenient place to get on to the towpath. A wooden bridge was thrown across

Dinghy racing on Belfast Lough

Dramatic Cave Hill overlooks
the city and its deep sea lough

Canoeing on the Lagan at Shaw's Bridge, Belfast

Carrickfergus Castle

the river here by a Captain Shaw to transport the guns of Cromwell's army in 1655. The present picturesque bridge with five arches was built in 1709. Close by, too close, a concrete bridge carries A55 ring-road traffic over the Lagan.

The nearby former mill village of **Edenderry** is hidden away in a bend on the river, a beautiful setting. Take the side road at the bridge (signposted) and turn right after 200yd to **Minnowburn Beeches** carpark. A $1^1/2$- mile walk along the bank will bring you to the village, or else you can drive.

The road ends in a group of small terraces with slate roofs, tall red chimneys, footscrapers and minuscule front gardens. Two twelve-house terraces front the quay where lighters (flat-bottomed barges) delivered coal to the weaving factory, once famous for damask linen, now derelict. Two slightly longer terraces lead to a tiny gospel hall. Wedged between the river and the hillside with no through road, Edenderry is a tranquil spot. It becomes animated on Orangemen's day, 12 July, when thousands of marchers from Belfast come this way to listen to religious and political speeches in an open field near the village.

A circular enclosure known as the **Giant's Ring**, a short walk across a meadow from Edenderry, is also approached via Ballynahatty Road (then signposted, large carpark). The enclosure is nearly 200yd in diameter, with an earthen bank 20ft wide and 12ft high, and a sort of dolmen in the middle. Refreshingly little is known about it. In the eighteenth century it was used for horse racing. A 2-mile race was six circuits and the punters stood on the ramparts. In 2,000BC it must have been a place for rituals too.

The towpath along the Lagan from Belfast to Lisburn starts in the university area. Joggers, birdwatchers, anglers, painters and boys on bikes are not quite so numerous as people out for a stroll. Even so, it must be the most crowded bit of the whole of the **Ulster Way**, a 500-mile footpath running all round Northern Ireland. The 9 miles of old locks and lock houses are the industrial archaeology of the Lagan Navigation that ran from Belfast to the shores of Lough Neagh where coal had been discovered. The Lagan was made navigable as far as Lisburn in the 1760s. In the 1790s the whole route was open. Its heyday was comparatively brief. Roads, and later the railway (1839), took much of the trade. Paradoxically, the canal provided the chief means of distributing coal imported through Belfast rather than moving Tyrone coal eastwards. It closed in 1958 and much of the waterway has disappeared under the huge rhubarb leaves of *Gunnera manicata* and the pink and white flowers of wild balsam.

A lock-keeper's house at **Drumbridge** dated 1757 has been

restored. Hidden below the level of the bridge, it is the only house designed by Thomas Omer, the Lagan Canal engineer, which is still lived in. There is a carpark here, across the road (B103) from the lychgate of **Drumbeg** church and the tombs of founders of the city. The church tower (1798) has a seventeenth-century bell. At **Drumbo** to the south-west is the stump of a twelfth-century round tower. (Reminder: *droim* means 'ridge'.) This village also has an attractive eighteenth-century parish church. Unusually it is nearly 2 miles away, at **Ballylesson**. In the graveyard is the huge tomb of a local worthy who rejoiced in the name Narcissus Batt. He rebuilt Purdysburn House nearby (now a health centre). He was only sixteen years old when he helped form the Belfast Chamber of Commerce in 1783. The fifty-nine founder-members were not stuffy city-suited gents. Many were active in the Volunteers, the liberal movement in Ireland at the end of the eighteenth century. Their first president was commander of the Belfast Volunteers, and some were United Irishmen. Several went to prison and the grandson of one founder was a leader of the United Irishmen, and went to the scaffold — Henry Joy McCracken. Narcissus Batt, more fortunate, died in his bed, rich and influential. Historically interesting, leafy and peaceful, this little backwater is only about 6 miles from central Belfast.

The road north to Carrickfergus and Larne runs through a quite different landscape. A wide (ten lanes) strip of motorway between the crag of Cave Hill and Belfast Lough soon narrows and turns towards the north-west and the international airport.

Carrickfergus (population 23,000) grew up round the massive **Anglo-Norman castle** built by John de Courcy in 1180 to guard the approach to Belfast Lough. Fishing boats and yachts bob about in the marina, with the four-storey, 90ft keep an impressive backdrop. The castle, shaped to fit the rocky spur on which it stands, was crucially important to the Anglo-Norman toehold on Ulster. In June 1690 William of Orange landed on the pier beneath the walls on his way to the Battle of the Boyne. A plaque at the end of the quay marks the spot.

More than half of the defensive **town wall**, which was built in the early seventeenth century, is still standing at its full original height. At that time Carrickfergus was the only place in the north of Ireland where English was spoken. Medieval banquets in the castle are a tourist attraction, and the town's Lughnasa Fair, an annual event, is held around the battlements. Lughnasa (1 August) was a quarterly feast of the old Irish year. Wrestlers, archers, minstrels and 'monks' tending braziers between the gun platforms lend sound and colour to this fine example of medieval military architecture. In 1760 it was easily captured by a French squadron which appeared in the lough,

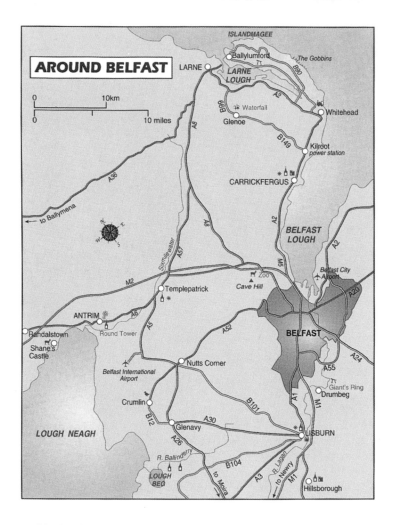

AROUND BELFAST

ISLANDMAGEE
Ballylumford
The Gobbins
LARNE
LARNE LOUGH
B90
0 10km
0 10 miles
A8
Waterfall
B99
Whitehead
Glenoe
A2
B149
Kilroot
power station
A36
CARRICKFERGUS
← to Ballymena
A2
Sixmilewater
A57
A8
BELFAST LOUGH
M5
A2
Zoo
Cave Hill
Belfast City Airport
A20
M2
Templepatrick
A5
ANTRIM
A52
BELFAST
Randalstown
Round Tower
A5
A24
Shane's Castle
Nutts Corner
A55
Belfast International Airport
Giant's Ring
Drumbeg
B101
A1
M1
Crumlin
B12
A30
Glenavy
A26
LOUGH NEAGH
LISBURN
R. Ballinderry
B104
A3
to Newry
M1
LOUGH BEG
to Mora
R. Lagan
Hillsborough

and had to be hurriedly recaptured. In 1778 the American privateer Paul Jones sailed blithely past the castle and carried off HMS *Drake* in what turned out to be America's first naval victory. It is said that Belfast citizens ran to the shore to cheer the attackers. Ulster Protestants were generally sympathetic to the American Revolution though the French one was less to their liking.

St Nicholas's parish church, off the market place, is contemporary with the castle, with late-twelfth-century pillars in the nave. The chancel was finished in 1305 and is out of alignment with the nave, an unusual feature. It was damaged and burnt many times down the years and much restored in 1614. The north transept contains the kneeling figures of Sir Arthur Chichester, his wife and infant son in

A traditional fisherman's cottage on Islandmagee peninsula

a marble and alabaster monument. Chichester was governor of Carrickfergus and, from 1605, Lord Deputy of Ireland. He was also the landlord of Belfast. A small effigy of his brother, Sir John, who had his head chopped off at **Glynn**, a small village near Larne, after a MacDonnell ambush in 1597, is part of the same monument. The Chichesters were the Earls of Donegall — a name which besprinkles the Belfast street directory. Their eventual bankruptcy coincided with the end of the great famine and allowed their tenants to become freeholders — a disaster for the family but a boon for the citizens of Belfast. Four stained windows are by Irish artists and the nave contains sixteenth-century glass.

A section of the old town wall beyond the church was excavated by Thomas Delaney, a young archaeologist who died in 1979. A stone in front of **Gill's Almshouses** commemorates his short but industrious life. A ghost is said to haunt seventeenth-century Dobbins Inn, still a hotel, in High Street. Some of the town's antiques shops occupy attractive old buildings, and the market house (1755) is a bank.

The handsome former **courthouse** is now the town hall. In 1710 a mass trial of witches took place inside. Eight young women, five of them named Janet, were sentenced to a year in prison, plus four sessions in the public stocks. Tucked discreetly behind the town hall is the entertaining **Knightride Monorail**, a time trip, not unlike the Jorvik Centre in York, through a thousand years of history in Carrickfergus.

Literary associations with Carrickfergus are interesting. William Congreve's father was a soldier and the future Restoration dramatist came to live in the castle in 1678 when he was eight years old and Carrickfergus was a busy port 'filled with English sailors, rough and jovial fellows'. He put one of them, Sailor Ben, into *Love for Love* (1695). Jonathan Swift's first job was at nearby **Kilroot** where he wrote *Tale of a Tub* between 1694 and 1696. Though born in Belfast ('between the mountain and the gantries'), the poet Louis MacNeice (1907–63) spent his boyhood here. His father was rector of St Nicholas's and the family lived first at 5 Governor's Walk opposite the castle and then in North Road at the rectory (demolished 1986). Another famous connection is Andrew Jackson, United States president, born in South Carolina in 1767. His parents emigrated from Carrickfergus in 1765. The **Andrew Jackson Centre**, a reconstruction of an eighteenth-century thatched cottage containing a little museum, stands near the site of their original home. Memorabilia of the **US Rangers**, the American equivalent of the Commandos, have also found a home in the centre. The first battalion of the Rangers, the US Army's most decorated unit, was raised in Carrickfergus in 1942.

Whitehead (population 3,500), a small resort with a pebbly beach and long promenade, is the base of the Railway Preservation Society of Ireland. The Portrush Flyer, a famous steam express, puffs out of the excursion station at holiday times. The port of **Larne** (population 18,000) is best viewed from a distance. To join a scenic road just outside Carrickfergus, turn left off the A2 opposite the chimney of Kilroot power station (Beltoy Road). At the top turn left (sharp turn) to go on up to **Glenoe** waterfalls (or to buy the delicious local ice cream) but turn right, along the old Carrickfergus road, for a bird's-eye view of shapely Larne Lough with a lighthouse on the tip of the peninsula. The three chimneys of **Ballylumford** (another, even bigger power station, which now burns North Sea gas), necklace-like Swan Island further up the lough and the dark shape of **Olderfleet Castle**, a sixteenth-century tower house down near the cluttered East Antrim Boat Club yard, are prominent features. A small ferry boat dashes across to Ballylumford on Islandmagee every hour or so, and the hoots of the roll-on roll-off ferries float up the ridge. The port is the terminus of the quickest sea crossing to Scotland.

Islandmagee is not an island but a 7-mile-long peninsula. It has a distinctive separate feeling about it. The witches tried at Carrickfergus in 1710 — the last witch trial in Ireland — were from Islandmagee. On the east side, wild basalt cliffs called the **Gobbins** were the scene of a gruesome incident in 1641 when soldiers from the Carrickfergus garrison threw the local inhabitants into the sea. The sea-level path cut in the face of the rock is dangerous in places. To reach the peninsula turn left off the A2 going back towards Belfast, and drive up the west side along the B90. There is very little traffic, lots of churches, signposts pointing to still more inland, some spotless public toilets, and good places for picnics or camping. Look out on the left for the **Ballylumford dolmen**, sitting for the past 4,000 years overlooking Larne Lough and now incorporated into the front garden of No 91 Ballylumford Road. The front door of the house is so close to this enormous Neolithic monument that the occupants find it more convenient to use a side entrance. The view across the lough is filled by container ships and ferries that dwarf the harbour buildings and a modern folly that looks like an Irish round tower. Fuel, groceries and fishing tackle are sold above the sandy beaches at Brown's Bay (campsite) and other beauty spots. The coast here is quite hilly, with windswept palm trees towards Muck Island, and **Portmuck harbour** on a promontory down a switchback road.

The old county town of **Antrim** has trebled in population (now 21,000) over the past 20 years, with housing estates, shopping centres and a ring-road bypass. A tenth-century **round tower** stands in Steeple Park, a mile from the centre. This was the site of an important sixth-century monastery called *Aentrobh*, abandoned in 1147. Though over 90ft high, the tower is rather obscured in summer by even taller trees. Over the lintel is an unusual cross-carved stone. At the base lies a giant two-hole 'bullaun' (hollowed stone). This tower and the twelfth-century one on Devenish Island are among the finest intact round towers in Ireland. These detached bell towers served as useful lookouts during the long centuries of Viking raids. Certainly a sentry monk on watch at the high windows could sound his handbell if strangers approached, and a rope ladder to the raised doorway, 7ft off the ground, could be pulled up and the door slammed shut.

One of several famous battles fought around Antrim was in 1798 when royal forces fought off and defeated 3,500 United Irishmen. The plantation castle built (1662) by Sir John Clotworthy (later Lord Massereene) was burnt down in 1922. Opposite the courthouse (1726, still in use) in Market Square, the estate's Tudor-style gateway leads to the magnificent gardens of **Massereene Demesne**, now a public park. They were first laid out at the end of the seventeenth century

and restored in the nineteenth century. Features include long ornamental fishponds flanked by high hedges, straight avenues converging on a round pool, a Norman motte with a hedged spiral path to the
top, elegant memorial urns to departed Massereenes, inscribed
stones to favourite dogs and horses, and a stone bridge over the
Sixmilewater river. The stables and coach house (built about 1840) are
used as an arts centre, Clotworthy House, with open-air theatre in the
yard.

Another historic building
in the town is an eighteenth-
century cottage in atmos-
pheric **Pogue's Entry** off
Church Street, birthplace
(1863) of author Alexander
Irvine, a newspaper boy who
became a missionary in the
Bowery, New York. His best
known work is *My Lady of the
Chimney Corner* set largely in
this carefully maintained cottage. He and his parents are
buried in the churchyard of
All Saints' parish church,
dating from 1596. The church
contains some Renaissance
stained glass and many
Massereene monuments. The
steeple was erected in 1816. In
summer there are cruises on
Lough Neagh leaving from
the marina. **Shane's Castle** estate on the Randalstown road was once
the seat of the Clandeboye O'Neills. The estate borders Lough Neagh
and is a venue for vintage vehicle rallies, field sports fairs and
suchlike events. Camellias are grown in the conservatory, designed
in 1812 by John Nash. Worth stopping for in **Randalstown** is the
delightful elliptical Old Presbyterian church of 1790. The interior has
a specially warm and friendly feeling about it.

At **Templepatrick** (population 1,500) on the airport road, **Castle
Upton stables** were designed in 1789 for Viscount Templeton by
Robert Adam. They have a battlemented archway and clocktower,
and another archway with a tower on top, leading to the rear
courtyard where horses are still kept. Castle Upton, a historic manor
house, is not open to the public. Near the stables but outside the

Above: Hillsborough market house
Opposite: Round tower in Steeple Park, Antrim

estate, the triumphal arch of the **Templeton Mausoleum** (National Trust) is also Adam's design, though unfinished. John Knox's grandson, Josias Welsh, who was chaplain at Castle Upton, is buried in this graveyard. Robert Adam never actually came to Ireland. A second Trust property at Templepatrick is the water-powered **Patterson's Spade Mill** built in 1919. You can watch all kinds of spades being made and buy one too.

North of Templepatrick, at **Doagh**, is Ulster's most visited monolith. Encircled by whin bushes on an isolated chunk of rock, the **Hole Stone** is a 5ft-high stone with a hole in it just big enough for a slim hand to pass through. Courting couples scramble up the rock to hold hands through the hole and enjoy the panoramic views.

West of Nutts Corner roundabout (where there is a big Sunday market) on the A52 at **Crumlin** (population 1,700) the walled garden of **Talnotry Cottage** provides a sanctuary for sick and injured birds, from jenny wrens to falcons, and is a natural habitat for many small native species which nest in the ivy. On side roads south of Crumlin are the Ballinderrys, 2 miles apart on a quiet little river of the same name. **Lower Ballinderry** has a Moravian church and manse under one roof — church at one end, manse (with chimneys) at the other. At **Upper Ballinderry** is a barn church with bull's-eye glass in the windows, built in 1666 for Jeremy Taylor, the famous Bishop of Down and Connor, a descendant of Dr Rowland Taylor who was burnt at the stake by Queen Mary. Jeremy Taylor was one of the great prose writers of the seventeenth century. Theological tussles with local Presbyterians apparently made his bishopric 'a place of torment'. He died aged fifty-four, the year before the Ballinderry church was consecrated and is buried in Dromore cathedral. At Upper Ballinderry antiques are sold from a large rambling warehouse, an Aladdin's cave of furniture, objets d'art and willow baskets — some made from the traditional unpeeled osier (*Salix viminalis*), often called the Sally Rod in Ireland.

On the Lagan upstream from Belfast, **Lisburn** (population 42,000) is an industrial town with a Tuesday market. Few buildings survived a devastating fire in 1707. One that did was the assembly rooms, now the **Lisburn Museum**. The building adjoins the **Irish Linen Centre**, an appropriate attraction for this town which was at the centre of the Linen Triangle (Belfast–Armagh–Dungannon), the source of half Ulster's whole linen output throughout the nineteenth century. Yarn from all over Ireland was brought to the bleach greens along the banks of the Lagan, a river with a good head of water in summer — essential for the bleaching process — and with access to export markets via Belfast port. The first bleach green in Ulster was established before 1626 at **Lambeg** a mile downstream, a hamlet with a pretty suspension bridge and church. The hamlet gave its name to the big drums which came to Ireland from Holland with the army of William III.

Louis Crommelin (1652–1727), appointed Linen Overseer of Ireland by William, also came from Holland. He found Lisburn an ideal headquarters. After the revocation of the Edict of Nantes in 1685, Huguenot families from Holland and France came to Ulster at Crommelin's invitation. Linen thread, made by twisting together two or more strands of yarn, is still made in the Barbour Threads factory at **Hilden** where John Barbour (a Scot from Paisley) set up Ulster's first hand-twisting mill in 1784. Nearby is a real ale brewery (visitors welcome).

Crommelin and other Huguenots who helped develop the industry are buried at **Christ Church** (1623, raised to cathedral status in 1662), which is only the size of a parish church. The slender octagonal spire was added to the tower in 1804. The interior contains some significant tablets and monuments. But how squeezed it all is! The cathedral is almost invisible from the street and the grave of Crommelin, who brought such prosperity to the town, is squashed into a churchyard no bigger than a pocket handkerchief. In the market place a bronze statue with a pistol in one hand and a sword in the other is General John Nicholson, killed in the attack on Delhi during the Indian Mutiny (1857).

The birthplace (1839) of **John Ballance**, a pioneer of the welfare state and prime minister of New Zealand 1891–93, is at Ballypitmave townland on the A30 north-west of Lisburn 2 miles before **Glenavy**, a tranquil village with a three-arch bridge spanning the river beside St Aidan's parish church. The war memorial commemorates all the Glenavy men who fought in the two world wars (and the Falklands war), carefully listing the dead and all the survivors too.

The village of **Hillsborough** (population 2,400) 10 miles south of Belfast, is something of a showpiece. Many of the pretty terraced houses along the steep main street are craft and antiques shops. Across the square with its Georgian townhouses and charming **market house** (built about 1760), the mansion visible through a pair of magnificent wrought-iron gates is Hillsborough Castle, formerly the residence of the governor of Northern Ireland, now used for visiting VIPs and occasional royal garden parties. The gates and screen (1745) came from Richhill Castle in County Armagh in 1936. On the other side of the square, beyond an oval lawn, **Hillsborough Fort** was built by Colonel Arthur Hill in 1650 to command the road from Dublin to Carrickfergus. The first Hill arrived in Ireland in the army of the Earl of Essex (sent by Elizabeth I to subdue the O'Neills). He founded one of Ireland's most powerful families. Bishop Jeremy Taylor lived with the Hills, his friends, in the 1660s and used to say his prayers in the fort. When it was remodelled for family feasts and parties, an ornamental gazebo was built in the middle of the north rampart in the bishop's memory. The windows resemble those of the **parish church** which he had consecrated in 1663.

Sir Hamilton Harty, called the 'Irish Toscanini' (1879–1941), is buried in the graveyard. Harty ran the Hallé Orchestra during its finest period, 1920–33, and wrote beautiful works for voice and orchestra such as 'Ode to a nightingale' and 'Children of Lir'. He was born in Ballynahinch Street and his father was church organist here for 40 years. Characterful side-streets to explore include **Arthur**

Street where terraces of one-and-a-half-storey cottages with slate roofs face each other in a cul-de-sac (1850). A lane behind the Shambles art gallery leads to a carpark beside the artificial lake and a wooded footpath up to the fort.

A prominent feature of the east and south approaches to Hillsborough is a 5-mile wall surrounding this lake and its adjoining forest. Built in 1841 by the third Marquis of Downshire, the wall has since acquired a concrete capping in parts. On a steep hill overlooking the town, an immense **Doric column** and statue of the said marquis appears to sprout from a cluster of bungalows. The present author ruined a pair of shoes going to examine the inscription *Per deum et ferrum obtinuit* on the base. It is the only ugly thing in this harmonious little place.

ADDITIONAL INFORMATION

PLACES TO VISIT

BELFAST

(Phone numbers are all Belfast exchange — dialling code 01232)

A free Belfast street plan showing the location of most places mentioned below and listing accommodation, plus walking tours of central areas of the city are available at the tourist information centre at 59 North Street (☎ 246609). Belfast sightseeing tours: coach trips with expert commentary start from the central post office, Castle Place.
Living History Tour 2-hour trip Thurs and Sun afternoon, plus Tuesday in summer.
City Tour 3¹/₂-hour trip, with numerous stops, Saturday afternoon, plus Wednesday in summer.
Phone for times ☎ 458484

Belfast City Hall
Free tours every weekday in summer, 10.30am, 11.30am, 2.30pm, plus Saturday 2.30pm. From October to June, Monday–Saturday, there is just one tour at 2.30pm, except on Wednesday when the tour is at 11.30am. Other times by arrangement. Please book.
☎ 320202 ext 2816

Botanic Gardens
Open daily until dusk. Palm house and tropical ravine open weekdays 10am–5pm, weekend 2–5pm; in winter (October–March) they close an hour earlier.

Belfast Harbour Office
Corporation Square. Advance booking essential. Weekdays only.
☎ 554422 ext 208

Cave Hill Heritage Centre
Belfast Castle. ☎ 776925
Open Monday–Saturday 9am–9pm, Sunday 9am–5.30pm.

Crown Liquor Saloon (NT)
Open pub hours.

Fernhill House People's Museum
Glencairn Road. ☎ 715599. Open Monday–Saturday 10am–4pm, Sunday 1–4pm. Reference library.

First Presbyterian Church
Rosemary Street. Open for Sunday service 10.30am and also on Wednesday 10.30am–12.30pm for interested visitors.

Harland & Wolff Shipyard
Access difficult unless you can demonstrate a professional interest. Write to Public Affairs Office, Harland & Wolff, Queen's Island, Belfast BT3 9DU. ☎ 458456

The Belfast City Tour includes Belfast docks.

Lagan Lookout
Donegall Quay. ☎ 315444. Open weekdays 11am–5pm and weekend afternoons. Shorter hours in winter.

Linen Hall Library
☎ 321707. Open weekdays 9.30am–5.30pm. Saturday to 4pm. Reading room and café. Prints and maps for sale.

Public Record Office
Balmoral Avenue. ☎ 255905. Public search room open weekdays 9.30am–4.45pm. Exhibitions.

Queen's University of Belfast
Grounds always open.

RUC Museum
65 Knock Road. ☎ 650222. Phone to arrange visit on any weekday. Roger Casement's pistol, poteen still (confiscated), IRA booby trap (disarmed), photos, uniforms and documents relating to the Irish constabulary since 1822 (Royal Ulster Constabulary created 1922).

St Anne's Cathedral
Lower Donegall Street. Always open. The tourist information centre is directly opposite.

Sinclair Seamen's Church
Corporation Square. Open Wednesday 2–5pm and for Sunday services at 11.30am and 7pm. For access at other times call ☎ 715997.

Ulster Museum
☎ 383000. Open Monday–Friday 10am–5pm, Saturday 1–5pm, Sunday 2–5pm.

Ulster Weavers
44 Montgomery Road. ☎ 404236. Tours of linen weaving factory, March–September. Shop, café. Telephone for appointment.

Van Morrison Birthplace
125 Hyndford Street. Plaque on house (private). From city centre take Newtownards road (A20), after 1 mile turn right (Beersbridge Road), ninth turning on the left is little Hyndford Street.

Belfast Zoo
☎ 776277. Open from 10am all year except Christmas Day. Latest admission 5pm (3.30pm in winter).

Wall paintings
West Belfast plus (nationalist) Ardoyne Avenue, off Oldpark Road. Lower Newtownards Road in east Belfast and Blythefield, off Sandy Row near International Youth Hostel for loyalist murals, frequently updated.

CARRICKFERGUS

Castle
☎ (01960) 351273. Open Monday–Saturday 10am–6pm, Sunday 2–6pm. Closes at 4pm October–March. Joint ticket with *Knightride Monorail* centre which has longer opening hours. ☎ (01960) 366455

President Andrew Jackson Centre & US Rangers Exhibition
☎ (01960) 366455. Open April–September Monday–Friday 10am–1pm, 2–6pm and weekend afternoons. Other times by arrangement.

ANTRIM

Antrim Castle Gardens
Massereene Demesne.
☎ (01849) 428000. Open to dusk. Telephone for details.

Pogue's Entry
☎ (01849) 428331. Cottage open Monday–Friday 10am–5pm, Saturday 10am–2pm. Shorter hours in winter.

CRUMLIN

Talnotry Bird Garden
☎ (01849) 422900. Open year round by arrangement. Telephone first.

DOAGH

The Hole Stone
Take B59 (Ballymena road) west from Doagh village. Signposted after 1 mile.

GLENAVY

John Ballance Birthplace
☎ (01846) 648492. Nine miles north-west of Lisburn, signposted off

A30. Open April–September Tuesday–Friday 11am–5pm and weekend afternoons.

GLENOE

Maud's Ice Cream Dairy
☎ (01574) 272387. Tours Monday–Friday 8am–4pm.

HILLSBOROUGH

Hillsborough Fort
☎ (01846) 683285. Open Tuesday–Saturday 10am–7pm, Sunday 2–7pm. Closes at 4pm October–March. The custodian will also admit visitors to the market house. Grounds always open until dusk.

LISBURN

Hilden Brewery
☎ (01846) 663863. Visitors welcome. Tours.

Irish Linen Centre
Market Square. ☎ (01846) 663377. Open Monday–Saturday 9.30am–5pm. Good linen/crafts shop.

TEMPLEPATRICK

Patterson's Spade Mill
751 Antrim Road. ☎ (01849) 433619. Open 2–6pm weekends in April, May, September and every afternoon (except Tuesday) June–August.

EVENTS

Belfast

Belfast Marathon (early May)

Lord Mayor's Show (May)

Royal Ulster Agricultural Society Show (mid-May)

Ulster Orchestra Symphony Concerts (mid-June)

Belfast/Dublin Maracycle (late June) Two huge teams pedal off to the other city.

Belfast Carnival (late June)

The Twelfth (12 July) Biggest of all the Orange parades starts city centre.

Rose Week (late July)

West Belfast Festival (early Aug)

Belfast Folk Festival (Sept)

Belfast Festival at Queen's (Nov)

Antrim

Game Fair (end June) Shane's Castle

Ballyclare

May Fair (late May)

Carrickfergus

Classic Sail (June) Parade of yachts, tall ships.

Lughnasa Medieval Fair (late July) Carrickfergus Castle.

Dundrod

Ulster Grand Prix (late August) International motorcycling.

Lisburn

Ulster Harp Derby (mid-July) Down Royal Racecourse.

TOURIST INFORMATION CENTRES

Belfast

St Anne's Court, 59 North Street ☎ (01232) 246609. Open all year Mon–Sat 9am–5.15pm. July & Aug Mon–Fri 9am–7pm, Sat 9am–5.15pm, Sun noon–4pm.

Antrim

16 High Street. ☎ (01849) 465156. Open all year Mon–Sat 9.30am–6pm.

Carrickfergus

Knightride, Antrim Street ☎ (01960) 366455. Open all year Mon–Fri 9am–5pm. April–Sept Mon–Fri 9am–6pm, Sat 10am–6pm, Sun noon–6pm.

Larne

Narrow Gauge Road. ☎ (01574) 260088. Open all year Mon–Fri 9am–5pm, plus Sat April–Sept. Until 6.30pm Thurs–Fri in summer.

Lisburn

☎ (01846) 660038. Open same hours as Irish Linen Centre (see above).

2

THE ARDS PENINSULA
& ST PATRICK'S COUNTRY

When St Patrick came to Ireland in AD432 he landed in County Down where the Slaney river flows into Strangford Lough. His plan had been to sail past the Ards, the long finger of land which separates this huge sea lough from the Irish Sea, but strong currents swept his boat through the tidal narrows and the historic landfall was made on the Down mainland.

The Ards stretches 23 miles from Bangor to Ballyquintin Point and varies in width from 3 to 5 miles. Crossing west to east at the narrowest place, from Greyabbey to the breezy beach at Ballywalter, you see how effectively the peninsula shelters the lough. The people in the fishing villages along the seashore, and in farms among the low hills, are mostly of Scottish descent. The accession of James VI of Scotland to the English throne coincided with the first phase of the plantation of Ulster, and some of his countrymen were quick off the mark to take full advantage. Elizabeth I had previously granted land patents on the Ards to Sir Thomas Smith, an Englishman, but he seems to have been tricked out of them. In 1605 the king divided a big chunk of north Down into three lots — one stayed with Con O'Neill of Clandeboye (the original owner), and two entrepreneurial Scotsmen, Hugh Montgomery and James Hamilton, got one lot each. The Scottish adventurers quickly divested Con of his share, and soon control of 'the whole Great Ardes' was split between Montgomery, later Viscount Ards, and Hamilton, who was created Lord Clandeboye in 1622 and who owned all the land on the west side of the lough down to Killyleagh.

Hamilton brought men from Ayrshire to build the town of Bangor where St Comgall had founded an abbey in AD558. **Bangor** (population 52,500) today hardly seems like part of the Ards proper, and its

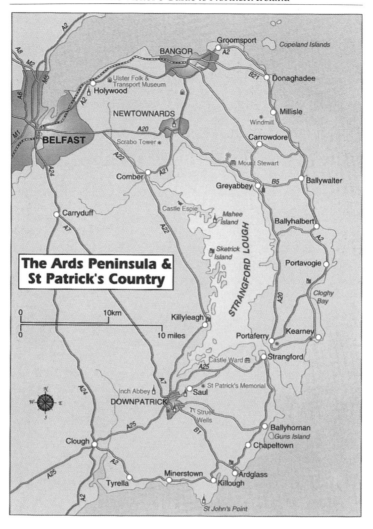

The Ards Peninsula & St Patrick's Country

strongly Scottish character has been diluted as the town has grown. A pleasant traditional seaside resort with a little light industry, it is also a commuter town efficiently linked by road and rail with Belfast 12 miles away. Boating and yachting (four yacht clubs), sea angling and golf are main leisure preoccupations. The **marina** here is the largest in Ireland. A plaque on the old pier records that in 1944 a convoy of battleships, cruisers and destroyers assembled off Bangor before sailing to the Normandy beaches for the D-Day landings. There are open-air band concerts in summer, amateur theatre, and an

Cycling at Cunningburn, Strangford Lough, near Newtownards

ice-rink. A tower house with Scottish corbelling was built as a **custom house** in 1637. You can get tourist information inside. Across the road, a restaurant in the attractive harbour master's office, recently restored, lures many of the sailing fraternity.

Nothing remains of Comgall's famous abbey, nor of two twelfth-century monasteries — except possibly the early sundial outside **Bangor Castle** and a fragment of wall near **Bangor Abbey parish church**. This church, which was altered in 1960, has kept its fifteenth-century tower and octagonal spire dated 1693. Memorials inside include a marble statue and cameo-busts of John Hamilton (died 1693) and his wife, Sophia Mordaunt, made in 1760 by Scheemakers. Most other buildings of any substance are Victorian — like the castle, which now has a heritage centre inside. The jolly clock tower with four faces on the esplanade was put up during World War I and paid for by Mr McKee, the borough's rates collector. Churches of many persuasions flourish in the town — from Baptist to Bahai.

The train from Belfast to Bangor stops here and there to deposit commuters in the evening, at **Holywood** (population 9,500) for instance, which is bypassed by the main Belfast road. The clock tower of its **old priory**, dating from the thirteenth century, is floodlit at night. An abbey founded in woods (*Sanctus Boscus*) here in AD620 by St Laiseran was connected with the larger abbey at Bangor. The Normans first destroyed and then replaced this Celtic church with one of their own. The small Franciscan monastery established in the sixteenth century was one of several, including Bangor, Grey Abbey, and Movilla at Newtownards, burned in 1572 by Sir Brian O'Neill in case English troops tried to garrison them. At the bottom of Church Street is a 70ft mast with a weathervane at the top which, although it does not look like one, is known locally as **'the maypole'**. Similar masts have stood here since a Dutch ship went aground nearby on the eve of May Day in 1700, though the tradition may go back even further. In High Street, a bronze statue of a boy playing an accordion, **'Johnny the Jig'**, is by Rosamund Praeger (1867–1954). Her brother was the distinguished naturalist, Robert Lloyd Praeger, whose home was in Holywood. Out on the main road, a Gothic mansion, now the Culloden Hotel, was formerly the Bishop of Down's palace.

Some trains (check which) stop at Cultra Halt for the **Ulster Folk & Transport Museum**. It has been developed over the past 40 years on the beautiful parkland estate of Cultra Manor and deserves an extended visit. Many of the buildings have been removed stone by stone from the Ulster countryside and re-erected in a setting as close as possible to the original landscape. There are two main areas in the **folk section**: a village which has slowly grown into a small Ulster town; and isolated farmhouses and the buildings of rural industries, including a flax mill from County Tyrone, a blacksmith's forge from Fermanagh, and a County Down bleach green watch tower — a conical stone hut where the watchman sat with his musket, guarding linen laid out to bleach in the sun.

The village has whole terraces carefully lifted from the streets of Belfast and the County Down town of Dromore, a school, a courthouse, a bank, a printing shop, a rectory and a church — all looking as if they have always been there. The houses from Tea Lane off Sandy Row in Belfast represent the oldest surviving terrace housing in the city. They were built in the 1820s. The oldest house in the park is the rectory of 1717, from Toomebridge. The parish church stood in Kilmore, County Down, from 1792 until it was dismantled, reassembled here in 1976 and re-dedicated. Each building has a guide inside, waiting to tell you about its history. The museum has a modern folk gallery and its large photographic archive includes the famous collection of 5,000 photographs of life in Ulster between 1901 and the late 1920s, taken by William A. Green. You can picnic anywhere in the open-air part, or go to the tea room in Cultra Manor — one building that started life in the right place.

Demonstrations of traditional farming methods go on all year. You may be lucky and arrive on a day when heavy horse harrowing is under way, or potato grubbing or wheat threshing. A road bridge across the main Belfast–Bangor road brings you to the **transport section** where the **Irish Railway Collection** is excellently presented. Other exhibits are a lifeboat, a three-masted schooner, a vertical take-off jet, and a full-scale model of the monoplane that Harry Ferguson flew across his father's farm in 1909. Ferguson is more famous for his tractors but he was also the first man in Ireland to fly.

The part-thatched Old Inn at **Crawfordsburn**, there since 1614, was the main watering place on an ancient track from Holywood to Bangor Abbey. Today the inn is a favourite stop-off for 'Narnia' fans visiting the haunts of C. S. Lewis (1898–1963), the Belfast-born religious and moral writer who wrote *The Screwtape Letters* and *The Problem of Pain*. Lewis brought his American bride here on honeymoon in 1958. The sandy beach here, and the one at **Helen's Bay**, are part of Crawfordsburn Country Park where a glen walk under a five-arch railway viaduct (carrying the Belfast train) leads up to a waterfall.

Inland, the wooded demesne of **Clandeboye**, seat of the late, last Marquis of Dufferin and Ava, is a popular venue for art exhibitions, sporting activities and other events. Three-storey **Helen's Tower** (built in about 1858), prominent on a hilltop at the far end, was erected in honour of Helen, Lady Dufferin, grand-daughter of Sheridan and composer of the ballad 'The Irish emigrant'. In 1915 and 1916, the 36th (Ulster) Division was camped at Clandeboye and drilled in sight of this romantic tower. A sad replica, called the Ulster Memorial Tower, was later erected on the Somme battlefield at Thiepval where nearly 6,000 Ulstermen were killed or wounded in July 1916. The **Somme Heritage Centre**, with a reconstruction of features of the battlefield — trenches and so on — opened here at Clandeboye in 1994. *Helen's Tower*, a biography of the first marquis by his nephew, Harold Nicolson, is one of the tower's many literary connections. Nicolson (1886–1968) belonged to the Bloomsbury Group.

On a hill, 3 miles across the valley, and twice as tall as Helen's Tower, **Scrabo Tower** was built at about the same time in memory of the third Marquis of Londonderry. It has 122 steps up to a good view of Strangford Lough and beyond (open in summer). Part of it was lived in until about 1970. There is a golf course round the tower, with bluebell woods on the south side (off A21).

Newtownards (population 24,500), a manufacturing and market garden town a bit inland from the head of the lough, dates from the thirteenth century when a **Dominican priory** was founded by Walter de Burgh. The ruins with a seventeenth-century square tower in Court Square incorporate the nave of Walter's church. The family vault of the Londonderrys, who succeeded the Montgomerys as

Ballycopeland Windmill, near Millisle

landlords of Newtownards, is in a corner. The nice old **market cross** at the end of High Street was smashed in 1653 and repaired in 1666 though not restored to its former height. A small chamber inside was used as a police cell.

The handsome **market house** (1765), now the town hall, has an outsize market square (Conway Square) with a life-size bronze statue of local man Blair Mayne (1915–55), commander of the first SAS unit, and a lively market on Saturdays. The harvest fair held here in September has been going strong since about 1613. Many of Belfast's fresh vegetables come from around Newtownards, including Comber potatoes, and the horticultural firm of Dickson's (established 1836) is famous for its roses. The mayor's chain of office is fashioned from twenty-six gold medals won by the Dickson nurseries. The Ulster Air Show takes place on the Newtownards aerodrome by the lough in June. A commercial radio station (Downtown) broadcasts from here.

The name of **Comber** (population 8,500) is synonymous with early potatoes, molly-coddled in the rich soil around here. In a mild spring they are in the shops in April. A **monument** to a swashbuckling soldier, Sir Robert Rollo Gillespie, occupies a large part of the central square. He was a native of the town and was shot in action in Nepa'

BE-964

Vintage car at the Ulster Folk & Transport Museum, Cultra

He died enunciating the words inscribed on the column: 'One last shot for the honour of Down'.

At **Groomsport** (population 900), where Marshal Schomberg landed with 10,000 Williamite soldiers in 1689, the harbour has a sandy beach on either side. Two of the fishermen's cottages that fringed the harbour in the eighteenth century have survived, one still with its thatch: **Cockle Row Cottages** are open in summer when there are craft demonstrations, and you can buy the paintings propped along the walls outside. Excursion boats go to the Copeland Islands in summer. Proximity to Bangor 3 miles west may account for the modern bungalows, and caravan sites. Some funny little brightly painted wooden prefabs with posh names at Fort Hill are holiday homes.

Donaghadee (population 4,800), an interesting seaside town with a lighthouse and a very big harbour, is the nearest Irish port to Great Britain. At a time when the only life insurance available on the Irish Sea crossing was said to be 'a bottle of claret to put the want of insurance out of your head', the shortest possible sea journey — namely the 21 miles from Portpatrick to Donaghadee — was obviously the most favoured. From the sixteenth to the nineteenth century Donaghadee was a major port that offered the only safe refuge from the treacherous reefs on this coast. In the expectation that the town would remain the mail packet station for Scotland, the harbour was greatly enlarged in 1820. It was a blow when the service was switched to the Stranraer–Larne route in 1849. Local fishermen kept an unofficial ferry service going long afterwards. On calm days they rowed people across to Scotland for £5.

At low tide, dulse-gatherers armed with small scythes go out in boats to cut at the purply fronds of this edible seaweed, *Palmaria palmata*. It is left lying on the slope at the back of the harbour, shrinking and drying in the sun. Fresh dulse turns green when fried in bacon fat. Mostly it is dried and sold in little paper bags for eating raw, a salty chew that is not to everyone's taste, but said to be so good for you that scientists at Queen's University, Belfast, are eager to establish its DNA composition. The **lighthouse** is the work of Sir John Rennie and David Logan (of Eddystone fame). The nineteenth-century castellated folly on top of a 140ft mound (the Moat) was used as a gunpowder store when the harbour was being constructed. Take the path to the top for the view.

Famous visitors landing here from Portpatrick were legion. James Boswell came in 1769, Keats came in 1818 (to walk to the Giant's Causeway but only got as far as Belfast). Daniel Defoe was acquainted with the town's hospitality, and so was Franz Liszt, who had a piano in his baggage, and was stuck here for some days in bad weather. The elderly Wordsworth made his cautious way back home via Donaghadee after a grand tour of Ireland in 1829. **Grace Neill's** Inn in High Street, now a pub, has been in business since 1611. A persistent claim on behalf of the old inn is that Peter the Great stayed there during his tour of western Europe (1697–98) to learn shipbuilding and other technical matters. It is a story Brendan Behan would certainly have heard in this atmospheric pub during his stay in the town. After World War II, the Commissioners for Irish Lights gave Behan the job of painting the lighthouse.

Biggest of the three **Copeland Islands** to the north-east is, appropriately, **Big Isle**, a mile offshore. Beyond it is **Cross**, or **Lighthouse Island** where there was once a rogue lighthouse — a beacon that burned over a ton of coal a night. It was suspected of actually contributing to some of the many wrecks in these waters. The present lighthouse, on **Mew**, the outermost island, went automatic in 1996 — the last manned lighthouse round Northern Ireland's shores. Cross Island is now an RSPB bird observatory visitable with National Trust permission. Garden herbs growing there are thought to have been part of a kitchen garden established by monks from Bangor Abbey.

On Big Isle in the eighteenth century there was a thriving fishing and farming community of 'God-fearing Presbyterians' who rowed across every Sunday to attend church in Donaghadee. By the 1860s the population had fallen to about forty but they had a church and a school. The new teacher had to sleep in the classroom (there only was one) until people got to know him. Then he lodged with each family in turn, a month at a time.

The last islanders moved to Donaghadee in the 1940s. Sheep graze Big Isle now, narcissus, roses and fuchsia grow wild and the empty houses are used by weekenders. There are swimming races across the mile-wide strait, and excursion boats from several places on the coast, including Bangor.

Windmill stumps are a familiar sight in County Down, especially around the Ards. There used to be over 100 windmills in the county. The cornmill at **Ballycopeland** is now the only windmill in working order left in the whole of Ulster. Built about 1790, it stands on a drumlin a mile inland from **Millisle** (population 1,530), an unpretentious bucket-and-spade resort of fish-and-chip shops and acres of caravan sites. Ballycopeland is a tower-type cornmill, with a movable cap turned by an automatic fantail so that the sails always face into the wind. It was used for milling oats and wheat, and for making animal feed, right up to 1915.

Pickie Fun Park, Bangor

Sailing on Strangford Lough

South from Millisle, the A2 runs along through a succession of coastal villages. At **Cloghy** it slants inland towards Portaferry. To visit the National Trust's nineteenth-century fishing village, off the beaten track at **Kearney**, with a pebbly beach and walks along the rocky shore, stay with the coast by leaving the A2 at Cloghy. Though distances here are small, the scarcity of places of refreshment on this whole stretch can be inconvenient, so plan your journey accordingly. After Kearney the road west will take you quickly to Portaferry, or continue south to the high grassy rath at **Tara Fort**, looking down over Millin Bay. From there it is 2 miles to Portaferry.

North-west of **Ballywalter** village (population 1,150) are the fragmentary ruins of medieval **Templefinn** ('white church') **parish church**. Three Norman grave slabs lie at the east gable. The home of Lady Dunleath, **Ballywalter Park** is a magnificent Italianate palazzo by Lanyon, built in the 1840s for Andrew Mulholland, a Belfast textile tycoon. It has an open day only very occasionally. Burr Point at **Ballyhalbert** (population 330) is the most easterly place in Ireland, though some say Burial Island, the islet offshore where seals bask on the reefs, ought to count as being even more easterly! **Portavogie** (population 1,500) has one of Northern Ireland's three main fishing fleets. There is a modern harbour, boat-building yards and a fish auction on the quay most evenings. Giant prawns, already peeled, are sold in the village. There is intensive farming round here and at harvest time everyone pitches in to bring in the potato crop.

A car racing circuit is a little inland, and at the north end of pebbly

Cloghy Bay, near the golf course, is **Kirkistown Castle**, built by Roland Savage in 1622. The castle is in fact a tower house, one of the fortified private homes built from the fifteenth to the early seventeenth century by local landlords — often as a protection from each other. This one has the remains of a bawn round it. The Savage family were the Norman landlords of the 'Little Ardes' and they built many of these small castles. Portaferry Castle is known to be an earlier one of theirs, erected in 1500.

Portaferry (population 2,300) has a beautiful site on the east side of the entrance to **Strangford Lough**. The long, low waterfront of cottages, terraces, pubs and small shops is best appreciated from the car ferry which takes you crabwise across the narrows to **Strangford** village in barely five minutes. It is a pity the crossing doesn't take longer since the views up the lough are worth savouring. Before the famines of the 1840s Portaferry was a busy coastal town with lively industries. Today it is a centre for yachting and sea angling — deep sea fishing outside the narrows and inshore fishing in the lough. Wreck fishing, for big conger eels and wrasse, is popular and there is a dive centre for wreck enthusiasts and underwater photographers. The lough is a great bird sanctuary and wildlife reserve. Queen's University, Belfast, has had a **marine biology station** here for the last 50 years, occupying two Georgian houses opposite the ferry slipway, and a marine aquarium, **Exploris**, is a recent attraction for tourists. The Vikings called the lough 'violent fjord' (Strangford). Four hundred million tons of water rush through the gap twice a day.

The very ruined **tower house** is a prominent feature of the town. A typical small Georgian market house sits in the middle of the sloping triangular 'square' which has some incongruous buildings round it. On the south side is a modest redbrick Orange Hall of 1870, and on the north side a fire station and an ultra-modern Roman Catholic church, St Cooey's Oratory. Two stones outside the belfry are from the ancient church of Templecowey which stood on the shore below **Tieveshilly Hill**, 3 miles south-east of Portaferry. If you go there look out for three holy wart wells under the thorn trees. Portaferry House, in parkland on the lough shore to the north, is owned by descendants of the Savages. From the stump on top of **Windmill Hill** (east of the centre) you get a good all-round view. Several small castles on the far shore are prominent landmarks.

The drumlins, small rounded hills that cover north Down, extend into the lough. Dozens of **drowned drumlins** turn up here and there, mostly near the shore. These islands give Strangford the appearance of a freshwater lake, especially at the sheltered north end. The wor drumlin, from *droim* meaning 'ridge', was coined in 1833 to describe 'low ridges of superficial debris in the North of Ireland'. There are thousands of these streamlined hillocks across the country. Many of the Strangford ones are breeding grounds for wildlife, including seals. The lough contains large tope and some really huge skate. Anglers catching one of these old and venerable creatures return it to the water after weighing. A flock of brent geese from Arctic Canada winters here, feeding on sostra grass; greylag and white-fronted geese visit from the Downpatrick marshes, and large numbers of surface-feeding ducks, like wigeon and pintails, dabble and up-end in the shallows. Many species of tern and gulls breed on the islands, there are oyster-catchers, redshanks and curlews on the mudflats, and sea hares, sun stars and curled octopus live around the shore. Predators include buzzards, sparrowhawks and short-eared owls.

Of the four Cistercian monasteries in medieval County Down, three were built round the lough — Grey Abbey, Inch Abbey and Comber. A stone in the parish church is all that is left of **Comber Abbey**. Inch (1180) and Grey Abbey (1193) have substantial remains, and there is a large stone fish trap at Grey Abbey. All three foundations had filial connections with England, and for nearly 400 years the monks carried corn, wheat, flour, fish and salt to the beleaguered English abbeys in Cumbria and Lancashire. Their boats, sixty-oar galleys, brought back Cumberland stone and iron ore.

Pause a while at **Kircubbin** (population 1,100), a boating and fishing village where you can gather clean mussels and cockles on the shore and there are always a few fishermen digging for lugworm. **Grey Abbey** ruins are further up the lough, on the edge of Greyabbey (population 700), a pleasant old post-town. Founded by Affreca, daughter of the king of Man and wife of John de Courcy, this was a daughter house of Holm Cultram in Cumbria. Affreca brought her monks from England, the usual Norman practice. The Irish Church's links with clan chiefs made it untrustworthy. The abbey was burned in 1572 but the Montgomerys later repaired the church and used it (interesting memorials) until they built a new one nearby in 1778 (above the carpark). The ruins of the abbey, in sheltered grounds with lawns and gardens, include triple lancet windows in the chancel and a fine west door, looking much like one from a late-twelfth-century English cathedral.

The National Trust property, **Mount Stewart**, on this same scenic loughside road (A20), is most famous for its lovely **gardens**, created by Edith, Lady Londonderry, from 1921, and ranked in the Trust's top six UK gardens. More historically interesting, it was the Irish home of Robert Stewart, Lord Castlereagh (1769–1822), foreign secretary of England during the Napoleonic Wars. Many treasures in the house, like the painting of Hambletonian by George Stubbs, were accumulated later but you can see some of Castlereagh's personal possessions, portraits of his political contemporaries, and objects connected with the great happenings in Europe during his brilliant career. These include the twenty-two original Empire chairs used by the plenipotentiaries at the Congress of Vienna (1814–15) which, after the defeat of Napoleon, established the 'balance of power' principle in international politics. They were brought from Vienna by the English ambassador, Castlereagh's half-brother, Charles.

Though his family was Presbyterian, Castlereagh was educated under the auspices of the established church, at the Royal School, Armagh, a prudent decision by his father since dissenters were still barred from military and civil office. Castlereagh was a model landlord. He endowed schools, built a chapel, houses for his tenants, and

The Exploris aquarium at Portaferry

a pier in front of the house for local fishing boats (aged seventeen, he survived a boating accident on the lough). He had an enigmatic and chilly personality and, despite his good works, hardly anyone seems to have liked him. As a politician, and an Irishman, who helped destroy the Irish parliament (Grattan Parliament) and who brought about the Act of Union (1801) he made himself one of the most disliked men in Irish history. Eighteen months after succeeding his father as second Marquis of Londonderry he committed suicide in mysterious circumstances.

Mount Stewart includes almost every style of gardening, and some of the inspiration of Gertrude Jekyll. Lady Londonderry, who had snake tattoes on her legs, introduced the stone figures of dodos, dinosaurs, griffins, platypuses and other mythological creatures which are dotted about the terraces. An Irish harp is among the garden's imaginative topiary art. **Special gardens** include a Spanish garden, Italian garden, sunken garden and a paved shamrock garden surrounding a 'Red Hand' of Ulster, planted seasonally with double red daisies, salvias and begonias. An octagonal garden building, the **Temple of the Winds**, was designed by 'Athenian' Stuart (1780). It has a spiral staircase and great views over Strangford Lough.

North-east of Mount Stewart, in the churchyard at **Carrowdore**, is the grave of the poet Louis MacNeice (1907–63). The wide main street

The ferry to Strangford village runs every 30 minutes

of the village (population 550) is closed off in September for a motorcycle race. The Northern Irish have a penchant for racing on their public roads. Apart from major occasions, like the Circuit of Ireland car rally, the Ulster Grand Prix motorcycle race and other big events, there are half a dozen small motorcycle races like the one at Carrowdore. The road surfaces in the host towns are said to be especially well maintained.

The west shore of Strangford, south of Comber, is a mass of small islands, submerged drumlins. A little beyond the waterfowl gardens of **Castle Espie** look out for the signposts to **Nendrum**. This primitive monastic site is on **Mahee Island** at the end of a twisting causeway linking several of the larger islands together. St Mochaoi was its fifth-century founder-abbot. Three concentric stone walls (cashels) on top of the hill were excavated and restored in the 1920s. A small on-site **museum** gives a good idea of life in a tenth-century Irish monastery. The inner wall contains a ruined church with an unusual sundial, a round tower stump and a graveyard; the second ring has the foundations of a rectangular schoolhouse and several little circular workshops. One was a smithy, another a pottery. The twelfth-century chancel in the church was built by Benedictine monks, brought from Cumbria by John de Courcy. You can leave your car at Nendrum carpark and walk back along the road to inspect a fifteenth-century ruined tower house, **Captain Browne's Castle**, at the west end of the island. The water level has changed since the days when the owners kept their boat locked up in a bay on the ground floor.

South of here, on **Sketrick Island**, the scanty ruins of a much bigger tower house also has a secure boat bay. The main reason for going to Sketrick, however, is the admirably sited pub–restaurant behind the castle — and the **Hen Island** race, a quaint competition in October when a fleet of oil drums, crates and home-made rafts are paddled between Sketrick and tiny Hen Island.

Going south on the A22 to **Killyleagh** (population 2,200) a startling skyline of romantic turrets comes into view just before the village. **Killyleagh Castle**, home of the Hamilton family since the seventeenth-century plantation, acquired its fairytale silhouette in the 1850s when the turrets were added, but it is mostly the same castle that the second Earl of Clanbrassil rebuilt in 1666. In a lurid intrigue over ownership, involving a wicked wife and a secretly burnt will, the earl was poisoned in 1675. One of the towers is Norman. The castle has a massive fortified outer wall (bawn) and a Victorian gatehouse. You can stay in it, self-catering. The grounds make a spectacular venue for open-air concerts in summer. A large stone at the gatehouse commemorates Killyleagh's most famous son, Sir Hans Sloane (1660–1753), physician to George II and founder of the British Museum.

Sloane was a native of Killyleagh and, encouraged by the ill-fated second earl, educated himself in the castle library. His collection of 50,000 books, 3,560 manuscripts and cabinet of curiosities was the nucleus of the British Museum. Sloane settled in Chelsea in 1712. He gave his name to a Circle Line station on the London Underground as well as to Sloane Square and Hans Place.

The whole of the **Lecale** region between Strangford and **Dundrum Bay** has associations with the patron saint of Ireland and is often called **St Patrick's Country**. By taking the ferry from Portaferry you approach the area by water — as Patrick did. The road to Downpatrick has a number of sites connected with the saint. However, there are other places of interest on the route, not least Strangford village. The **tower house** that overlooks the small double harbour and ferry landing in **Strangford** (population 550) shared with Portaferry Castle the task of controlling traffic between the two shores and sea traffic through the narrows. South of the village is an early 'gatehouse' tower house, **Kilclief Castle**, which was the summer home of John Cely, Bishop of Down from 1413 until he was sacked in 1443 for living adulterously in the castle with one Lettice Savage, a married woman. No such colourful story attaches to three other **tower houses** nearby — **Walshestown** (sixteenth-century), **Audley's** (fifteenth-century), and **Old Castle Ward** (late sixteenth-century) standing in the farmyard on the National Trust estate of Castle Ward. There are more tower houses down the coast at Ardglass.

The designer of **Castle Ward** is unknown. Whoever he was, he did as he was told. The house was built after 1762 by Bernard Ward, later the first Lord Bangor, and his wife Anne, daughter of Lord Darnley. Ward favoured the Palladian style of architecture, Lady Anne preferred the Strawberry Hill Gothic which was fashionable at the time. The result is a compromise. The **entrance front** is in the classical idiom, with a pillared pedimented portico, and the **garden front** facing Strangford Lough is gothic, with seven bays of pointed windows and urns on the battlements. Inside, each style keeps strictly to its own side of the house — the exception being the classical staircase, in the middle. Mr Ward got that. His rooms have Doric columns and restrained panelling, hers have quatrefoils, pointed doorways and amazing plaster fan vaulting in the boudoir. The **stable yard** contains a Victorian laundry and a converted barn for concerts and opera. A saw mill, cornmill and slaughterhouse are among stone buildings in the pleasant farmyard. Landscaped in the eighteenth century, the

Lady Anne's Boudoir,
Castle Ward

Mount Stewart
Gardens are a fine
example of 1920s
garden design

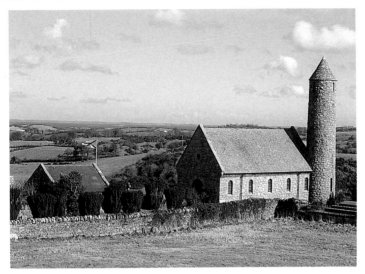

The church at Saul, built on the reputed site of St Patrick's first abbey

demesne has a classical temple/summer house, a wildfowl collection, sunken garden and, down by the lough, a bird hide. The Wards continued not seeing eye to eye and later separated.

St Patrick was probably born in Scotland or Wales, the son of a Roman centurion, and was taken to Ulster as a boy slave. He escaped and returned to preach the gospel after years of studying with Martin of Tours in Gaul. The Slaney river where he is said to have landed in the fifth century is now a stream near the townland of **Ringbane** north of Saul. The chieftain of Lecale at that time was Dichu who was apparently quickly converted and gave Patrick a barn (*sabhall* in Gaelic, pronounced 'saul') for holding services. In the 30 years up to 461 when he died in the abbey at Saul, he preached throughout Ulster and is said to have travelled over the whole country, converting the Irish. According to the eighth-century 'Hymn of St Fiacc', St Patrick received his last communion from St Tassach. The slight ruins of **St Tassach's church**, one of Ireland's earliest Christian buildings, are behind a row of houses at **Raholp** (townland) on the A25. Footpaths signposted **St Patrick's Way** link St Tassach's, Slieve Patrick, Saul and other places associated with the saint. (Pubs at Raholp and Saul are convenient for parking the car.)

At **Saul** itself, a Celtic-revival-style Anglican church (with a round tower adjoining the chancel) on the site of an important twelfth-century monastery is where St Patrick's abbey is thought to have been. In the churchyard is an early Christian mortuary house. Built in

1932 by the Church of Ireland to commemorate the fifteenth centenary of the saint's landfall, the church contains a thirteenth-century
font basin and a small, informative permanent exhibition. The statue
of St Patrick, prominent on **Slieve Patrick**, a high hill across the
valley, was designed by Francis Doyle-Jones for the Roman Catholic
Church. It too was erected in 1932. A 10-minute walk up to the statue
to examine the bronze panels round the base has the bonus of a fine
view over Strangford's islands.

According to the precious Book of Armagh (AD802), now in Trinity
College Library, Dublin, Patrick is buried on the great hill at
Downpatrick. The reputed **St Patrick's Grave** near the site of an old
round tower in the churchyard of Down cathedral is a place of
pilgrimage. So much earth was scooped up from the grave and
carried away that a granite monolith was placed over the top in 1901
to protect it. Pilgrims strew daffodils on the stone on St Patrick's Day
(17 March). John de Courcy claimed to have dug up the remains of
Ireland's other two great saints, Columba (died Iona 597) and Brigid
(died Kildare 523), and to have put them in St Patrick's grave.

Downpatrick (population 10,250) takes its name from the dun
(fort) where a sixth-century monastery, an Augustinian church, a
Benedictine church and several versions of Down cathedral, were
built — not to be confused with the other great earthworks called the
Mound of Down on the edge of the Quoile marshes. The strong
association with St Patrick brought many medieval religious orders
to Downpatrick and the monasteries established here grew into the
regional capital which, by extension, gave its name to County Down.

As was the norm in Ulster, the **cathedral** was pillaged, burnt and
rebuilt on several occasions. An earthquake damaged it in 1245, and
in 1538 Lord Deputy Grey used it as stables — a sacrilege that counted
towards his execution not long afterwards. The chancel was restored
1790–1818 and a tower added in 1829. The interior has a tall elegant
Georgian organ case. The organ was given to the cathedral in 1802 by
George III. Some of the carved capitals are fourteenth- or fifteenth-
century, others are eighteenth-century restorations. The coats of arms
of the county's leading families, post-plantation, are ranged round the
upper walls. There is a slab in the porch to the governor of Lecale,
Lord Edward Cromwell, and his grandson Oliver Cromwell. These
Cromwells, ennobled to the Earls of Ardglass, were direct descendants of Thomas Cromwell, secretary to Henry VIII and chief architect
of the dissolution of the monasteries. The Lecale Cromwells were
Royalists. Oliver Cromwell, the Lord Protector of England, was
distantly related to Secretary Cromwell.

Outside the cathedral a worn tenth-century **high cross** faces into

English Street which runs down the hill to meet Scotch Street and Irish Street at the bottom. This enclosed and hilly town has some interesting Georgian buildings. In English Street the former county gaol, built 1789–96, houses **Down County Museum** which has a section devoted to St Patrick. It also contains the prison governor's house and a three-storey cell block where convicts were held before transportation. The museum is interesting for Australians who think they may have a convict ancestor from Ulster. Without one, it is said, you are hardly a dinky-di Australian! Troops were billeted here in both World Wars. The United Irishman Thomas Russell, who survived the 1798 uprising but was implicated in the Emmet conspiracy in 1803, was hanged at the entrance gate. The inscribed stone over his grave, in the churchyard of the **parish church** (1737) lower down the street, was put there by Mary Ann McCracken.

Up the side street next to the museum, the 'new' gaol, opened in 1835, has a very imposing gatehouse. It was last used in 1891. The redbrick alms house and school of the **Southwell Charity** opposite the museum was established in 1733 to support six old men and six old women and to educate ten poor boys and ten poor girls. Now used as flats for elderly people, the buildings are rather spoilt by the high level of the road, raised 15ft in 1790. **Denvir's Hotel** (1642) at the bottom of English Street had a sanctuary for debtors in the back yard and also in the recess at the front. Creditors had to wait outside. One Georgian building is now used as club rooms by the Downe Hunt, the oldest hunt club in the British Isles. The T-shaped Non-subscribing **Presbyterian church** of 1710, **Stream Street**, has preserved intact its original pews and high pulpit.

North of Downpatrick the ruins of **Inch Abbey** overlook the Quoile river. There was a monastery here in AD800. It was plundered in 1001 by Vikings, destroyed again in 1149 and founded as a Cistercian abbey by John de Courcy in 1180. The whole of the foundations have been excavated. The most striking feature still standing is the tall triple east window. Traces of a hospital and a bakery, with a well, lie between the church and the river. It is a lovely position, within sight of the cathedral and the Mound of Down. A nature reserve runs along the river banks from **Quoile Bridge** to the flood-control barrage. Built in 1957, the barrage has artificially converted the saltwater estuary to a slow-moving freshwater lake which has resulted in some unusually rich colonisations by insects, fish and vegetation.

Taking the Ardglass road (B1) south from the town, past the enormous red-and-yellow hospital (1834), **Struell Wells** is signposted. The miraculous healing powers of the water in this rocky valley, where yellow whin grows in ridges, were first mentioned in written records of 1306. The wells are built along the course of an underground stream. The roofed **men's bath house** has an anteroom with seats and a sunken bath. The **women's house**, a bit smaller and minus its roof, is near a large sycamore tree. There is a **drinking well** and, in the centre of the enclosure, an **eye well** with a pyramid roof. Pilgrims carry the magic away in bottles.

West of Struell on the Ballyhornan road the acres of concrete at the old RAF base of **Bishopscourt** have been converted to a motorcycle race track, attracting large and enthusiastic crowds. The usually quiet village of **Ballyhornan** — it can be rowdy at holiday times — faces **Guns Island**, which you can get to at low tide. Rare seaside and lime-loving plants, including orchids, grow in the **nature reserve** at **Killard Point** north of the village. To the south, on the A2, the little

St Patrick's Grave in the cathedral churchyard at Downpatrick

Chapeltown Roman Catholic church of 1791 has a life-size pre-Reformation stone statue of the Virgin and Child in a niche in the east gable.

Ardglass (population 1,650) was once the busiest seaport in Ulster. You can catch codling, pollack and coalfish off the quay at the deep double harbour, and the town is still an important fishing port, now with a new marina at **Phennick Cove**. Built on a hill — the name means 'green hill' — Ardglass is full of interesting perspectives and surprising panoramic views. What is most striking is the way castles pop up everywhere. Between the fifteenth and sixteenth century a ring of tower houses and fortified warehouses was built to protect the harbour. **Jordan's Castle** (fifteenth-century) in the middle of the town was besieged in about 1600 but held out for three years. It was bought and repaired in 1911 by a Belfast solicitor, F. J. Bigger, who filled it with antiques and left it to the government in his will. In summer you can inspect this well-preserved four-storey tower house from the inside. It was Mr Bigger who put the stone over St Patrick's Grave in Downpatrick. A curious row of fortified warehouses, now used as a golf clubhouse, has a tiny tower house (Cowd Castle) at the end. Other well-kept fortified buildings include a circular battlemented tower on top of a small tower house (No 7, Green Road) and two early-nineteenth-century castellated structures, Isabella's Tower and King's Castle.

Killough (population 800) is a quiet backwater. The main street, unbroken façades of single- and two-storey early Victorian houses, is lined with tall sycamore trees. The village has a pretty parish church on the wall of the silted-up harbour and almshouses built by Lanyon, Lynn & Lanyon in 1868. There is little work here, since the brickworks closed. You could park past the windmill stump near the coastguard station, and walk to **St John's Point** along a rather rough coastal path. Alternatively, drive to the point, where there is a **lighthouse** and a ruined **tenth-century church** and afterwards walk towards the beaches of Minerstown and Tyrella Strand along the edge of Dundrum Bay for ever-improving views of the Mournes.

ADDITIONAL INFORMATION

PLACES TO VISIT

ARDGLASS

Jordan's Castle
Open July and August daily except
Monday and Sunday morning.

BANGOR

North Down Heritage Centre
Bangor Castle, Castle Park Avenue.
☎ (01247) 271200. Open Tuesday–
Saturday 10.30am–4.30pm, Sunday
2–4.30pm, also Mondays in high
summer.

COMBER

Castle Espie
Wildfowl & Wetlands Trust.
☎ (01247) 874146. Open daily
10.30am–5pm (from 11.30am
Sunday).

Nendrum Museum
Mahee Island. Open all year
Tuesday–Saturday 10am–4pm
and Sunday afternoon. Closes
7pm April–September.

CULTRA

Ulster Folk & Transport Museum
☎ (01232) 428428. Open all year
Monday–Saturday long hours,
plus Sunday afternoon.

DOWNPATRICK

Inch Abbey Ruins
Always accessible.

Holy Wells
Struell — 1½ miles east of town
off B1. Always accessible.

Saul Church
Site of St Patrick's first abbey.
Open daily.

Quoile Countryside Centre
National nature reserve off A25
1½ miles north of Downpatrick.
☎ (01396) 615520. Open April–
September 11am–5pm daily, and
weekend afternoons in winter.

Down County Museum
☎ (01396) 615218. Open most
weekdays plus bank holidays and
weekend afternoons. Town trails
available.

St Patrick's Grave
In cathedral old graveyard.
Always accessible.

GREY ABBEY

Abbey Ruins
Open Tuesday–Saturday 10am–
7pm, Sunday 2–7pm. Physick
garden and visitor centre not open
in winter.

GROOMSPORT

Cockle Row
☎ (01247) 458882. Open weekends
in May and every afternoon in June.
Visitor information, crafts.

MILLISLE

Ballycopeland Windmill
☎ (01247) 861413. Open April–
September Tuesday–Saturday
10am–7pm, Sunday 2–7pm. To visit
out of season: ☎ (01232) 543033.

NEWTOWNARDS

Mount Stewart (NT)
☎ (012477) 88387/88487
Gardens open daily 11am–6pm
April–September plus some
weekend afternoons in March and
October. House open May–
September daily 1–6pm except
Tuesday, plus weekends in April
and October. Shorter hours for
Temple.

Somme Heritage Centre
233 Bangor Road. ☎ (01247) 823202.
Open Monday–Thursday 10am–
4pm, plus weekend afternoons
April–September, and Friday in
high summer.

Scrabo Tower
☎ (01247) 811491. Signposted from Newtownards town centre. Open June–September 11am–6.30pm daily except Friday, and by arrangement. Country park always open.

PORTAFERRY

The car ferry — ☎ (01396) 881637 — between Strangford village and Portaferry runs every 30 minutes daily all year except Christmas Day. Last ferry from Portaferry 10.45pm (11.15pm Saturday). Last ferry from Strangford 10.30pm (11pm Saturday).

Exploris Aquarium
☎ (012477) 28062. Open Monday–Friday 10am–6pm, from 11am on Saturday and from 1pm Sunday. Closes at 5pm in winter.

STRANGFORD

Castle Ward (NT)
☎ (01396) 881204 . House 1–6pm April–October weekends, also weekdays (except Thursday) May–August.

EVENTS

Bangor

Yacht racing (July)

Cultra

Year-round events programme at Ulster Folk & Transport Museum. ☎ (01232) 428428 for details.

Downpatrick

Jameson Ulster National (early March) Steeplechase.

St Patrick's Day (17 March) Pilgrimage, parades.

Horse Trials (late April)

Motorcycle racing (early October) Bishopscourt.

Killyleagh

Open-air concerts (early May)

Portaferry

Regatta (late June) Galway hookers and other traditional Irish sailing boats.

Sketrick Island

Hen Island Boat Race (October) All craft are home-made.

TOURIST INFORMATION CENTRES

Bangor

34 Quay Street. ☎ (01247) 270069. Open all year Mon–Fri 9am–5pm, Sat 10.30am–4pm, longer hours in summer plus Sunday afternoon.

Downpatrick

74 Market Street. ☎ (01396) 612233. Open all year Mon–Sat 9am–5pm, longer hours in summer plus Sunday afternoon.

Newtownards

31 Regent Street. ☎ (01247) 826846. Open all year Mon–Sat 9.30am–5pm.

Portaferry

The Stables, Castle Street. ☎ (012477) 29882. Open Easter–Sept Mon–Sat 10am–5pm and Sunday afternoon.

Rowallane Gardens, near Saintfield

3

THE MOURNES &
MID-DOWN

Deciding which way to drive through the **Mournes** can present something of a dilemma since they are beautiful from every direction. The ancient Kingdom of Mourne, isolated but well populated, is hidden away behind the bare eastern summits which, from the north, appear as an unbroken line of steep and shapely hills. South

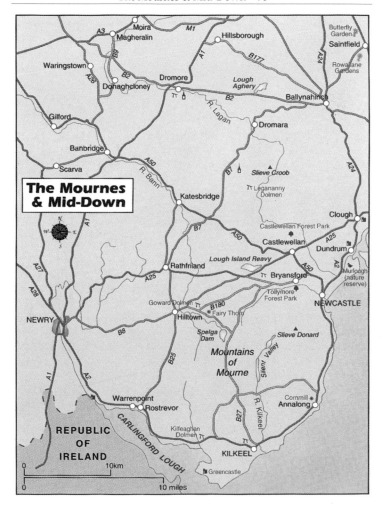

Down is dominated by these much painted, much walked mountains and whichever route you take south from Belfast, there they are, in front of you. The melody and words 'Where the Mountains of Mourne sweep down to the sea' of the popular song have made the Mournes the best- known mountains in Ireland. In this compact range, 15 miles long and 8 miles wide, only a dozen of the sixty or so individual summits rise above 2,000ft, with **Slieve Donard**, at 2,796ft, the highest peak in Ulster.

Saintfield (population 2,150) was the scene of the first of two County Down battles in the 1798 rebellion. The local Presbyterian minister, the Rev T. L. Birch, was active in the United Irishmen Society, founded in Belfast in 1791 to win religious equality and parliamentary reform, and he established a branch in the town. The rebels managed to hold Saintfield for a few days but were defeated at Ballynahinch soon afterwards. The long grassy graveyard of Mr Birch's church contains the headstones of his slain parishioners and a memorial plaque (**First Presbyterian church, Main Street**). Many residents now commute by car to offices in Belfast. The old railway station (closed 1950) has been preserved.

A mile south, **Rowallane** is well known for its tremendous show of rhododendrons and azaleas. The big house on the estate, now the National Trust's headquarters in Northern Ireland, was inherited in 1903 by Hugh Armitage Moore, a distinguished plantsman who spent the next half-century creating and working in the 50-acre garden. Two hundred feet above sea level, the garden is encircled by a windbreak of Australian laurels, hollies, pines and beech trees growing in the thin layer of soil covering the little glacial hills — drumlins — of County Down. The spectacular massed plantings of rhododendrons flourish in the light acid soil, sharp drainage, gentle rain and even temperature. Plants in the **walled gardens** include rare primulas, blue Himalayan poppies (mecanopsis), plantain lilies (hostas), roses, magnolias and autumn crocuses (colchinums). There is a big handkerchief tree 50ft across, many viburnums and chaenomeles, and a natural rock garden fringed with more mecanopsis. The estate has attractive stone farm buildings.

The wide streets of **Ballynahinch** (population 5,200) were laid out in about 1640 by the Earls of Moira, whose former seat, Montalto, is to the south. From the stump on Windmill Hill you can see across the valley to the wooded demesne of Montalto. The last and biggest battle of the United Irishmen's rebellion was fought in this valley. If the rebels had taken Ballynahinch, right in the middle of the county, their strategic advantage would have been considerable. As it turned out, the rebel force of some 7,000 men was driven back to **Slieve Croob** mountain, south-west of the town, and the battle was lost. A handful of the leaders were executed, including the Lisburn linen draper Henry Munro, and Henry Joy McCracken who had been defeated at the Battle of Antrim a few days earlier. The rest of the survivors were pardoned and went home. Lord Kelvin's father, Dr James Thomson, was in the rebel camp on the night before the battle and described it in the *Belfast Magazine* years later (1825). The ghostly face of Betsy Gray, a young girl shot for riding out to join the rebels, gazes from a large **mural** near the central carpark.

Like Saintfield, this town was badly damaged in 1798 and at

various times since. St Patrick's church (Catholic, 1843) has an interesting classical interior, with a baptistry under the gallery stairs and rich Victorian stained glass. The rear of the nearby parish church of 1772 looks on to the river valley and the Montalto woods. Harris's cornmill near the bridge on the Newcastle road grinds corn and barley for animal feed. The large waterwheel, made in 1816, is powered by the Ballynahinch river.

At **Spa** crossroads (on the B175) are the buildings of the once fashionable spa, popular from about 1770. The old assembly rooms, formal gardens (laid out as a maze) and chalybeate water springs went out of style at the outbreak of war in 1914. **Seaforde Nursery**, a mile north of Clough on the A24, has a well-kept hornbeam maze though the main attraction is the **butterfly house**.

Signposted off the A24, 4 miles south of Ballynahinch, are the three little ruined **churches of Loughinisland** — the island lake (now reached by a causeway). The oldest of the three is thirteenth century. This beautiful spot was a burying place of the MacCartans who had a stronghold nearby. The doorhead of the smallest church is carved with the initials PMC, for Phelim MacCartan, and the date 1636 — a time when it was unlawful to build Catholic churches. The authorities may have felt able to overlook so small a church.

Clough Castle, a few yards off the A24/A25 crossroads, is a good example of a motte and bailey castle, built during the early phase of the Anglo-Norman conquest of Ireland. The stone keep on top of the big hill is late-thirteenth-century. To appreciate mottes and baileys you have to concentrate on the grassy mounds, even when the stone buildings on top look rather more interesting. The motte, a flat-topped artificial earthwork with a ditch round it, had a lower level enclosure (bailey) as the first line of defence. The bailey at Clough is a kidney-shaped mound. If the castle came under attack, those on the motte could isolate themselves from the bailey by pulling away the ladder bridging the ditch. A hail of arrows from the wooden palisade on top of the motte would, with luck, see off unwelcome visitors.

These motte and bailey castles were the first things the Normans built in Ireland. There are about forty in County Down alone, and County Antrim has almost twice as many. The early Normans made rather little impact on the Mournes, though there is a strategic motte at Hilltown, one of a string of mottes from Belfast down to the Crown Mound near Newry. On the A1 south of Lisburn **Duneight motte** is signposted, and 6 miles on, at **Dromore**, is a very impressive **motte** with an oblong bailey. Most mottes were only about 60ft across, cramped and uncomfortable places to live, and the Normans soon abandoned them and moved into decent stone castles like Dundrum,

Dundrum Castle

3 miles down the road.

Up a steep turning off the A2 and surrounded by tall trees, ruined **Dundrum Castle** stands on a rock above Dundrum inner bay. King John captured it in 1210, the Magennises occupied it in the fourteenth century, and Cromwell's troops damaged it in 1652. The massive

circular keep has a spiral staircase and two latrines are built into the curtain wall. It is one of a line of castles that controlled this coast from Greencastle, on Carlingford Lough, to Carrickfergus. Communications between them were usually by sea. Shelduck nest in old rabbit burrows down around the bay, and there are long-tailed ducks and red-throated divers. The birds, and the seals sunning themselves on the point, seem unperturbed by the popping from a nearby army rifle-range across the narrow channel at Ballykinler. About 1½ miles beyond Dundrum village, turn inland at a small carpark and toilets, and over a stone bridge to see the handsome **Slidderyford dolmen** in a field on the left. Returning to the A2 you reach the sand dunes of **Murlough nature reserve** (National Trust) after 200yd. The Normans farmed the dunes as a rabbit warren, and warrening (for meat and skins) was an important local trade for centuries. There is an interesting interpretive centre near the carpark.

Approached from Dundrum, the resort of **Newcastle** (population 7,200) seems quite spacious, with a curved raised beach. At the south end it squeezes on to a ledge up against the mountain, with room for the road and not much else. The caravan sites are all at the wide end, invisible from the long promenade that stretches from an outsize redbrick Victorian hotel (appropriately named after the province's biggest mountain) round to the harbour bars and yacht club yard. The blue mountains are a backcloth to a raised beach where horse-riders come for a morning canter on the sands. Songwriter Percy French (1854–1920) celebrated Newcastle 'where the Mountains of Mourne sweep down to the sea' and the grateful town built him a **memorial fountain** in the promenade gardens.

A large **inscribed stone** in the promenade wall near the warm seawater pool commemorates Harry Ferguson's flight in a home-made monoplane along the beach in 1910. The town gave him £100 as a reward. Ferguson was the inventor of the four-wheel drive system, and he sued the Ford Motor Company for $250 million for infringing patents for his most famous invention, the modern tractor.

The most distinctive building in the town, a 1960s Roman Catholic church with a green copper parasol roof, is visible from far off. At the south end of the promenade an odd Victorian cottage with a drinking fountain in front is the Annesley estate office. **Donard Park**, behind the town, tends to be overshadowed by the proximity of the forest park of Tollymore but it has fine walks from the capacious carpark up the tumbling Glen river. The championship courses of the Royal County Down golf club are at the north end of town. Evening entertainment and plenty of restaurants help make this a lively place.

Visitors to **Castlewellan** (population 2,250) are mostly heading for one or other of the two forest parks nearby but this agreeable market town deserves more than a passing glance. It has **two squares, two market houses** and **two attractive churches**. Like other villages in the Mournes, it had been a stronghold of the Magennis clan dispossessed in 1642. In 1741 it was bought by William Annesley, descendant of an Elizabethan army captain, the same Annesley who purchased Newcastle a few years later. He laid out Castlewellan to a spacious street plan on a ridge near his demesne. The market house-cum-courthouse was built in 1764 but its church-like tower with a large clock face was added later. Tall St Malachy's church (Roman Catholic,1884) is close to the other market house. The Annesleys had their own private entrance to St Paul's, the early Victorian Anglican church, and their own large pew — out of sight of the congregation.

Many prehistoric and early Christian monuments in the Mournes have vanished in extensive quarrying, but there are still numerous stone-walled cashels in these rocky uplands including, near Lough Island Reavy at **Drumena**, a well-preserved oval-shaped one with a souterrain you can go inside (signposted off the A25 to Rathfriland, 2 miles south-west of Castlewellan). Dressed Mourne granite has been exported since the late eighteenth century, and the granite base of the Albert Memorial in London's Hyde Park came from a quarry west of Castlewellan.

The outstanding feature of **Castlewellan Forest Park** is the **national arboretum** dating from 1740, and developed in the 1870s by the fifth Earl of Annesley. The present arboretum is ten times the size of the old walled garden but the original south-sloping Annesley garden with two ancient Wellingtonias at the entrance remains the showpiece. The largest of three greenhouses, about 100ft long, has aquatic plants growing in ponds and a collection of small tropical birds flying around freely inside. There is a spring garden, rhododendron wood, dwarf conifer beds and, along the edge of Castlewellan lake, a wood planted for autumn colour. Visitors using the carpark at the end of an avenue of tall limes (café and shop adjacent) will see a range of early-eighteenth-century stable and farm buildings with three courtyards and a dovecote. A **3-mile trail** round the lake passes various modern sculptures, including one conveniently shaped like a chair ('Arboreal Throne') which you can sit on!

Tollymore, the province's first forest park (opened 1955) belonged first to a Magennis and passed by inheritance to the Earls of Roden in 1798. The Roden mansion has been demolished but the demesne is celebrated for its follies, gateways and bridges. The main entrance, **Barbican Gate**, with chunky round castellated turrets and quatrefoil loopholes, and **Bryansford Gate** (the exit), with a gothic arch, pinnacles and flying buttresses, well reflect the extravagant follies inside. These include a gateway with stone acorns and strange bobbles like buns (or baps) on top, a pair of immense gate pillars with spires and baps, a melancholy grotto or hermitage, and at least eight handsome bridges, some studded with large stone bobbles, over streams and close to waterfalls. An **information centre** and café are housed in what looks like a gothic church but is actually a barn. Himalayan cedars, a 100ft Wellingtonia, a Monterey pine, silver firs and beeches are among outstanding trees. Most of the modern timber forests (conifers) are away on the other side of the river. The Mournes mountain rescue service operates from a log-cabined mountain centre on the Hilltown road.

Tollymore is a convenient departure point for walks into the heart of the Mournes, and there are marked paths to follow. The footpath west joins up with the **Hare's Gap**, the path south-west follows the course of the Spinkwee river up to Slievenaglogh and the Diamond Rocks. Up here you can see not diamonds but smoky quartz and black mica crystals in cavities in the granite. Topaz, beryl and tourmaline are said to have been found hereabouts. Silver jewellery set with semi-precious Mourne stones, and ornaments made from polished granite, are sold in Kilkeel.

The coast from Newcastle south to Greencastle was notorious for smuggling and still has many coastguard lookout points. Whenever it paid, especially in the eighteenth and early nineteenth century, wines and spirits, tobacco, tea, silk and soap were brought across from the Isle of Man in small boats, landed at lonely beaches and carried on ponies through the mountains along the **Brandy Pad**, an old smugglers' trail, to Hilltown in the western foothills, the main distribution centre.

The **Kingdom of Mourne** has very precise limits, clearly marked on the three main roads through it. It comprises the southern uplands and the coastal plain of south-facing farms with potato fields enclosed in dry-stone walls, centred on the market town and fishing port of Kilkeel. One 'welcome' sign is up on the B27 from Kilkeel towards Hilltown, another is at Cassy Water on the A2 5 miles west of Kilkeel. A third sign is 2 miles south of Newcastle, before Maggie's Leap, where the A2 turns in slightly. St Patrick is said not to have ventured beyond a small stream here. The task of making Christians out of the men of Mourne was left to St Donard (died 506) who lived inside a stone cell on top of the mountain now named after him. **Bloody Bridge** carpark, just inside the kingdom boundary, is a convenient place from which to climb Slieve Donard, although not the most attractive because of quarrying. Scene of a massacre by the

The Mountains of Mourne from near Dundrum

Magennises in 1641, Bloody Bridge is where the Brandy Pad begins, running up the side of the river.

The water authority allows vehicle access to the south end of the **Silent Valley** reservoir, two artificial lakes which supply Belfast with 30 million gallons of 'soft' water a day — Belfast's kettles never need descaling. Erosion damage by thousands of pounding boots ended the annual Mourne Wall Walk which used to bring walkers from far afield every June to walk the length of the **22-mile wall** surrounding the reservoir. This huge wall of rough stone 5ft high runs up and down fifteen mountains and provided work for unemployed men in the Mournes from 1910 to 1922 every spring and summer. While the

Walking in the Mountains of Mourne

reservoir was being built (1923–33) a temporary rail link with Annalong brought cement up the mountain. Quickest access is up the B27 from Kilkeel — after 4 miles go right, up Head Road (1.7 miles) to the Water Commissioners' big red gates (open 10am–6.30pm). (Note: entering Kilkeel from the Annalong direction turn right just before the traffic lights.)

An exhilarating walk hereabouts is to the top of **Slieve Muck** (2,198ft) starting from the small carpark at the B27/Attical Road junction. Walk north for 2 miles until you hit the Mourne Wall and stay with it up the slope to the summit. The views are lovely.

The road into the pretty fishing village of **Annalong** (population 1,950) is lined with dull modern houses. Turn down quickly to the marine park and harbour where a cornmill is working away at the river mouth. The panoramic backdrop of craggy **Slieve Binnian** with a patchwork of small fields running up the mountain slopes appears in hundreds of landscape paintings. The main stone-working district was above Annalong and the picturesque harbour was enlarged in the 1880s to cope with increased granite exports. The large stone-coasters that crowded out the fishing boats have gone and there is more than enough room now for the few inshore herring skiffs. A stone-dressing yard, navigation mark with a stone bobble, fisher-men's cottages with flowery gardens and a friendly hostelry serving fresh fish are all part of the harbour scene. Across the bridge, the restored cornmill is powered by a waterwheel and a 1920s Marshall 'hot-bulb' engine. Behind the visitor centre is a herb garden. A good way to climb Binnian is to walk up the west side of the Annalong river.

Going south through **Ballymartin** (population 470) it is easy to miss the small beach well below road level. Black Rock at Point Sands is a popular diving spot. Approaching Kilkeel on the east side, there is an 8ft-high dolmen, called the **Crawtree Stone** (on a private road). The harbour at **Kilkeel** (population 6,100), bustling country town with the province's largest fleet, is busiest during landings and at auction time when fish, including herring, is sold on the quay. There are fish-processing factories around the port, pleasure angling off the piers and miles of lobster pots along the coast. The town has winding streets, terraced shops and houses with stepped pavements, and a bend in the middle round the ruins of the **Old Church**, a fifteenth-century church with a sixth-century predecessor from which the town took its name — *Cill Caol* ('church at the narrows'). The Church of Ireland moved to a new church in 1818 and the Old Church became a Free School, for all denominations. The water in the granite bullaun (hollowed stone) in the churchyard will only cure a wart if you first drop a pin in it.

The megalithic tomb of **Dunnaman**, a court grave with a long gallery, is at **Massforth** on the A2 west of Kilkeel, just inside the speed limit, behind **St Colman's church**. An unobtrusive sign on the parochial house indicates the path between clipped hedges. St Colman's is typical of the huge nineteenth-century Roman Catholic churches with acres of adjacent carparking which occupy sites on the edge of towns or out in the country miles from anywhere. Designed by O'Neill and Byrne of Belfast, St Colman's serves the people of Upper Mourne. It needed to be big since, when it opened in 1879, it had 5,000 parishioners. From 1540 when the Catholic priests who controlled the Old Church in Kilkeel were expelled, until the relaxation of the penal code in the 1770s, the Catholic clergy ministered to their flocks in private houses or out in the open at mass rocks. Even in the mid-nineteenth century there were so few Catholic churches in Ireland that an average congregation was 3,000. The Presbyterians and other nonconformists had also been subject to the penal laws though to a lesser extent, and they too had few churches — one for every 1,500 Presbyterians in 1834. However, all of them have made up for lost time since. St Colman's is gothic squared granite. The pinnacles were added in 1910. The T-shaped interior has rich stained glass with stations of the cross by Mayer of Munich. The church at **Attical** (population 130) in the mountains is its small sister (1890).

About 3½ miles west of Kilkeel **Kilfeaghan dolmen**, clearly signposted off the A2, is at the end of a half-mile single track, with parking near a bed-and-breakfast sign. The dolmen has a gigantic capstone weighing 35 tons. Access is beyond the round gate pillars through small gates in the dry-stone walls.

The ruined royal fortress of **Greencastle**, with a formidable jagged rock-cut ditch, looks across narrows to another Norman pile guarding the opposite shore of **Carlingford Lough**. After 1495 the same constable (who had to be an Englishman) controlled both castles. Unlike Carlingford, Greencastle village was never much more than a hamlet of scattered farms, though it had a famous Ram Fair until about 1880. The remains of a medieval church are in a field between the massive ruins and a motte behind the coastguard station. The views are worth the short run from Kilkeel (4 miles). There are bird sanctuaries on the islands off **Cranfield Point** which has dunes and a sandy beach where the water is said to be the least cold in Ulster.

Staying with the B27 from Kilkeel, the road runs close to **Pigeon Rock Mountain**, where there is a popular rock climb called The Thing. Tors on Hen Mountain at Kinnahalla also attract rock climbers. Stop for the view at the carpark above the **Spelga Dam**, which supplies water to Banbridge and Craigavon and has good trout fishing.

One mile west of Kinnahalla, a few yards from the road at **Bush Town**, is the **largest fairy thorn** in Ulster, an ancient sprawling tree immune from the axe. Farmers are careful to plough round sacred thorns, a familiar feature of the Irish countryside, standing alone in potato fields. To cut one down invariably brings bad luck, and they are a potent image in Irish myth and magic. The Ulster poet Samuel Ferguson (1810–86) wrote a poem 'The fairy thorn' about a group of young girls going at twilight to dance round one of these trees. Overcome by the intensity of the experience, they are seduced by the fairy folk:

> Soft o'er their bosoms' beating — the only human sound,
> They hear the silky footsteps of the silent fairy crowd,
> Like a river in the air …

At the T-junction the ruins of **Clonduff church** contain a Magennis gravestone (gate may be locked).

The many pubs of **Hilltown** (population 1,000) — eight in the high street — are a legacy from eighteenth-century smugglers who shared out their contraband here. The village has a livestock market on alternate Saturdays, a picturesque sheep fair and festival in early July and a large sale of rams in September. The Georgian **market house** opposite **St John's** parish church (1766) adjoins the **Downshire Arms**, an old hostelry which is now a pub/restaurant with self-catering holiday apartments in the courtyard. The weathervane on the pretty cupola is a fish, a reminder of the good fishing in the Bann and its tributaries. The forge at Katesbridge 10 miles downstream has

Greencastle

The Silent Valley

Annalong Cornmill,
above the harbour

a similar vane.

The more recent (1844) of the two Roman Catholic churches was built on land given by Hilltown's Protestant landlord. Small impoverished Catholic communities were often dependent on such gifts, which were not uncommon after emancipation. To visit the **Goward dolmen**, cross Eight Mile Bridge where Redmond O'Hanlon, a famous highwayman, was slain in 1681, and take the B8 east. The dolmen is signposted on the right after 2 miles. The track ends after less than a mile at a carpark close to the dolmen — called locally Pat Kearney's Big Stone.

From the square at **Rathfriland** (population 2,150) on top of a steep hill, five streets with stepped terraces fall away sharply on all sides. Before the combustion engine, the cheery residents usually walked home, getting out of their traps and carts to spare the ponies. The all-round views from such a position are likely to be good, and so they are. The town has a midweek variety market in the square and three livestock sale days a week. During the nineteenth-century potato famine, the **market house** (1770) was used as a soup kitchen though Rathfriland was spared the worst, since cereals as well as potatoes were grown locally. Four substantial Presbyterian churches are testimony to past differences of opinion. The old Quaker meeting house is now a scout hall, and the small shop with pointed windows on the first floor was originally the town's Methodist chapel. A very prominent funnel-shaped water tower occupies the high point in the riverless town, near the site of a sixteenth-century Magennis castle, now vanished.

This part of County Down has distinguished connections with pioneer Canada. The intrepid Catherine O'Hare, mother of the first European child born west of the Rockies (delivered by Indian midwives in 1862), was herself born in Rathfriland in 1835. She and her husband, Augustus Schubert, joined 200 Overlanders who went west in search of gold, and blazed the trail for the Canadian Pacific Railway. Rathfriland has not yet erected a memorial to this remarkable woman, though the city park in Kamloops, British Columbia, is named after her, and Armstrong also has a monument.

The scenic Dromara road (B7) from Rathfriland passes **Drumballyroney** parish church and school (interpretive centre) where Patrick Prunty, father of the novelists Charlotte, Emily and Anne Brontë, was parish schoolmaster before he moved to England, became a clergyman and refined his name. Several other places connected with him or his family are signposted (Brontë homeland drive). These include ruined **Magherally Old Church** which, however, is more interesting as the burial place of the scholar and author Helen Waddell (1889–1965). Best known for the phenomenally successful novel *Peter Abelard*, her reputation was built on some passionate renderings in English of secular ninth- to twelfth-century Latin lyrics. The noble many-arched stone bridge at **Katesbridge** (population 170) is said to have withstood the weight of several Churchill tanks during World War II. It is a good spot for fishing (salmon, trout, pike). Although he has a new electrified forge, the blacksmith keeps the old forge and handbellows in good repair in case there is a power cut while he is shoeing.

There are various mottes around **Ballyroney** village, an enormous Presbyterian church, a lough with an island in the centre and, signposted on the right, the side road to the **Legananny dolmen.** This elegant tripod is the best known, most photographed of Northern Ireland's dolmens — partly because of its theatrical setting on the southern slope of Slieve Croob and also for its unusually tall and slender uprights. It has genuine star quality. Continuing along the B7, St Michael's church, at a kink in the road at **Finnis**, is next to a **mass house** of 1760, now an outhouse of the parochial house, which this large Roman Catholic church replaced in the 1830s. The architect, Thomas Duff, also designed Newry cathedral which was started the same year, though St Michael's took a decade to complete. There are many old mass sites in this area where a small tributary runs into the infant **Lagan**, only 2 miles from its source on Slieve Croob. A mile north is the village of **Dromara** with nice hump bridges over the broadening river. The scenic road from Dromara to Castlewellan gives views across Dundrum Bay to the Mournes.

Banbridge (population 12,500) is the industrial centre of this district. It was an important stop on the Dublin–Belfast road. The underpass which slices down the middle of the broad, very steep, main street was cut out in 1834 to assist Royal Mail coaches to go through the town centre. Ironically the coach inn had to be demolished to make room for the coach underpass. In **Church Square** the statue of Captain Francis Crozier RN, who discovered the North-West Passage in 1848, is flanked by four large and friendly-looking polar bears. A blue plaque on a large Regency house nearby records his birth here in 1796. Banbridge's other blue plaque is to hymn writer ('What a friend we have in Jesus') and benefactor of Port Hope, Ontario, Joseph Scriven (1819–86), born at 91 Dromore Road.

The distinguished sculptor F. E. McWilliam (1909–92) was born in Banbridge. His *Legs Static* stands outside the **Civic Building** in Downshire Road and a special museum to house the town's extensive McWilliam collection is planned. Though he lived mostly in London he drew powerfully on what he called his 'roots of memory'. The well-known *Princess Macha* (1959) at Altnagelvin Hospital, Derry, is one of many commissions he received for public spaces. Best known of all his works are the *Women of Belfast*, victims of terrorist bomb blasts, created when he was in his sixties from memories of earlier 'troubles'. These poignant bronzes may be seen in the Ulster Museum.

To see **double damask linen** being made, take the Scarva road from Banbridge to the factory of Thomas Ferguson, one of a number of thriving linen manufacturers in this part of County Down who enjoy showing visitors round their works. A visit to a linen factory is on the itinerary of the **Irish linen tour** (see page 93) which also takes in a **scutch mill**, McConville's of Dromore. Scutching or beating the flax was the first stage of traditional linen manufacture.

At **Tullylish**, on the road from Banbridge to **Gilford** (population 1,650), part of the old mill is used as a pottery, and there is a restaurant. John B. Yeats, a celebrated portrait painter and father of the poet W. B. Yeats, was a native of Tullylish.

A dramatic **motte and bailey** and a modest **Anglican cathedral** underline the past importance of **Dromore** (population 3,700), a market town on the Lagan where St Colman founded an abbey in the sixth century. Every building of significance was destroyed in 1641. A Celtic cross built into the cathedral graveyard boundary wall and a single stone (St Colman's Pillow) in the south wall of the chancel, are the only relics of early times. Two outstanding bishops of Dromore, both men of great literary distinction, Jeremy Taylor (1613–67) and Thomas Percy (1729–1811), are buried in the cathedral. If it is not open ask at the rectory. Taylor, who rebuilt the cathedral in the 1660s, was the author of *Holy Living* (1650) and *Holy Dying* (1651), two wonderful prose works of 'rules and exercises' for Anglicans who were deprived of the ordinary care of their priests in the days of the Cromwellian Republic. Percy, who enlarged the cathedral, is best remembered for his *Reliques* of ancient English poetry — a collection of old ballads that was a main literary influence on the poetic revival signalled by Wordsworth's *Lyrical Ballads* (1798). The **stocks** outside the town hall are occasionally used — for brides and grooms before their wedding. A huge **viaduct** south of the town once carried the Banbridge and Lisburn railway. The local running club sometimes holds races on the third Saturday in August in memory of Sam Ferris who ran in three Olympic marathons but did not win any. There is a horse fair in the town in late September.

Between Dromore and Lough Neagh, the Lagan meanders down through meadowland, under eighteenth-century whinstone bridges and past small country towns founded in the plantation period. A feature of the area is **yeoman planters' houses** (late-seventeenth- to eighteenth-century) and massive **round gate pillars** with conical tops marking the entrance to farms and fields. Taking the B2 west from Dromore for 5½ miles, a white late-eighteenth-century slated farmhouse stands on the B9 crossroads. From here you are 1½ miles from each of three villages. Go south for Donaghcloney, straight on for Waringstown, north for Magheralin.

The former factory village of **Donaghcloncy** (population 750), where kerbs and bridge parapets are painted red, white and blue, has a solid redbrick parish church with a war memorial in front. It is an odd combination of church and house — net curtains at the windows and a television aerial on the roof.

Half a mile west of the B2/B9 crossroads, the turning to Waringstown is marked by a huge pair of gate pillars at a delightful thatched yeoman's house built about 1680. A second pair flanks the farmyard. The founder of **Waringstown** (population 1,850) built himself a two-storey Jacobean-style gentleman's house, one of the first unfortified houses in Ireland (1667). A third storey was added later. A flaky pink-painted mansion with tall Tudor-revival chimneys, it looks solid enough but is actually built of mud and rubble and without foundations. Across the road are seven curious terraces in sets of three and four houses, with scalloped garden walls and railings — some of

Katesbridge

Waring's seventeenth-century cottages rebuilt in 1930s mode. The Waring fortune was founded on linen, and Dutch-style houses were built along the main street for the weavers, most of whom came from Flanders. The present white-washed houses with flowerbeds, though modern, have a certain harmony. A yeoman's house built in 1698 (now a restaurant) stands on a high bend in the road. Waringstown cricket club, founded in 1851, fields a strong team — as does Donaghcloney. The **big house** and the **parish church** (1681) had the same designer, James Robb, chief mason of the king's works in Ireland. The church's Jacobean interior is largely of ancient oak — roof, panelling, choir screen and a notable pulpit.

There is fishing at New Forge Bridge near Drumcro House on the B9 near **Magheralin** (population 1,100). Big trees, meadows, planters' houses and old cornmills make an attractive approach to this blink-and-miss village. Stained glass in the Victorian parish church includes windows by Irish artists depicting scenes from the lives of Irish saints. The eighteenth-century memorials came from the church of 1657 up the road, in use until 1845, now ruined but well tended. To see the stained glass, ask at the rectory (pointed door in wall opposite, always open). John Macoun, naturalist and explorer of the Rockies, was born in Magheralin in 1831. He was the surveyor for the Canadian Pacific Railway.

Though **Moira** (population 2,750) has grown in size, the village centre has retained a feeling of intimacy and completeness, with a town hall (former courthouse, built about 1800), a wide main street lined with red-berried rowans and eighteenth-century blackstone houses divided by carriage archways. Sausage connoisseurs travel from far afield to buy from a Moira **master butcher** who has to open his shop at 8am — 7am on Saturday — to cope with demand. Built mostly by Sir Arthur Rawdon, whose famous formal gardens have vanished, the town has a habit of winning civic flower awards. For most of the year the place is a mass of flowering shrubs, roses, flowerbeds and hanging baskets. On the north side, a long grassy avenue terminates in **Moira parish church**, a top-heavy but appealing building of 1723 where William Butler Yeats, the poet's grandfather, was curate in the 1830s. The communion rails came from the staircase of the Rawdon mansion. Looking down from the church, the lawns seem to continue, unbroken, into the flowerbeds and trees of the old Rawdon demesne but they are in fact bisected by the busy A3 trunk road. The road opposite Station Road leads to **Berwick Hall**, a thatched yeoman's house of 1700. Moira was the scene of a victory in AD637 by the king of Tara over Comgall, king of Ulster.

ADDITIONAL INFORMATION

PLACES TO VISIT

ANNALONG

Cornmill
☎ (013967) 68736. Open February–
November Tuesday–Saturday
11am–5pm. Guided tours/
demonstrations.

BANBRIDGE

Irish Linen Tour
May–September only. Departs
Banbridge Gateway Centre 10am
every Wednesday (except July
factory holidays). Tour ends 4pm.
To book: ☎ (018206) 23322.

Ferguson's Linen Factory
☎ (018206) 23491. Tours Monday–
Thursday 11am and 3pm, Friday
11am only.

BRYANSFORD

Tollymore Forest Park
☎ (013967) 22428.
Open 10am to dusk.

CASTLEWELLAN

Forest Park & Arboretum
☎ (013967) 78664 (head forester).

Legananny Dolmen
Like most prehistoric monuments,
always accessible.

DROMORE

Cathedral
Ask at rectory opposite for access.

DUNDRUM

Castle Ruins
Open April–September Tuesday–
Saturday 10am–7pm, also 2–7pm
Sunday.

Murlough Sand Dunes
☎ (013967) 51467. Permanent
access to nature reserve. Guided
walks. NT interpretive centre
open July to mid-September
daily 10am–5pm.

GILFORD

Tullylish Potteries
59a Banbridge Road, Tullylish.
☎ (01762) 831765. Ceramics and
pottery gallery. Tours by arrangement on Saturday afternoon and
Tuesday and Wednesday evenings.
Shop open until 9pm every day
(Sunday 11am–2pm).

HILLTOWN

Fairy Thorn
1 mile west of Kinnahalla.
Visible from main road.

KILKEEL

Greencastle Ruins
Open July–August Tuesday–
Saturday 10am–7pm, Sunday
2–7pm.

MOURNE MOUNTAINS

Silent Valley
☎ (01232) 741166. Open daily
10am–6.30pm, closes 4.30pm in
winter.

RATHFRILAND

Brontë Homeland Interpretive Centre
Drumballyroney.
☎ (018206) 31152/23322.
Open March–October
Tuesday–Friday 11am–5pm
and 2–6pm weekends.

SAINTFIELD

Rowallane Gardens (NT)
☎ (01238) 510131. Open weekdays
11am–6pm, Saturday and Sunday
2–6pm; weekdays only in winter
(until 5pm).

SEAFORDE

Butterfly House
☎ (01396) 811225. Open Easter–
September Monday–Saturday
10am–5pm, Sunday 1–6pm.
Signposted on A24 south of
Ballynahinch.

EVENTS

Annalong

Fish Festival (mid-August)

Castlewellan

Horse Fair (1 May)

Dromore

Horse Fair (second Saturday in September)

Mourne Mountains

Hilltown Booley Fair (early July) Sheep fair, shearing, traditional music.

TOURIST INFORMATION CENTRES

Banbridge

Gateway Centre, 200 Newry Road. ☎ (018206) 23322. Open all year Monday–Saturday 10am–5pm, plus Sunday afternoon. Longer hours in summer.

Kilkeel

6 Newcastle Street. ☎ (016937) 62525. Open all year Monday–Saturday 9am–5.30pm.

Newcastle

10 Central Promenade. ☎ (013967) 22222. Open all year Monday–Saturday 10am–5pm, Sunday 2–6pm. Longer hours in summer.

Lough Neagh has a great-crested grebe colony and, in winter,
100,000 waterfowl

4

COUNTY ARMAGH & NEWRY

S t Patrick made Armagh the centre of his mission in Ireland in the
fifth century. He might have built his church among the ruins of
Emain Macha (Navan Fort), destroyed in AD332, but he settled for a
high hill 2 miles east. Long before the coming of Christianity, the
House of the Red Branch ruled all Ulster (*Uladh*) from the stronghold
at Navan Fort, a great earthworks off the A28 near Armagh city which
appears as *Isamnium* in Ptolemy's second-century world atlas. Irish
vernacular literature, by far the oldest and richest north of the Alps,
had its greatest flowering in this part of Ireland.

The M1 from Belfast to Dungannon runs along the top of County
Armagh, across the flat countryside of Lough Neagh's south shore.

LOUGH NEAGH

The main recreation area for north Armagh is Lough Neagh around **Oxford Island** and Kinnego marina. Anglers come here in hordes to fish the **Bann** up to Portadown. The lough is fished commercially for freshwater herring (pollan), and dollaghan (a kind of huge salmon-trout) is caught around Washing Bay, **Maghery** and in the Main river flowing into the lough near Shane's Castle. But Lough Neagh, which covers 153 sq. miles, is most famous for its wild eels. Millions of elvers (young eels) swim up the Bann from the north coast but about 20 million lucky ones are saved the trouble. They are trapped at Coleraine and transported by tanker south to the lough to grow to maturity. In the spring and early summer there are as many as 200 boats line-fishing for eels.

The shores of this inland sea and its handful of islands have large bird populations, especially at the southern end. Swans breed on Croaghan Island, a colony of great crested grebe nest in the reed beds of Oxford Island, with a heronry on Raughlan peninsula opposite. Tours of the nature reserve start from the **Lough Neagh Discovery Centre**, Oxford Island. The ruined keep and holy well on wooded **Coney Island**, a bird sanctuary at the Blackwater estuary, can be reached by boat from the small marina at Maghery or from Kinnego. A hand-operated car ferry across the Upper Bann was a convenient way to explore the marshy land round here but now there is no one to work it and you have to go round the long way.

The level of the lough was lowered in 1846 and twice since, the last time in 1959, but drainage round the edge is still not adequate for arable farming. US troops used the area as a training and assembly ground in preparation for the invasion of Europe (1942–45) and Langford Lodge, known as 'Station 597', near Gartree Point recalls the days fifty years ago when this was the main USAAF repair base in Europe. A private airfield nearby is used for testing Martin Baker

Although not the most picturesque introduction to this delightfully rural county, the motorway gives fast access to the Lurgan/Porta-down area — the comparatively industrialised north-east corner. **Craigavon** is very thoroughly signposted from the M1. Turn off at junction 11 for a look at the province's first 'New Town', designated in 1965, and named after James Craig, Lord Craigavon (1871–1941), first prime minister of Northern Ireland.

ejection seats for aircraft. Sir James Martin (1893–1981), born in Crossgar, County Down, invented all kinds of components for aircraft — but his ejection seat is the star, with at least 6,000 airmen having ejected safely, to fly again, since 1946.

Pieces of petrified wood, altered by silica salts, are sometimes washed up on the shore of the lough. Belfast street hawkers used to sell them as knife sharpeners with the cry:

Lough Neagh hones! Lough Neagh hones!
You put them in sticks, and you take them out stones!

Be prepared for the nuisance of the Lough Neagh fly (chironomid midge) which has a spectacular emergence at certain times in spring and summer. These harmless non-biting midges descend in clouds on windless days and get into everything.

Sand and gravel extraction from the lough is long established, and lignite is becoming big business. An estimated 200 million recoverable tons of this brown coal, half the price of imported coal, has been identified at **Coagh** on the west shore, twice that amount at **Crumlin** near the airport, and an even thicker seam directly underneath Ballymoney town. The only natural energy source discovered in significant quantities in the province, lignite is a focus of future energy development.

For unusual peaty landscapes visit **Peatlands Park** where wooded drumlins stick up through the flat bog of cut-over peat (M1 exit 13). The Department of the Environment has a narrow gauge railway here with locomotives formerly used for peat extraction. **The Birches**, 4 miles due east (or take M1 exit 12), was the ancestral home of 'Stonewall' Jackson, the great Confederate general killed in 1863 at Chancellorsville in the American Civil War. A blue plaque in the pretty courtyard of Waugh's farm records the connection.

The plan was for the existing towns of Lurgan and Portadown to develop towards each other in linear fashion, taking overspill from Belfast and growing to a population of 180,000. The mayoral chairs from Lurgan and Portadown, removed to the **civic centre**, stand outside the council chamber. However, the town is still waiting for the people to arrive. Large isolated buildings stand in a landscape of manmade lakes, dual carriageways, roundabouts and bridges, at the

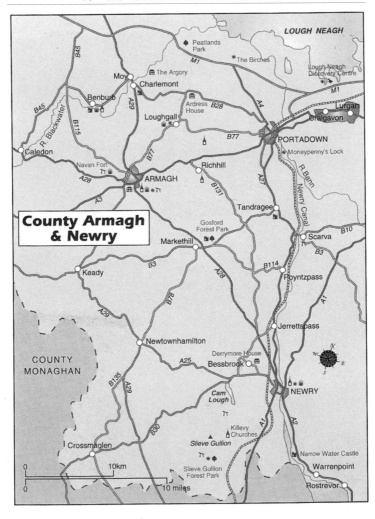

end of a stumpy little motorway, the M12. The Belfast–Dublin railway line runs between two **'balancing' lakes** which help drain this part of the Lough Neagh basin. Only about 6ft deep, the lakes are much favoured by swan families and are used for boating and other watersports in summer. Outside Craigavon's uncompromising essay in town planning, the scenery soon reverts to a pastoral landscape of small dairy farms and winding leafy lanes.

An unpretentious town with an agreeable broad main street,

Lurgan (population 22,000) was granted to the Brownlows of Nottingham (later Lords Lurgan) after 1607. The place did not really get going until the end of the century when Samuel Waring introduced linen-damask weaving to Ulster.

> I'll ne'er despise the weaving trade
> The shuttle's lighter than the spade

sang the rhyming weaver John Dickey, and you can see weavers' cottages, with projecting front parlours built to accommodate the loom, if you go looking for them around **Bownes Lane**. Textile firms and clothing manufacturers are still important here. Though the

Lough Neagh Discovery Centre, Oxford Island

official Lurgan Town Trail makes no mention of him, the parish's most famous personality is undoubtedly **Master McGrath**, the coursing greyhound which won the Waterloo Cup three times between 1868 and 1871. Behind the pulpit in the eighteenth-century parish church in the town centre, a **stained glass window** bears his image. A local bard composed a ballad to him, and the council placed his effigy at the top of the town's coat of arms. His proud master, the second Lord Lurgan, raised an imposing monument on the canine grave outside the Brownlow mansion. He received yet one more posthumous accolade in 1993 when Major William Brownlow, his master's descendant, unveiled a **statue** of this noble Irish hound in a ceremony at Craigavon civic centre.

The precious Book of Armagh, oldest of the great illuminated Irish manuscripts (now in Trinity College Library, Dublin), was 'lost' for 200 years among the books of Arthur Brownlow, a seventeenth-century antiquarian. The manuscript somehow found its way into Brownlow's library after being pawned in 1680 for £5. **Brownlow House** is a romantic honey-coloured Tudor-style mansion of 1836 with tall chimney-pots and lanterned tower, designed by the Edinburgh architect William Playfair (1783–1857). It is now the headquarters of the grandly named Imperial Grand Black Chapter of the British Commonwealth, close cousin to the Orange Order. The grounds, landscaped in the eighteenth century, are a public park, with a lake and golf course. The mansion's present owners have renovated the interior and occasionally open the house to the public.

Distinguished Lurganites include James Logan (1674–1751), scholar and scientist. Son of a Quaker schoolmaster, he helped found Pennsylvania, becoming president of the infant state's council. A **plaque in High Street** on one of the gate pillars of the Quaker meeting house marks his birthplace. Lurgan had the first meeting house in Ireland (1653). Field Marshal Sir John Dill, who liaised between the British and US governments in World War II, was a Lurganite (died 1947, buried Arlington National Cemetery, Washington), as was Lord Dugan, governor of South Australia until 1939 and of Victoria until 1949. The poet, painter and polemicist George Russell ('Æ') was born in William Street in 1867 and there is a bust of him in the **town hall**. He shared with W. B. Yeats an interest in mysticism and the supernatural, was much involved in the Gaelic revival, and edited the influential *Irish Homestead* and *Irish Statesman* for nearly 30 years.

The creation of the waterway from Newry to Lough Neagh in the 1730s brought prosperity to **Portadown** (population 21,500). A pleasant walk along the towpath from Shillington's Quay brings you to an atmospheric little spot, **Moneypenny's Lock**, the last lock before the Newry Canal joins the Upper Bann river. The lock-keeper's house has been restored and the life and times of the lightermen who made their living on the canal is recorded. Like Lurgan, this busy textile and manufacturing town developed with the linen industry, which gave way to synthetic fibres in about 1950. Today it has factories making carpets, industrial ceramics, jam and traditional Irish breads. Potato farls and barmbracks from Irwin's bakery go to England, boxed speciality cakes (McCann's) are eaten everywhere from Norway to Australia, and Belgians like a nice Portadown wheaten with their paling-'t-gruen — eels in green sauce. Roses appear on the town's old coat of arms, a reminder of the days when Portadown rose grower Sam McGredy carried off all the trophies, starting in 1905 with 'Countess of Gosford', a huge pink rose. In the heyday of rail, Portadown was a major junction with large marshalling yards. There is a big cattle market on Fridays when streets in the area are parked up with farmers' Volvos and Mercedes. A covered market is held on Saturday in the William Street halls.

The wide sloping main street has a triangular 'square' at either end. More than a dozen denominations have built churches and chapels in one small central area. A Baptist church stands adjacent to a convent, nearby is a small Elim Pentecostal chapel and a Presbyterian church, a blackstone Catholic church in William Street looks across at a Methodist church which has an imposing façade but is all blackstone 'potted meat' behind. In front of **St Mark's** (Anglican), the bronze statue of a nineteenth-century Ulster Unionist Party leader is adorned with an Orange sash in July when Portadown Orangemen commemorate the Battle of the Boyne. There are plenty of other places of worship too: up near the A4/B28 roundabout, next to an older, ruined church, the grey concrete exterior of the Catholic church of **St John the Baptist**, Garvaghy Road, conceals a harmonious interior.

Sir Robert Hart (1835–1911), who created the Chinese Post Office and founded their lighthouse service, was born in Woodhouse Street. Hart's house has been knocked down to make way for a supermarket but he appears in street and school names and is commemorated in St Mark's vestry. Queen's University, Belfast, has his voluminous diaries of 54 years in China. He also introduced the Chinese to the music of the brass band — one of his less-fêted achievements. This was a fitting service from a native of Portadown, since the town goes in for bands in a big way — including silver, flute, pipe and accordion bands — and has a good male voice choir. It is a vigorous kind of place, with courteous people in the banks and shops.

Newry Town Hall

The Armagh/Down county border south of Portadown follows the line of the Upper Bann/Newry canal. Settlements benefiting from the construction of the 18-mile canal included Scarva, Poyntzpass and Jerrettspass. Anyone attending the Sham Fight pageant at **Scarva** (population 300) on 13 July (see page 16) will tell you about the seventeenth-century significance of the three passes of Scarva, Poyntz and Jerrett. These sleepy places are heavy with history. However, the importance of Scarva is of much greater antiquity. It was a part of the huge defensive earthworks and ditches known as **Black Pig's Dyke**, sometimes called the Dane's Cast and, sometimes, the Dorsey, meaning 'gates'. A section of these earthen defences, built in the fourth century BC by the Ulster kings after their retreat east from *Emain Macha* (Navan Fort), is clearly visible in the grounds of **Scarva House**, a two-storey house of about 1717 with a charming courtyard. A **visitor centre** in Main Street, Scarva, has interesting background on the village. The large raths, or forts, of **Lisnagade** (1¼ miles east of Scarva village) and **Lisnavaragh** (½ mile west of Lisnagade on a bend in the road) are believed to mark the north end of the defensive frontier.

The cathedral town of **Newry** (population 23,000) is well placed at

View down Carlingford Lough from Flagstaff Hill

the head of the **'Gap of the North'**. Through this pass between two ranges of hills the men of Ulster sallied forth to harry the tribes of Leinster in the days of the Fianna legends. Because of its strategic position, the town was repeatedly destroyed in the wars for the control of the North. Newry is named from a yew tree said to have been planted by St Patrick himself. An abbey on the east bank of the Clanrye river was colonised by Cistercians in 1153. In the sixteenth century Sir Nicholas Bagenal, marshal of Ireland and founder of the town, used it as his residence. All trace of it has vanished. One stone castle after another was built near the abbey. The third and last one was destroyed in 1566 by Shane (the Proud) O'Neill. In 1578, Bagenal built the **first post-Reformation** (ie Protestant) **church** in Ireland on top of the steep hill 500yd due east of the town hall. The church has kept its original tower, despite a battering in 1641, and Bagenal's coat of arms is on a tablet in the porch.

There is a good view of Bagenal's church from the garden of the **Poor Clares'** tall pink **convent** in High Street. The convent garden almost encircles the burial ground of the town's first Presbyterian (Unitarian) congregation, established in 1650. Republican and author John Mitchel (1815–75) is buried here. (If the graveyard is locked, ask at the convent about access.) Transported for the offence of treason-felony he came back to Ireland 28 years later and was elected MP for Tipperary. Mitchel's best-known book is the famous *Jail Journal*, a classic of Anglophobia but quite readable. He was an early advocate of the 'physical force' school. His **statue** stands in the pedestrianised shopping centre.

The A1 dual carriageway slices through the east side of Newry over the site of the abbey and divides this old quarter from the rest of the town. Newry's considerable prosperity in the eighteenth century stemmed largely from its ingenious waterway, the earliest **inland canal** in the British Isles. It has fourteen locks, and a single carefully preserved **swing-bridge** survives at the bottom of Monaghan Street. The town's mercantile past is reflected in names such as Buttercrane Quay, Sugar Island and Sugarhouse Quay, close to the six-storey redbrick Sands's Mill (1876) with rounded windows. Tall eighteenth-century warehouses line the quays. The main downstream (export) traffic was linen, Tyrone coal, Mourne granite, farm produce — and early emigrants who bought passage on American flaxseed ships returning to New York and Philadelphia with Irish linen. Started in 1730 and finished in 1742, the canal was extended down to **Carlingford Lough** as a ship canal in 1761. By the 1840s, however, trade had declined. The last vessel passed through the locks in the 1930s.

The characterful **town hall**, half in Down, half in Armagh, straddles the river which runs in parallel with the canal. A marble bust of Charles Russell, Lord Russell of Killowen, stands in the foyer. Born in 1832 at 50 Queen Street (now Dominic Street), Russell was leading counsel for Parnell in 1888 and Lord Chief Justice of England (1894–1900). The bust was a gift from the English Law Society. The **museum** and an **arts centre** are across the road. The autumn arts festival attracts international names.

Since about 1750 Newry has been the cathedral town of the Catholic diocese of Dromore, and the Tudor-gothic **cathedral of St Patrick and St Colman** occupies a prominent position. Thomas Duff was the architect (1825) though the tower and transepts were added in 1888, and the cathedral's rich stained glass and mosaics more recently still. Duff designed the classical **courthouse** with glass dome (1841), and had a hand in the Anglican church of **St Mary's**. The Unitarian church of 1853 is the work of his pupil, W. J. Barre, also of Newry.

No 1 Trevor Hill, a five-bay granite house, is the oldest (1775) in a row of handsome late Georgian houses built for the gentry and their clergy. They include a fine mansion occupied by the Bank of Ireland for the past century, designed in about 1826, possibly by Francis Johnston. Atmospheric crumbly corners of old Newry include River Street (south of John Mitchel Place) — a row of tiny houses with eagles over the doors, and Ballybot ('poor town') beyond the former cattle market. At one time the universal roofing material was slate from the North Wales quarries, and many Newry houses are still roofed with 'Bangor blues'. The town is a main shopping centre, with a general market on Thursday and Saturday. An open-air market on Sunday, a few miles south at **Jonesborough**, draws big crowds from both sides of the border.

Four miles from Newry, along the fast A2 towards Warrenpoint, picturesque **Narrow Water Castle** stands on a rock, jutting into the estuary. It was built in about 1560 to guard the entrance to the Clanrye river which flows into Carlingford Lough a mile south. King John's army crossed the lough by pontoon bridge in 1210, close to the mound of a late-twelfth-century castle, about 400yd further on.

Warrenpoint and Rostrevor are small resorts, 3 miles apart, on the lough's sheltered north shore. The port at **Warrenpoint** (population 5,600) handles container traffic and substantial coal, timber, paper and grain tonnages, with a regular service to Rotterdam. When Newry port closed in the 1970s, this harbour was enlarged, and the town has a long promenade and an interesting local history display at the old National School at **Burren**, 2 miles north of Warrenpoint, well signposted from the town.

Rostrevor

The road into **Rostrevor** (population 2,250) winds past a tall granite **obelisk** erected in memory of Major General Robert Ross (1766–1814). He was commander of a small British force which captured Washington in 1814 after unexpectedly defeating the Americans at Bladensburg. He and his officers burned the White House after eating a hearty dinner in President Madison's abandoned dining room. Ross was killed at Baltimore soon afterwards. Palm trees and mimosa flourish in the mild climate of Rostrevor. There are oak trees in the square, nice old houses, and a long seafront. Natural oakwoods make a fine show in autumn when the leaves turn. Behind the town, on the wooded slopes of Slievemartin, the **Cloghmore** ('great stone') is a geological curiosity. To see this enormous glacial erratic block weighing 40 tons, follow the forest drive to the carpark, then walk to the viewpoint (½ mile) beyond the pines and on up to the stone. Camping in **Kilbroney Park** and Rostrevor Forest is popular.

The bronze bell of Rostrevor's **Catholic church** was rescued from the ruins of Kilbroney church a mile up the mountain road (B25) where St Bronach, patron saint of seafarers, founded a monastery in the sixth century. A granite cross survives from the early foundation.

From the top of Slieve Gullion the whole of the **Ring of Gullion** is laid out below — a ring dyke of wild and rugged hills about 7 miles in diameter, rising to over 1,000ft. Often shrouded in mist, the mountain dominates the Gap of the North and is rich in myth and legend. Like Navan Fort, it features in the fourth-century prose epic *Táin Bó Cuailgne* ('The cattle raid of Cooley'), from the famous Ulster cycle of stories dating from the Iron Age, in which the chief hero of the men of Ulster is Cuchulain, who lived around Slieve Gullion. The central theme of the epic is Cuchulain's battle against invaders from Connaught who have come to claim a brown bull belonging to Conor, King of Ulster (ruling at Navan Fort). Writing was introduced to Ireland in St Patrick's time, when the *Táin* and other sagas were written down. The region's vanishing folklore is also well documented. Just in time, it found a popular chronicler, Michael J. Murphy (1913–96), who collected enough Irish folk stories and superstitions ('pisthogues') to fill 300 volumes.

The southern end of Slieve Gullion is a **forest park**, with a steep drive up to the top. Wild goats move along the ridges and a Neolithic **passage grave**, known as the House of Calliagh ('old witch') Birra, crowns the south summit (1,894ft). The water of a lake on the bare north summit, close to a round cairn, makes excellent tea. It is also said to turn hair grey and to cure toothache.

The **Killevy churches**, on Gullion's south-east slope (signposted from A1 and B113), are the back-to-back ruins of two rectangular churches, one tenth-century, the other thirteenth-century, joined together but with no way through from one to the other. The many **O'Hanlon graves** nearby are a reminder that Armagh was O'Hanlon country for centuries. A striking feature is the massive lintelled door of the earlier church (west side). The pointed window of the other (east) church dates from the fifteenth century. Killevy is the site of an important fifth-century nunnery founded by St Monenna, also called St Blinne who (like St Bronach) was a patron saint of sailors. A granite slab in the graveyard is traditionally this lady saint's grave, and a **holy well** associated with her is further up the mountain. The Vikings raided the nunnery in 923 but it was in use as an Augustinian convent until the dissolution (1542).

Well-signposted prehistoric monuments around Gullion include **Ballymacdermot cairn**, near **Bernish viewpoint**, which was slightly damaged when an American tank bumped into it in World War II; and **Ballykeel dolmen**, between Slieve Gullion and Camlough. The eighth-century **pillar stone of Kilnasaggart**, with thirteen crosses and a long Irish inscription carved on it, is 1¼ miles south of Jonesborough. A ruined tower near the pillar stone was part of **Moyry Castle**, built by the English in 1601 to control the pass below.

The A25 runs between two waters at the north end of ribbony Camlough lake which supplies the taps of Newry and is a good angling spot. The south Armagh hills peter out at the border in small rock-strewn, stone-ditched fields fringed with yellow whin, beyond the Dorsey (the pre-Christian defensive earthworks contemporary with Navan Fort), down towards **Crossmaglen** (population 1,600). This remote village has an exceptionally large market square (with a variety market on alternate Saturdays), an army base and a reputation for, among other things, horse breeding and handmade lace. The graveyard at **Creggan** parish church was a burying place for a branch of the O'Neills from about 1450 when Hugh 'of the Fews' O'Neill came from Tyrone to settle in south Armagh. The Ulster O'Neills were very fierce. Their arms featured the Red Hand of Ulster and they were said to carve their chess sets from the bones of Leinster warriors. Their vault at Creggan is close to the wall of the church. Nearby are **tablet-memorials** to eighteenth-century bards, the bandit–poet Seamus Mór MacMurphy (1720–50) and Art McCooey (1738–73) among them.

The landscape north-west of here, around the once-busy linen centre of **Keady** (population 2,500) is scattered with relics from Ulster's linen heyday, including many mills beside the region's little lakes and rivers. The old flax **scutch mill** below **Tassagh railway viaduct**, for example, was powered by the Callan river.

One of the earliest of the model villages associated with the Industrial Revolution, the mill village of **Bessbrook** (population 3,150) was founded in 1845 by John Grubb Richardson, a Quaker linen manufacturer, to house workers at his huge flax mill. Solidly built houses with slate roofs are ranged in terraces round two squares, each with a green in the middle, linked by a broad road. The Richardsons built schools, a butcher's shop, dairy, dispensary, savings bank, village hall and several churches but no pub, pawnshop or police house, these last three being deemed undesirable and/or unnecessary. Everything was built of granite quarried nearby, and flax for the mill was grown locally in large quantities. An eighteen-arch **viaduct**, built in 1851, still carries the Belfast–Dublin railway (trains stop at the small station between here and Newry). Later, in 1885, a narrow gauge electric tram (maximum speed 12mph) brought workers in from Newry 3 miles away. The linens of the Bessbrook Spinning Company were world famous. After World War II, the industry declined and the tramway closed. The big mill (which operated until 1972), its pond, weirs and sluices, and smaller mills along the line of the old tram, are substantial exemplars of Ulster's industrial archaeology. Earlier than Saltaire in Yorkshire (1852) and

Port Sunlight in Cheshire (1888), Bessbrook was the inspiration for the Cadbury garden village of Bournville near Birmingham.

Derrymore House, a delightful eighteenth-century thatched cottage orné-style manor house just outside the village, was built by Isaac Corry (1755–1813), MP for Newry and last chancellor of the Irish Exchequer. As chancellor, he imposed the window tax, was involved in a number of duels with pistols, and supported union between Ireland and Britain. He was a friend of Lord Castlereagh, and the Act of Union was drafted in the pretty drawing room in 1800. The house is in National Trust care.

Livestock markets 3 days a week bring bustle to aptly named **Markethill** village (population 1,350). But the main attraction for visitors is nearby **Gosford Forest Park** which has a **castle** in the middle. The first Norman-revival castle in the British Isles, Gosford (1819) was designed for the Achesons, Earls of Gosford, by Thomas Hopper who later built Penrhyn Castle in Wales. It is a huge sprawling building with a square keep, round tower with a circular drawing room, and extremely thick walls. The fourth earl sold the furniture in 1921 to pay his debts. In World War II, when writer Anthony Powell was billeted here, the castle was in military use, and at one time it housed a circus, including the lions.

The castle replaced a manor house (burnt in about 1805) where Jonathan Swift spent many months as a guest of the Achesons, his friends, between 1728 and 1730. Several of the nature walks round the estate were devised by him. **Dean Swift's Chair**, a half-moon seat hedged with yew in the arboretum, is where Swift sat in fine weather composing poems, some of them about Markethill. The Achesons were indulgent hosts but Sir Arthur Acheson was greatly offended when Swift instructed staff, in Sir Arthur's absence, to cut down a fairy tree outside the main gate. Swift's poem, 'On cutting down the old thorn at Markethill', explains why he did it. Close to the ruined house are the original farm buildings, waterwheel and laundry. Below a pretty bridge with waterfall is Swift's Well. A miniature round tower, with a distinctly Teutonic look about it, was built by German prisoners-of-war. The forest park is used by caravanners and campers all year round. It has some fine old walnut trees and a walled cherry garden.

The main street at **Tandragee** (population 2,850), on the Cusher river, curves up the steep hill to a baronial-style castle built in about 1837 by the sixth Duke of Manchester. In the 1950s it became a **potato crisp factory**. A tour of the factory provides an opportunity to see the inner courtyards — and to learn something about the potato, Ireland's staple food from the mid-seventeenth century. An earlier O'Hanlon

The Mall, Armagh

castle on the site was confiscated at the plantation of Ulster, but the O'Hanlons recaptured and destroyed it in 1641. Outlawed Redmond O'Hanlon, killed at Hilltown in 1681, is buried at Relicarn (2 miles south-east). The ninth-century Bell of Armagh, now in the National Museum, Dublin, was discovered near his grave in the eighteenth century.

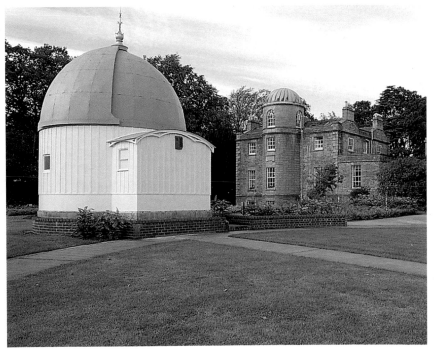

Armagh Observatory

The City of Armagh and Surrounding Area

Spiritual capital of Ireland for 1,500 years, **Armagh** (population 14,650) has preserved an air of quiet dignity and refinement against considerable odds. The city is the seat of both the Anglican and the Roman Catholic archbishops of Ireland. The twin-spired Catholic cathedral is on a hill north-west of the city. Two marble archbishops standing on plinths outside the entrance look mildly across to the Anglican cathedral which crowns the ancient rath where St Patrick built his stone church in AD445. Steep streets, climbing and intersecting, follow the curve of the ditches and banks which ringed the rath and its church. Parking around the Anglican cathedral is not feasible but down the hill there is usually space on the **Mall**, a pleasant, green, tree-lined promenade where cricket is played in the summer.

The Mall used to be the city's racecourse, and many of the Georgian townhouses along its length have large balconied first-floor reception rooms which would have given a good view of the starting and finishing posts. Archbishop Richard Robinson (1709–94) ejected the punters and turned the course into a mall. The moving spirit behind the city's fine eighteenth-century architecture, Robinson was patron of the celebrated Francis Johnston (1761–1829), who left his mark on his native Armagh and, later, on Georgian Dublin.

The sombre **gaol** (disused) at the south end of the Mall had gallows outside until 1866. The fine classical **courthouse** closing the north end is by Francis Johnston (1809). On the east side the **Armagh County Museum**, in an Ionic schoolhouse of 1833 with a small lawn of its own, is a rewarding visit. Its art gallery, natural history and folk collections and library are notable. Self-portraits and other works by 'Æ' (George Russell — 1867–1935) and James Sleator (born Armagh 1889) are on display. At the north-east corner, the **Sovereign's House** (1810) contains the infrequently open museum of the Royal Irish Fusiliers. On the west side, an extravagant small church with a campanile is a gospel hall of 1884.

The local building stone, used to good effect, is warm-coloured carboniferous limestone. The buildings in Charlemont Place, the courthouse and the house called Patrick's Fold (36 Scotch Street) are good examples. The colour varies from grey to pink, yellow and red. The brighter stone came from quarries south of the city and is called 'Armagh marble'. It was polished and used for pavements, doorsteps and mantelpieces.

The planetarium, in the grounds of **Armagh Observatory**, has 'star shows' in a domed theatre, a full-scale mock-up of a Gemini space-craft and original equipment used by American astronauts. Opened in 1968 — its first director was Patrick ('Sky at Night') Moore — the planetarium grew out of the observatory which was founded in 1790 by Archbishop Robinson as part of his plan for a university. The building, by Johnston, was not finished until 1825. It has astronomical books and instruments of great interest. Some of these are on public display in the planetarium and include a Herschel Newtonian mirror and Gregorian telescope by Adams, and a 20-inch radius quadrant belonging to George III which were presented to the observatory by Queen Victoria in 1840. Across the road (A3) from the planetarium are the red castellations of the **Royal School**, founded by James I in 1608 and rebuilt by Robinson in 1774.

In AD447 St Patrick ordained that his church in Armagh should have pre-eminence over all the churches of Ireland. Since then, about eighteen successive churches have occupied the hill top. The **Anglican cathedral** of St Patrick has a medieval core, and was restored in 1765 by Archbishop Robinson. However, its present sandstone exterior is later. The cathedral was brand new when Thackeray visited it in 1842 and admired the **eighteenth-century**

monuments inside. These include a statue of Sir Thomas Molyneux by Roubiliac, one of Dean Drelincourt by the Flemish sculptor Rysbrack, and a bust of Archbishop Robinson by Nollekens. Note the fine kneeling figure of Primate William Stuart by Chantrey, a brass tablet to the archaeologist and historian Bishop Reeves (who retrieved the lost Book of Armagh), a broken eleventh-century market cross, and a collection of pagan stone figures in the north transept (chapterhouse) where seventeenth-century memorials to the Earls of Charlemont are set in the west wall. The Royal Irish Fusiliers' chapel is in the south transept.

Outside, a small door at the east end leads to Archbishop Patrick O'Scanail's **thirteenth-century crypt**. Note grotesque medieval stone heads high up round the exterior walls and a sundial of 1706. A slab in the north transept west wall marks the position of the **grave of Brian Boru**, high king of Ireland, who defeated the Norsemen at Clontarf in 1014. Brian, aged 73, and his son Murchard were killed in the battle and their bodies brought to this place for burial. Here, in 1004, Brian had formally acknowledged the primacy of Armagh. A scion of the Munster house of O'Brien, Brian Boru was considered a usurper of the Irish throne. Because of this, no northern contingents helped him at Clontarf but he still won, thus ending two centuries of Viking supremacy in Ireland.

The **Robinson Library** (1771) was the first public library in Ireland outside Dublin. It contains a copy of *Gulliver's Travels* corrected in Swift's hand and the *Claims of the Innocents* (pleas to Oliver Cromwell). The registers of archbishops of Armagh from 1361 are in the Public Record Office, Belfast. One of these archbishops, the learned James Ussher (1581–1656), primate from 1624, is remembered for a statement in his 1650 diary that the world was created on 23 October in 4004BC. An adjacent infirmary (like the library, founded by the generous Robinson) is now the **Armagh campus** of Queen's University, Belfast. Stones from an early-twelfth-century Augustinian abbey (St Peter and St Paul) on this site were used for the Presbyterian church (1722) lower down Abbey Street. Dean Swift passed the church (now disused) during construction and observed stone masons 'chiselling popery out of the very stones'. **Vicar's Row**, opposite the cathedral's west door, is a terrace of small houses for clergy widows. Nos 1–4, the earliest in the row, started in about 1720, have tiny windows. The end house, No 11, is the birthplace of Charles Wood (1866–1926), composer of organ music, string quartets and anthems.

The **Catholic cathedral**, also dedicated to St Patrick, was begun in 1840. Building stopped during the great famine and for years

Navan Fort

afterwards. The walls were only about 15ft high when J. J. McCarthy resumed construction, changing the style from Duff's comparatively modest perpendicular gothic design to lofty decorated gothic. The outside was finished in 1873. The finest view of the twin spires is from the city's west and north-west approaches. The pope and many of Europe's royal families helped with the builders' bills but mostly the cash was raised through collections, bazaars and raffles. A **grandfather clock**, a prize in the 1865 bazaar, is still waiting in the sacristy for the lucky winner to collect it. The two archbishops, whose statues flank a long flight of steps up to the grand entrance, were the incumbents under whom building began (Primate Crolly) and ended (Primate McGettigan). Cardinal Logue later beautified the interior, a dazzle of mosaic, painting, stained glass, Italian marbles and red 'Armagh marble'.

The old Irish game of road bowls is popular in Armagh. Competitions are held regularly on the wiggly B115, out past the Catholic cathedral. Players hurl a 28oz iron ball along the road, cutting corners and flying over hedges to complete the course in as few throws as possible. Armagh's main rivals are Corkmen, and betting is brisk.

The fine house at **36 Scotch Street** (until recently a bank, now flats), set back from the present building line, was designed for Leonard Dobbin, the Bank of Ireland's agent, by Johnston in 1812. It is said to be the site of a church built by St Patrick in AD444, the year before he obtained the prime site up the hill. **No 40 English Street** is the city's tourist information office now. Tucked in behind it is a heritage centre, **St Patrick's Trian**, where a giant Lemuel Gulliver lies pinioned in the 'Land of Lilliput'. To visit the remains of the longest friary church in Ireland (163ft), you have to cross the busy A28. The ruins are just beyond the gates of the former bishop's palace demesne and are all that survives of a **Franciscan friary** established in 1263 by Archbishop O'Scanail. From here, you can see a large obelisk raised by Archbishop Robinson, and looking back towards the city, the bawn-like modern **St Malachy's church** (Roman Catholic). St Malachy was born in Armagh (1094) and was archbishop in 1129–48.

The Anglican **archbishop's palace** (at present used as council offices) was built in 1770 by Thomas Cooley. Johnston added a third storey in 1786 and also designed the beautiful, delicate interior of the **primate's chapel**, a detached Ionic temple to the right of the main entrance. The **palace stables** contain a heritage centre, with café, gift shop and so on, and there are horse-drawn carriages for hire.

Navan Fort is signposted off the Caledon–Killylea road (A28) 1½ miles west of Armagh. This was the chief stronghold of the Celtic kings of Ulster from about 700BC until its destruction in AD332. Queen Macha's palace (*Emain Macha*) crowned the summit, and her hospital ('house of grief') tended the sick; Deirdre of the Sorrows first encountered her lover, Naisi, on the ramparts; Cuchulain practised feats of arms below the palace, and the deeds of the Red Branch knights were celebrated in song. Later a huge Celtic temple, 120ft wide and 40ft high, was erected on the top. All that remains of this fabulous kingdom is a grassy enclosure 250yd across, with a large mound inside, and some prehistoric sacrificial lakes. The area is protected as an archaeological park and has a modern **interpretive centre** concealed, or nearly concealed on the south side of the enclosure. Prehistoric finds from the site are on display. From the breezy top of the mound is a fine view of the cathedrals of Armagh, somewhat spoiled however by a large limestone quarry.

The big house with curvilinear Dutch gables at **Richhill** (population 2,700) was built after 1664. Its magnificent wrought-iron gates, made in 1745 by the Thornberry brothers of Armagh, were moved to

Hillsborough Castle in 1936. From time to time the Richhillians petition the authorities to return them. A mile south-east at **Aghory** (take B131) the Presbyterian church commemorates the father-and-son founders of the Disciples of Christ, a huge indigenous American fundamentalist church which now has over 1½ million adherents. Thomas Campbell had a small farm and bible teaching school here. He emigrated from Richhill to the Pennsylvanian backwoods, followed shortly (1809) by his son Alexander, known as the 'Sage of Bethany'. The **tower** and **memorial window** at Aghory were a gift from American church members. Another interesting church near here is at **Kilmore** where a medieval **spiral staircase** is built into a massive square tower.

This area, north-east of Armagh, is Ireland's apple orchard country. The bulk of the crop is the tangy Bramley Seedling cooker, harvested in October and sold on the fresh market in Belfast and Dublin. (The apple pies of Ireland have lost out lately to pavlovas and other cold comforts of the sweet trolley.) The seventeenth-century settlers came here from Worcestershire and their orchards were laid out on the same pattern as in the Vale of Evesham. Round-roofed houses dotted about are lucrative mushroom production tunnels. Soft fruit growing has declined though strawberries are still sold by the road in summer.

Loughgall (population 300) is surrounded by 5,000 acres of apple orchards, prettiest at blossom time (May/June). **Loughgall Manor**, at the end of an avenue of mature lime trees, is a picturesque gabled mansion with a lake. It is now a government horticultural research centre, visitable on open days and by appointment. The yew walk was planted over 300 years ago by the Cope family who settled here in 1610.

The Orange Order was founded by Protestant farmers in 1795 in Loughgall at **Sloan's House** (now a museum) after a fight between Peep o' Day Boys (Protestant) and Defenders (Catholic). In the aftermath many Catholics fled from Armagh to the west of Ireland. The bucolic battle was fought at **The Diamond** crossroads, near Quaker farmer–weaver **Dan Winter's Cottage**, 3 miles north-east of the village. Lead shot from the fighting remains lodged in the roof of the cottage, now a protected building, its ancient thatch and flagstones intact.

Ardress House and the Argory are two National Trust properties barely 3 miles apart, and it is easy to see both houses in an afternoon, though opening days are very restricted except in July and August. **Ardress House** has a long imposing front, with urns on the parapets and a pedimented porch. It was a modest seventeenth-century farmhouse until its witty architect-owner, George Ensor, enlarged it in about 1770, adding a wing at one end and, to balance it, a wall with dummy windows at the other. The beautiful decoration of the drawing room, with exquisite plaques representing the four seasons, is by Michael Stapleton, the Dublin stuccodore who was the leading Irish plasterer of the time. Behind the house is an eighteenth-century working cobbled **farmyard** with piggery, smithy, chicken houses, and a well in the middle.

The Argory, a large neoclassical house of about 1820, overlooks the Blackwater river. Its owners, the McGeough-Bonds, were much preoccupied with heating and lighting. A handsome cast-iron stove in the front hall heated the central part of the house, and in 1906 the family installed an **acetylene gas plant** for lighting. On the first floor is an unusual **cabinet barrel organ** (1824). The house has a cheerful lived-in feeling, full of furniture, pictures and bric-à-brac. The gas plant, one of very few surviving in the British Isles, can be inspected in the laundry yard. Piped to the light fixtures, the gas gives a warm yellow light. A herd of Moilies, a rare native Irish breed of red-and-white cattle, is kept on the estate.

At the B28/A29 junction outside Moy, 2½ miles south of the Argory, is ruined **Charlemont Fort**, built in 1602 by Lord Deputy Mountjoy (not signposted but do not be deflected from your goal which is opposite Millars Hill Orange Hall, in College Lands Road). Right on the Armagh/Tyrone border, the star-shaped fort faced across the Blackwater into the territory of Hugh O'Neill. In 1598 he had resoundingly beaten the English at Yellow Ford, a few miles from Charlemont, and his power had increased. A campaign by the Earl of Essex had been a miserable failure and Elizabeth I now sent Charles Blount, Lord Mountjoy, to crush O'Neill once and for all. The fort was an important part of the English strategy.

The gatehouse entrance is visible from the road (B28) at the end of a short avenue of trees. Go through the farm gate 50yd up the road to see the ramparts, in the shape of a star, stretching down towards the river (take care not to dislodge masonry). The main accommodation inside was thatched cottages. One wonders how well the garrison slept in this isolated and dangerous place, so close to Tyrone territory. The people across the river had good reason to hate and fear Mountjoy, Elizabeth's toughest and most effective general. The Lord Deputy campaigned all year round. He swept off the cattle, burnt crops, destroyed the peasants' looms and distaffs, and starved O'Neill into submission in 1603. Another approach to the fort, which was finally burnt down in 1921, is via stone steps on Moy bridge.

Top: Ardress House
Above: The Argory, two National Trust
mansions in County Armagh

ADDITIONAL INFORMATION

PLACES TO VISIT

ARMAGH CITY

Anglican Cathedral
☎ (01861) 523142. Open 9am–4pm daily. At other times ask at 3 Vicar's Row.

Armagh County Museum
☎ (01861) 523070. Open 10am–5pm Monday–Saturday, closed most bank holidays.

Armagh Friary Ruins
Always accessible.

Catholic Cathedral
Always open.

Navan Fort (Emain Macha)
Off A28, always accessible. The Navan Interpretive Centre is open all year weekdays 10am–5pm (until 6pm in summer) and from 11am at the weekend.
☎ (01861) 525550

Observatory Grounds
☎ (01861) 522928. Open Monday–Friday 9.30am–4.30pm.

Palace Stables
☎ (01861) 529629. Open Monday–Saturday 10am–5pm, Sunday 2–5pm, longer hours in summer.

Planetarium
☎ (01861) 523689. Hall of astronomy open Monday–Friday 10am–4.45pm, weekends from 1.15pm. Star shows at 3pm.

Robinson Library
☎ (01861) 523142. Open Monday–Friday 9am–1pm, 2–4pm.

Royal Irish Fusiliers Museum
☎ (01861) 522911. Open weekdays, limited hours.

St Patrick's Trian
☎ (01861) 521801. Open 10am–5pm Monday–Saturday and Sunday afternoon, longer hours in summer.

LOUGHGALL

Dan Winter's Cottage
The Diamond, Derryloughan Road. Inside yard of the Winter family farm. ☎ (01762) 851344. Open Monday–Saturday 10.30am–8.30pm and Sunday from 2pm.

MARKETHILL

Gosford Forest Park
Open 10am–dusk.
☎ (01861) 551277

MOY

Ardress House (NT)
Seven miles west of Portadown.
☎ (01762) 851236. Open April–September weekends 2–6pm, also June–August daily 2–6pm. Closed Tuesday.

The Argory (NT)
Signposted at Moy. ☎ (01868) 784753. Open April–September weekends 2–6pm, also June–August daily 2–6pm. Closed Tuesday.

MULLAGHBAWN

Folk Museum
Thatched roadside farmhouse on B30 between Crossmaglen and Camlough. ☎ (01693) 888278. Open daily 11am–7pm (ex Sunday am). In winter the museum is open only on Sunday 2–7pm.

NEWRY

Newry Museum
☎ (01693) 66232. Open Tuesday, Thursday and Friday. Telephone for times.

Derrymore House (NT)
Off A25, 4 miles west of Newry.
☎ (01693) 830353. Open May–August Thursday–Saturday 2–5.30pm, and over Easter.

Killevy Churches
Free access always.

Slieve Gullion Forest Park
☎ (016937) 38284. Open Easter–
September 10am–dusk.

OXFORD ISLAND

Lough Neagh Discovery Centre
☎ (01762) 322205. Open April–
September daily 10am–7pm. In
winter, shorter hours and closes
Monday and Tuesday.

PORTADOWN

Moneypenny's Lock
2-mile walk, marked Ulster Way,
from Shillington's Quay carpark,
Castle Street. ☎ (01762) 322205.
Exhibition open Easter–September
Saturday–Sunday 2–5pm.

SCARVA

Visitor Centre
Main Street. ☎ (01762) 832163.
Open Tuesday–Friday 11am–5pm
and weekend afternoons. Closed
November–February.

TANDRAGEE

Tandragee Castle
Entrance off A51. ☎ (01762) 840249.
Free tours of the Tayto crisp factory
Monday–Thursday at 10.30am and
1.30pm. Morning tour only on
Friday. Closed Easter and July.

WARRENPOINT

Burren Heritage Centre
Bridge Road, Burren, 2 miles above
the town. ☎ (016937) 73378.
Open Tuesday–Friday 10am–5pm
and Sunday afternoon. October–
March Monday–Friday.

EVENTS

Armagh

St Patrick's Day (17 March)
Parades, pilgrimages, musical
events.

Apple Blossom Festival (early May)

All-Ireland Road Bowls Finals (early
August)

Fintona

Ecclesville Horse Show (late May)

Keady

*Bard of Armagh Humorous Poetry
Competition* (early November)

Newry

Drama Festival (March)

Newry Canal Festival (early June)

Ulster Coarse Fishing Championship
(May)

Oxford Island

Irish Wildlife Fair (September)
Coincides with arrival on Lough
Neagh of overwintering birds.

Rostrevor

Fiddler's Green Folk Festival
(early August)

Scarva

Sham Fight (mid-July)
200-year-old pageant with horseback joust between two seventeenth-
century kings.

TOURIST INFORMATION CENTRES

Armagh

40 English Street. ☎ (01861) 521800.
Open all year Monday–Saturday
9am–5pm, Sunday 2–5pm. In
summer longer hours on Sunday
(1–5.30pm).

*Tourist information is also available
from*:

Civic Centre, Lakeview Road,
Craigavon. ☎ (01762) 341199

Community Centre, The Square,
Crossmaglen. ☎ (01693) 868900

Town Hall, Newry.
☎ (01693) 68877

Cascades Leisure Complex,
Thomas Street, Portadown.
☎ (01762) 332802

5

FERMANAGH LAKELAND &
THE CLOGHER VALLEY

It is only in the last 30 years or so that Fermanagh's beautiful lakeland has been developed as a holiday area. Easy access to the south-west corner of Northern Ireland began when the motorway was built from Belfast and opened up a fast land route. The limestone caves at Marble Arch, in the south-west of the county, were opened to the public in 1985. Then in 1994 came the reopening of the old canal that links the Erne to the Shannon system, and now there are 500 miles of navigable water from Limerick to Belleek, the longest leisure waterway in Europe. However, for the present, Fermanagh is still agreeably empty of crowds and visitors on cruising holidays are enchanted to find so much water for so few boats.

A long sinuous waterway, 50 miles from end to end, **Lough Erne** is divided in two by a constriction in the middle where the small county town of Enniskillen stands. The highway between the ancient provinces of Ulster in the north and Connaught in the south went across the narrows at this point, and the area is exceptionally rich in Celtic and early Christian antiquities. The lower lake, navigable down as far as Belleek, is 5 miles wide in places, with quite big waves when the wind gets up. The shallow upper lake is a jigsaw of heavily wooded islands and has few open stretches. Even good map readers, armed with the navigation guides of the Ordnance Survey, can get happily confused by the maze of look-alike islands and headlands.

In the Middle Ages there was a chain of island monasteries down the lake — convenient stopping places for the endless stream of pilgrims on their way to St Patrick's Purgatory, an important shrine on Lough Derg, County Donegal. Water transport was the main way of travelling around. Bishop Chiericati, a papal nuncio who passed through Fermanagh in 1517, found the county 'full of robbers,

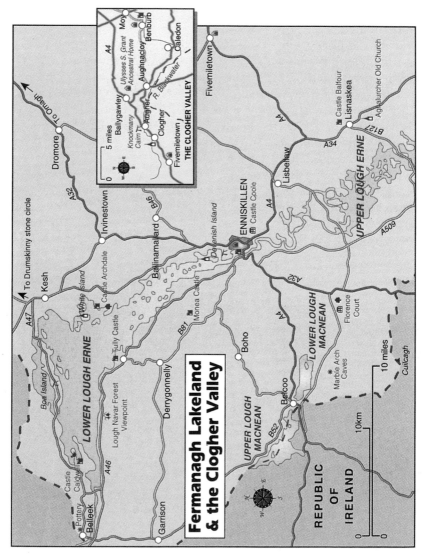

Fermanagh Lakeland & the Clogher Valley

woods, lakes and marshes'. The lakeside is high and rocky in parts, and overland travel was hard-going. The Maguire clan, chieftains of Fermanagh, policed the lake with a private navy of 1,500 boats which were stationed at Enniskillen Castle and Hare Island. Many of the ecclesiastical sites around the lake can be visited by car, and Fermanagh's ruined castles and historic houses open to the public are conveniently close to main roads. Sooner or later, however, you will find yourself on a boat heading out to see the island monasteries and high crosses.

The quickest route to Fermanagh, once so remote from the rest of the province, is via the M1 motorway and then through south Tyrone and the **Clogher Valley**. The quiet villages of this part of County Tyrone, along the meandering course of the Blackwater river, deserve more than a cursory inspection.

Moy (population 850) was laid out in the 1760s for the Volunteer Earl — the patriot and aesthete James Caulfield, Earl of Charlemont (1728–99) — opposite Charlemont Fort across the Blackwater. The formal rectangular market place, with lawns and horse-chestnut trees, was inspired by the square at Marengo in Lombardy, admired by the arty young earl during his grand tour of Europe. Houses round the sides are mostly eighteenth-century though all the four churches are later. **St John's parish church** (1819) used to open on to the market place but after one of the Charlemont ladies objected to the draught in her pew, the front door was walled up and the church has a peculiar

The neat eighteenth-century marketplace at Moy

blind look about it. In the nineteenth century the Charlemont seat was at Roxborough Castle, a huge Grand Hotel-style mansion facing across the river to Charlemont Fort. Though the house was burnt in 1921, two heavy, black-painted **gates** and a fine **screen** surmounted by red dragons, still mark the castle entrance near the river.

A local riding school is the last vestige of the days of the great Moy horse fair, held once a month and lasting a whole week. For over 100 years, Moy supplied the best cavalry and carriage horses in the British Isles. The village had stabling for 2,500 horses. World War I records of one Moy dealer are an indication of the scale of the operation: a standing weekly order from the Army for 100 troopers and chargers, plus a horse which had to weigh an imperial ton. These noble beasts were destined to pull the gun carriages across the battlefields of Europe. In the 1920s the fair dwindled to a two-day event and ceased altogether by 1950. The Ulster poet Paul Muldoon, who grew up here, has written memorably about the fair at 'The Moy'. The local library has a small permanent **exhibition** on the explorer John King, the only survivor of the 1860 Burke Willis expedition across Australia. He was born near Moy in 1838.

The centre of **Benburb** (population 300) is dominated by the precincts of a large Victorian redbrick mansion which has been a **Servite Priory** since 1948 — the first community of this monastic order to be established in Ireland. The Victorian ballroom is now a chapel and the stable block is a shop. You can see here a stone replica of the O'Neill inauguration stone ceremonially broken by Mountjoy at Tullahoge in 1602. The monks built a turbine on the Blackwater which generates their electricity. The fast rapids attract canoeists, and fishing is good.There is a fine view from the priory lawns down the gorge to the Blackwater where a ruined castle stands on a rock 120ft above the water. Sir Richard Wingfield (Viscount Powerscourt) built **Benburb Castle** in 1615, on the site of an O'Neill fort. An **exhibition** in the west flanker tower includes an informative map of the numerous seventeenth-century churches and Celtic crosses scattered along the Blackwater valley. Inside the castle's bawn is a small house with a television aerial on the chimney and a burglar alarm. In the village street, tiny cottages used for years as apple peeling sheds have been repaired and are homes once again. They date from the seventeenth century.

Clonfeacle parish church (1618), outside the priory gates, is one of the oldest churches in regular use in the province. Basically a hall (the belfry tower was added in 1892), the church has a seventeenth-century font and bell, and a monument to Captain James Hamilton. He was one of 3,000 Scots killed at the battle of Benburb in 1646.

Led by Major General Robert Monroe, the Scots were routed in a disastrous encounter with Owen Roe O'Neill, charismatic nephew of the great Hugh O'Neill. The Irish are said to have lost only forty men. For access to the church ask at the redbrick rectory opposite.

A massive, most impressive Celtic cross, known as the **Clonfeacle cross**, is in the yard of a Catholic church 1½ miles from Benburb on the Blackwatertown road. **Eglish cross** is signposted off Milltown Road, Benburb. A scale model of the battle of 1646 is displayed at the **Benburb Valley Heritage Centre**, a nineteenth-century weaving factory still bulging with linen-making equipment, further along Milltown Road, beside the old Ulster Canal. Afterwards you can walk back to the village along the bank.

The tidy village of **Caledon** (population 390) takes its name from the Earls of Caledon. Their mansion, designed by Thomas Cooley (1779) and enlarged by John Nash (1810), is the fourth great house to be built here. It has a beautiful Regency drawing room and library, and the fourth earl kept black bears in the park. His third son, born in 1891, was Field Marshal Earl Alexander of Tunis. On the estate is the ruin of a strange **folly** made out of the knuckle bones of cattle. It was built in the eighteenth century by Lord Orrery who hoped, he said, to 'strike the Caledonians with wonder and amazement'. The butchers and tanners of Tyrone supplied the bones, though their opinions of the 'bone house' are not recorded. The village street has some appealing nineteenth-century buildings. Archbishop Robinson built the eighteenth-century **Anglican church** and the needle spire was added by Nash.

Caledon was one of thirty-six villages and halts which were joined by the **Clogher Valley Railway**. This line, 37 miles long, from Tynan in County Armagh to Maguiresbridge in County Fermanagh, closed in 1941. The picturesque well-built redbrick stations are now private houses and some have been turned into shops and offices.The one at Augher is a tea shop, and the station house at **Aughnacloy** (population 600) is a masonic hall and carefully maintained.

A fine position on a high ridge, with beautiful views across the valley towards **Slieve Beagh**, gives the border village of Aughnacloy a special appeal. Georgian houses and old hotels lining both sides of **Moore Street**, the wide main street, have undergone some sympathetic recent restoration. On the north side —'even' numbers — is a bank, several restaurants and pubs, a tiny sweet shop, a post office with red pillar box, and the pretty pink market house of 1810, now restored. 'Odd' numbers include two eighteenth-century churches, several more restaurants and pubs, and right at the top of the village opposite the petrol station, a **panoramic view** from a small paved garden with an ancient water pump. A National School of 1886 and a row of gabled almshouses built with a £10,000 endowment from a Dublin doctor, lend distinction to the lower end of the village. An elaborate numbering system marked out along Moore Street is for the benefit of stall holders at the big street market held here twice a month (first and third Wednesdays).

The **ancestral home** of American president **Ulysses Simpson Grant** has been rebuilt and is signposted off the A4 east of Ballygawley. His place in history was won as commander of the victorious Federal armies in the American Civil War. Robert E. Lee surrendered the Confederate forces to Grant on the Appomattox river, Virginia, in 1865. John Simpson, Grant's maternal great-grandfather, was one of many young County Tyrone men who left for America in the eighteenth century. He was born in the thatched cottage in 1738. An adjoining visitor centre tells the Grant story and has an interesting exhibition on the American Civil War. Grant came to Ulster on a visit in 1878 at the end of his two terms as president (1869–77).

Antiquities near **Ballygawley** (population 650) are a passage grave at **Sess Kilgreen** (a mile north-west), and a fifteenth-century ruined church dedicated to St Kieran overlooking the Clogher Valley at **Errigal Keerogue** (3 miles west). The romantic castle of Spur Royal across the lake at **Augher** (population 450) incorporates part of an early-seventeenth-century bawn. The old railway station house is now used as a tea shop and craft centre.

A preserved cottage at Springtown, a mile south of Augher, was the childhood **home of William Carleton** (1794–1869), author of many stories of Irish peasant life, some sad, some humorous. *Traits and Stories of the Irish Peasantry* was followed by numerous popular novels, including a bleak tale of the potato famine *Black Prophet* (1847). Youngest son of a Gaelic-speaking tenant farmer, Carleton went to a 'hedge' school, an unlicensed open-air school, and became a hedge schoolmaster himself briefly. Intended for the Catholic Church, he was put off by a visit to St Patrick's Purgatory, a renowned pilgrimage centre in Donegal, and soon escaped to a literary life in Dublin. The cottage where he and his thirteen brothers and sisters grew up is down a winding track shaded by trees (ample turning space at the house, where there is a plaque). His parents are buried in the graveyard of **St MacCartan's church** in Ballynagurragh townland a short distance away.

Inside the church, a **stained glass window** commemorates Archbishop **John Joseph Hughes**, first archbishop of New York, baptised here in 1797. Hughes worked as a gardener at the Favour Royal estate nearby before emigrating in 1817. An authoritarian figure, he was an

Clogher cathedral

energetic pamphleteer and politician who championed the cause of the immigrant Irish in America and built St Patrick's cathedral on Fifth Avenue. Carleton's Cottage and St MacCartan's church are both signposted from the A4. A path from the river in **Favour Royal forest** leads to St Patrick's Well and Chair at **Altnadaven** (signposted from A28), an atmospheric mossy little place which is the venue for Bilberry Sunday, a local festival in late July.

Knockmany Hill, 2 miles north-west of Augher, is topped by a large **passage grave** with stones incised with swirling patterns. The spiral motives are similar to those at Newgrange in County Meath. A cairn was built over the top in 1959 to protect the Knockmany grave, which appears above ground in old photographs. To get inside the tomb visitors need to plan ahead (see Additional Information). There is a general view of the stones through a locked iron grid. The mythological mother goddess, Áine, loved by the warrior Finn

McCool, is traditionally buried on top of this hill which commands a magnificent view of the surrounding countryside.

Clogher (population 550) was the fifth-century seat of the diocese of Clogher, the oldest bishopric in Ireland, and gives its name to two dioceses, Protestant and Catholic. The diocese corresponds roughly with Fermanagh, south Tyrone, and County Monaghan in the Republic. The twelfth-century Cross of Clogher, made of oak and clad in bronze with red enamelling on the arms, is on display in Monaghan county museum just across the border. The first bishop of Clogher was St MacCartan (died 506), a disciple of St Patrick. In medieval times there were endless power struggles between the bishops of Clogher and the vicars general of the deanery of Lough Erne. Pope Sixtus IV made several appointments to the see but the bishop was rarely able to take possession. When the Blessed Oliver Plunkett, primate of Armagh, visited Clogher in 1671 he inspected the old diocesan register which catalogued all the bishops. These included Bishop Eoghan (died 1515) who lost a finger on his left hand 'in defence of his church'. The first Protestant bishop, Myler MacGrath, was appointed in 1570 by Elizabeth I. Only three years earlier he had been appointed bishop of Down and Connor — by the pope. Even in the sixteenth century this was unusual!

The little **Anglican cathedral**, rebuilt in purply blue stone in 1744, preserves a fine early sculptured slab cross, a gallery of portraits of sixteenth- to eighteenth-century bishops, and some good stained glass. The tower gives a view right down the Clogher Valley. Ask at the deanery for access.

In the churchyard are seventeenth-century monuments and two **high crosses** as well as some mournful memorials of Ulster's more recent past. This is the older of two Anglican cathedrals in the diocese. The other, at Enniskillen, was raised from parish church status in 1924. Both are dedicated to St MacCartan (though the Enniskilleners insist on spelling theirs 'Macartin'). An impressive **earthworks** in the park behind Clogher cathedral was the seat of the old kings of Oriel, ancestors of the Maguires. Driving south from the village, you cannot avoid seeing, on the left, a tall nineteenth-century hilltop tower known as **Brackenridge's Folly**. The local squirearchy of the time steadfastly refused to admit Mr George Brackenridge to their midst. He remedied this injustice by building the tower as his own mausoleum, thus obliging the county bigwigs who looked down on the living Mr Brackenridge to look up to him when dead. The locals are still amiably rude about him. Sepulchral humour of this kind is not untypical of Northern Ireland.

Blessingbourne House, outside Fivemiletown, is an agreeable

Elizabethan-style manor looking on to a small round lake. It was built in the 1870s. The stable yard is divided into holiday flats popular with pike fishermen, and a small **coach and carriage museum** can be visited by appointment. **Fivemiletown** (population 1,100) is so called because it is 5 Irish miles from Clogher, Brookeborough and Tempo (1 Irish mile − 2,240yd). Its simple **parish church** was built the same year as St James's in Aughnacloy (1736). Old photographs showing the railway running down the middle of the main street are displayed in the **library**. Ask here for directions to houses where lace is made — a local cottage industry.

After Fivemiletown, the road enters Fermanagh, passing **Colebrooke Park**. This was the ancestral home of Field Marshal Lord Alanbrooke (1883–1963), chief of the British Imperial General Staff during World War II, and also the home of Lord Brookeborough, prime minister of Northern Ireland 1943–63. The two houses in the grounds are Colebrooke, a large classical mansion of pinkish sandstone, now partly run as a guesthouse, and Ashbrooke, a dower house. **Aghalurcher** church (Anglican, 1762), prominent on an adjoining hill, contains Alanbrooke's banners of the Orders of the Bath and Garter and monuments to many other battling Brookes, including a young dragoon killed at Waterloo.

The A4 bypasses quiet **Brookeborough** village but a signpost indicates this is where to turn to see a fascinating **vintage cycle collection** at 64 Main Street. Pennyfarthings, tandems, bikes made for the butcher's boy and the postman, and an ancient model with levers from the 1870s are among the 60 specimens on show.

A distinctive long, flat mountain about 20 miles directly ahead is the ridge of the **Cuilcagh mountains** rising to 2,188ft and marking the south-west extremity of Fermanagh. An indirect approach to the lakes is by minor roads south off the A4 through an attractive area of forest and little lakes. The main road runs into Enniskillen, passing the bell tower of **Lisbellaw** parish church and Castle Coole stately home.

A glance at the map shows virtually all major roads in Fermanagh converging on **Enniskillen** (population 11,400) on its island between Upper and Lower Lough Erne. The result is considerable congestion around the town. The loop roads and improved bridges of the traffic engineers, and housing estates on neighbouring hillsides, have effectively deprived the casual visitor of any sense of being on an island. However, as a good shopping centre, with first-rate angling facilities, a lively cultural scene (including a large lakeside theatre) and friendly people, Enniskillen makes a convenient base for exploring this lovely watery part of the province.

The long main street changes its name half a dozen times as it curves and wiggles from East Bridge to West Bridge, up and down two slight hills. **Enniskillen Castle** at the west end was in turn a Maguire fort, plantation castle and, from the late eighteenth century, artillery barracks. The English first captured it in 1594. The Maguires got it back briefly but were expelled again in 1607, after which the whole of Enniskillen was granted to Sir William Cole. As constable, and captain of the king's long boats, Cole enlarged the castle, built the fairytale **Water Gate** and created the plantation town. The Water Gate, which is really just a short length of wall flanked by two towers with nothing behind it, is best seen by boat, approaching from the upper lough. There are always a few anglers under its romantic towers, pole fishing for eels, roach and bream from the river bank.

Enniskillen was the only stronghold in Fermanagh to escape destruction in the seventeenth century. Cole's garrison successfully defended it against Roderick Maguire during the 1641 rising, and again resisted in 1688 when the town rallied to William of Orange. The Enniskilleners were able to stop Jacobite troops at Belleek and prevented a large Irish force from joining the attack on Londonderry, and they formed William's personal guard at the Battle of the Boyne.

The Water Gate at Enniskillen

The extensive waterways of Fermanagh are popular for cruising holidays

Two famous regiments, the Royal Inniskilling Fusiliers and the Inniskilling Dragoons, originated from this time (the town later changed the I for an E). Napoleonic battle trophies and other militaria of the Inniskilling regiments, both long since merged with other regiments, occupy several floors in the **castle keep**. The ground floor of the keep, which dates from the castle of Hugh the Hospitable (died 1428), contains objects from the county museum's collection, including an ogham stone and grotesque stone idols (originals) and copies of the mysterious carvings on White Island, Lower Lough Erne.

At the east end of the town is a delightful Victorian **town park** of humpy hillocks squeezed on to the slopes of Fort Hill. In the middle

continued on page 136

THE ISLANDS OF LOWER LOUGH ERNE

Devenish Island, 2 miles downstream from the town, is the site of a sixth-century monastery founded by St Molaise (died 563), one of the 'twelve apostles of Ireland'. Arbitrator in the quarrels of the Ulster chieftains, and mentor of St Columba, Molaise had 1,500 students attached to Devenish. The monastery was raided by Vikings in the ninth century and burned in 1157 but then remained an important religious centre until the early seventeenth century. The island's greatest treasure, the *Soiscél Molaise*, an early-eleventh-century book shrine, is in the National Museum, Dublin. Follow the path up from the east jetty, and you will pass a remarkable succession of ecclesiastical remains.

• Ruined *Teampull Mór*, the lower church, dates from about 1225 and has a fine south window of that period. It was greatly extended in about 1300 and was in turn a Culdee monastery and the parish church of Devenish. The Culdees (*Céli-Dé* — Companions of God) were a strict Celtic anchorite order founded at the end of the eighth century. Killadeas, a small angling and boating resort down the lough (east shore), is named after the Culdees. The arms of the Maguires of Tempo appear in two places outside their sixteenth-century burial chamber here, and the graveyard below the church contains some interesting stones, including an eleventh-century cross-carved slab.

• St Molaise's House is a tiny twelfth-century church with thick walls which once had a stone roof. Though much ruined, it still has a sturdy look about it.

• The perfect round tower (also twelfth-century) has a site as beautiful as any in Ireland. Over 80ft high, with a decorated cornice round the conical cap, it has five floors which are ascended by interior ladders. The four windows at the top gave the sentry an all-round view of strangers approaching over the water, and time for him to sound his bell in warning. The door of the tower, 9ft off the ground, faces the entrance to St Molaise's House and so the monks — having snatched up books and relics from the church — could hurry to the safety of the tower, pull up the outside ladder and hope for the best. A few yards away are the foundations of an earlier round tower which may have been destroyed by Vikings who arrived on Lough Erne in 837 and established a base at Belleek. Their long boats had no difficulty in reaching the island monasteries.

• Beyond the round tower are the ruins of St Mary's, an Augustinian priory, built by the master mason Matthew O'Dubigan in 1449 when, according to an inscription on the south wall, Bartholomew O'Flanagan was prior. The O'Flanagan sept supplied the last prior of St Mary's too, and also many of the priests for Inishmacsaint. The most notable feature is the north door to the chancel which has elaborate carvings. The east window was taken to the Anglican parish church at Monea (B81/C443 junction, 1 mile south-west of Monea Castle) where it was reset in 1890. The **site museum** preserves a female head from the west door into the nave. Note the unusual design of a pretty fifteenth-century cross in the graveyard. The Augustinian priory and the Culdee monastery down the hill co-existed in apparent harmony until both were abandoned in 1603 at the dissolution of monasteries in Fermanagh.

Inishmacsaint Island also had a sixth-century monastery — one of the thousands that sprang up all over Ireland in the generation after St Patrick's death. This one was founded in about 523 by St Ninnid who, like St Molaise, studied under St Finian at Clonard. The island has an ancient rath or prehistoric hillfort, a ruined twelfth-century church, and a striking tenth-century 14ft-high cross with splayed arms and a broad shaft. It lacks the usual Celtic circle and looks as though the stone carver was called away before he could finish it.

White Island has seven stone figures, lined up on the far wall of a roofless twelfth-century church, and they are first glimpsed through a Romanesque doorway as you walk through trees from the jetty. Dating from the ninth or tenth century, these Christian statues have a distinctly pagan mien and their significance has been much de-bated. The builders of a later church used them as ordinary masonry stones but sockets on the heads indicate they were intended as supports. From left to right: a female fertility figure (*sheela-na-gig*) with a wide suggestive grin; a seated man holding a book; an abbot with bell and crozier; another priestly figure scratching his chin; a man with a kiss-curl fringe holding two griffins by the scruff of their necks; a second curly-haired man with sword, shield and a big brooch; the seventh figure is unfinished. An eighth stone, a medieval sour-faced mask, is unconnected with the others. Look out for an eleventh-century gravestone in the church. Three large earthworks west of the church remain from an early monastery.

UPPER LOUGH ERNE ISLANDS

The maze of islands in the shallow, reedy upper lake are better known for their natural beauty and wild birds than for their eccles-iastical sites. Most of them are uninhabited, some with ruined man-sions and abandoned cottages, others with heronries, or wild goats who run up and steal your picnic sandwiches. However, a few islands still retain traces of the religious communities that flourished here in early Christian times. Three which can be reached by either car or boat are Inishkeen, Cleenish and Galloon.

Inishkeen (accessible by causeway 3 miles south-east of Enniskillen off A4) has a rath at either end, and strange carved stones in old St Fergus's cemetery — a god's head with antlers and an angel sitting in a boat, or it could be a devil boiling in a cauldron. The Annals of Ulster report that, in 1421, Hugh Maguire slew the three sons of Art Maguire on Inishkeen. Opposite the northern tip of the island, across the picturesque reach used by the rowing club, is the site of **Lisgoole Abbey**. A battlemented tower, now incorporated into a Georgian house, dates from the twelfth-century monastery which passed from Augustinians to Franciscans in the sixteenth century. At Lisgoole, in 1631, Brother Michael O'Clery and other learned friars compiled the Book of Invasions, an ingenious synthesis of pagan myths and Christian beliefs.

is a fine cast-iron bandstand with a clock tower and cupola. Nearby a statue to Sir Galbraith Lowry Cole (1772–1842), one of Wellington's generals in the Peninsular War, stands on top of a Doric column. Sir Galbraith is holding a fearsome-looking cavalry sabre in his left hand and has a panoramic view of the lakes. A spiral staircase (108 steps) to the top of the monument is accessible in summer, on weekdays and weekend afternoons.

The **Anglican cathedral** on the main street contains a full-length martial portrait of this same general, still brandishing his sabre. The cathedral tower, which survives from a seventeenth-century church on the site, contains a bell cast from cannon used in the Battle of the Boyne. Colours of the Inniskilling regiments hang in the light and airy late Georgian interior. Notable features are the seventeenth-century font and a stone tablet to William Pokrich (died 1628) with half the inscription upside down. Across the narrow street is a very tall and thin nineteenth-century Catholic church, **St Michael's**, with a long

Cleenish (reached across a metal bridge south-east of **Bellanaleck**) had a celebrated abbot, St Sinell, tutor to St Columbanus, the austere Irish missionary who went to Europe in 589 and founded famous Celtic monasteries in France (Luxeuil) and at Bobbio near Milan. The island has some distinctive carved gravestones. The father of Field Marshal Sir Claude Auchinleck (died 1981) was a native of Cleenish. On **Inishrath**, a small island further upstream, Hare Krishna devotees have turned an 1840s mansion into a **Hindu shrine**. The wooded demesne of **Crom Castle**, home of the Earls of Erne, occupies a long headland west of Galloon. The romantic ruin of a plantation castle (1611) is down by the shore (jetty) where two huge yew trees, planted in 1669 and grotesquely misshapen, survive in the abandoned garden. The family's present home, New Crom Castle, is a nineteenth-century castellated mansion half a mile away (private).

Galloon (3 miles south-west of Newtownbutler) supports a small farming community and whooper swans are common round here. The churchyard contains fragmentary remains of two very weathered tenth-century crosses and some fine eighteenth-century grave slabs carved with skull and crossbones, coffins, bell and sand timer. The Adam and Eve cross in Lisnaskea market place is thought to have come from Galloon, and similar grave slabs are at **Aghalurcher Old Church** (south of Lisnaskea), many of them in a covered vault. The church itself was abandoned in 1484, the year a Maguire slew a kinsman on the altar.

nave and steep roof. A window in the south aisle portrays St Molaise, the abbot founder of Devenish monastery, holding the Devenish Gospel Shrine. **Blake's Of The Hollow** (1887) down the street is Enniskillen's best-known musical pub. At this point there is a pronounced dip or hollow in the road, hence its name. It has a characterful Victorian shop-front and pine-boarded snugs inside. Further along, on the **town hall** tower are niche statues of a fusilier and a dragoon. Go into the lobby to see a brass plate commemorating brave Captain Oates of the 6th Inniskilling Dragoons, who walked out into a blizzard on Scott's tragic return journey from the South Pole in March 1912. In the **convent** below Fort Hill the chapel contains modern stained glass by Irish artists.

Enniskillen was the most important of a ring of castles — Crom, Portora, Tully, Archdale, Crevenish and Caldwell — which the planters built round the lough shore to control this huge waterway. Ruined **Portora Castle** (built about 1613), which commanded the

Two great houses of Fermanagh, both in National Trust care:
Castle Coole (*top*) and Florence Court (*above*)

The caves at Marble Arch

entrance to the lower lough, is now in the grounds of **Portora Royal School**, founded by James I in 1608 and moved to this site above the river in 1777. The castle's ruinous state is partly the result of an experiment by the chemistry class of 1859. A large oil painting of Oscar Wilde (1854–1900), the school's most famous old boy, adorns the entrance hall. Other pupils included Henry Francis Lyte (1793–1847), the divine who wrote the hymn 'Abide with me', and the dramatist Samuel Beckett (1905–89). Nurse Edith Cavell, the English patriot, was a friend of the headmaster's wife and occasionally ministered to boarders in the school sanatorium. A matron in Brussels during World War I, she was shot by the Germans in 1915 for helping Allied soldiers escape over the Dutch frontier.

The rivers and small lakes around **Lisnaskea** (population 2,450) are rich fishing waters. The town's main street is crowded with pubs, and the library preserves a local publican's folk collection. A carved market cross and ruined **Castle Balfour** (about 1618) are noteworthy. The **Share Holiday Village**, to the south, is a remarkable lakeside activity centre for both disabled and able-bodied people. Groups from many countries come to participate in supervised activities like canoeing, sailing, indoor riding and camping. From the Share centre, a good road (B127) crosses Upper Lough Erne via bridges at either end of Trasna Island, joining the main Enniskillen road at **Derrylin** hamlet. Look out for Derrylin's weird black-and-white stone man, with a pudding-basin hairdo, bow tie and dinner jacket next to Blake's public house. The craggy outline of **Knockninny Hill** is a striking feature on the upper lake. The hill is a well-known beauty spot and, although only 600ft high, gives a fine view of the islands from the top (3 miles north of Derrylin).

Florence Court and Castle Coole are two fine properties owned by the National Trust near Enniskillen. The magnificent neoclassical mansion at Castle Coole, the most palatial of Ireland's late-eighteenth-century houses, is the more famous but the setting of **Florence Court** is memorably dramatic. The house stands in a natural amphitheatre of mountains — the hump of Benaughlin to the south, Cuilcagh and the Leitrim hills to the west, and Mount Belmore on the north side. Former seat of the Earls of Enniskillen (descendants of planter–constable William Cole), Florence Court is a three-storey early-eighteenth-century house joined by long arcades to small pavilions (added in about 1770 by Davis Ducart). Sumptuous **rococo plasterwork** (about 1755) by the Dublin stuccodore, Robert West, is the most notable feature of the interior.

The surrounding woodlands, now a **forest park**, shelter the original **Irish yew**, progenitor of the columnar tree now found throughout the world (*Taxus baccata fastigiata*). Discovered as a seedling on the rocky slopes of Cuilcagh in the mid-eighteenth century, the tree can be propagated only by cuttings. A great number of cuttings have been taken from the old mother tree which stands, exhausted and gaunt, at the edge of a clearing. **Cuilcagh** (2,188ft) can be climbed from Florence Court, if you have 7 hours or so to spare, and the right boots. The top is very steep and rugged.

The first big house at **Castle Coole** was a plantation castle which was destroyed in 1641. Two more houses, each bigger and better than the last, came and went before the present masterpiece was completed in 1798. Designed by James Wyatt for the Lowry-Corry family, Earls of Belmore, it has a beautiful Palladian main front, 275ft long, with pillared colonnades and elegant pavilions at each end. Silvercoloured Portland stone, imported at great expense by boat and hauled here by ox-cart, was used for the façade. Art historians describe the splendid interior of the house in tremulous tones of emotion. The garden front overlooks a lake, where a large breeding colony of greylag geese has lived since 1700, and the park has some noble beeches and a four-row avenue of ancient oaks. The stables and the head gardener's house were built in the 1820s by Richard Morrison. A young French émigré, the Chevalier de Latocnaye, who visited Castle Coole in 1796, ventured the opinion that Lord Belmore's new palace was rather too grand for a private individual. 'The temples should be left to the gods,' he said.

During his visit to Fermanagh the Chevalier went into the underground caves at **Marble Arch** and got lost when his candle blew out. Until structural engineering work was completed in 1985, only geologists, cavers and a few adventurous individuals went down into the caves. Now they are a big public attraction. The entrance is signposted up the **Marlbank Loop** road, immediately west of Florence Court. Apart from the things one expects to see in caves, like stalagmites, there are subterranean lakes and rivers fed by surface streams rising in the Cuilcagh mountains. A boat trip across the lower lake is a highlight of the guided tour. The 'marble arch' — a detached limestone arch 30ft high — is above ground, at the lower entrance to the caves in a flowery glen where the Cladagh river rushes out from under the ground and flows beneath the arch.

These show caves are only a fraction of the extensive cave systems of County Fermanagh. Caves on the moors around **Boho** hamlet (due north of Marble Arch) include **Noon's Hole**, the deepest pothole in Ireland (nearly 300ft). **Knockmore Cliff**, an 800ft-high sheer reef of limestone with a fine view, has several visitable caves (north-west of Boho). Generally speaking, however, it is not advisable to go exploring round here without a guide. When leaving the Marble Arch carpark, turn right to complete the scenic run along the wild Cuilcagh plateau, passing first a small bridge where the Sruh Croppa river suddenly vanishes into a crevice called the **Cat's Hole**. After 2 miles the loop rejoins the lower road (turn right, back to Florence Court). Two nearby lakes, the **Macneans**, are full of heavyweight pike which anglers come to do battle with — in particular German and Swiss anglers, who are partial to poached pike.

Guesthouses and bed-and-breakfast places with views over the lake punctuate the shore route from Enniskillen to Belleek (A46). The road runs through **Ely Lodge Forest**, especially pretty in autumn when the leaves turn. Ely Lodge, the Irish seat of the Duke of Westminster, is on a promontory beyond (visible from the lake). An earlier house on the site was blown up by its owner, a nineteenth-

Lough Melvin is noted for its salmon and unusual kinds of trout

century Hooray Henry, to celebrate his 21st birthday.

Turn inland to see **Monea Castle**, a superb ruined castle surrounded by bog, overlooking a lake at the end of a long avenue of great beech trees. Built in 1618 by Malcolm Hamilton, Rector of Devenish, later Archbishop of Cashel, Monea has an impressive entrance front — two glowering circular towers with square turrets supported on Scottish-type corbels at the top. The 1641 insurgents captured it (one wonders how) but the Hamiltons soon got it back. The governor of Enniskillen, Gustavus Hamilton, who was one of William III's generals at the Boyne, lived in the castle. After the battle, and now raised to the peerage, the new Viscount Boyne moved out of Monea and built a grand country residence not far from the battleground (in County Meath) and called it after himself — Boyne House.

Belleek's basket-weave pottery has been made since 1857

Derrygonnelly (population 700) is an 1830s village with a harmonious main street lined with two-storey houses, shops and musical pubs such as **Corrigan's**, where the fiddle, the tin whistle and the accordion can be heard for the price of a pint of Guinness. Just north of the village is a small ruined church that combines medieval and Renaissance features, built in 1627 by Sir John Dunbar. His arms are over the doorway. The B81 from Derrygonnelly runs north to Tully Bay where the ruin of a small castle overlooks Lower Lough Erne. Built in 1613 by Sir John Hume, **Tully Castle** was burnt by the ousted Maguires in 1641. The Maguires were in a particularly vengeful mood. Though they spared the Humes they killed everyone else in the castle and, since the garrison was away, these were mostly women and children. A small herb garden, recently created in formal seventeenth-century style, is a poignant reminder of the domestic duties and pleasures of the short-lived household.

The most interesting, certainly the most strenuous, route to one of the best panoramas in Ireland is a steep zigzag path from the A46 (carpark and waymarked Ulster Way) up 1,000ft to **Lough Navar forest viewpoint**. If you insist on driving, the forest entrance is opposite Correl Glen nature reserve on the C446 road, and you can drive right up to the map table. All Lower Lough Erne lies below, with the cone of Errigal (2,467ft) in County Donegal north-northwest, and Ben Bulben (1,730ft) due west.

Belleek (population 550) is on the border with the Republic (a little bit of the village is actually in the South) and also marks the end of the Erne navigation. The current at the low bridge opposite the famous pottery reaches 6 knots on occasion, and a sluice here controls the level of Lough Erne. Half a mile beyond are the dams of the Erne hydro-electric scheme, after which the river plunges down to the Atlantic at Ballyshannon. There are nice waterside holiday chalets in Belleek and the village hosts an annual fiddle festival when fiddlers from all over Ireland arrive for a weekend of traditional Irish music-making. There is more accommodation 5 miles away in **Garrison** (population 320) at the head of **Lough Melvin**, notable for early salmon and three unusual species of trout: the gillaroo, the sonaghan and the ferox, a very big trout with strong jaws.

The **pottery** was started when local deposits of felspar were discovered at Castle Caldwell in 1857. The porcelain is especially coveted by Americans, and some of the exquisitely glazed early pieces sell for large sums. Cream-coloured lattice-worked baskets, decorated with pink and yellow rosebuds, blue cornflowers or daisies, are characteristic of the Belleek style. These 'woven' baskets are definitely not for putting things in but the pottery also makes a wide range of tableware and less fragile ornaments. A tour of the works is of great interest. Some delectable extravaganzas from the early days are on display in a small **museum** in the visitor centre where there is also a shop. The felspar is now imported from Norway.

Castle Caldwell estate, in the fork of a double-pronged peninsula east of Belleek, is a nature reserve and a popular haunt of bird-watchers. The two prongs are managed as state timber forest, and the deep bay between them is fringed with rare fen and reed-swamp vegetation. Nature trails run down each prong. Crossbills nest here and sparrowhawks breed nearby. Old Castle Caldwell, first built in 1612, passed in 1662 to the Caldwell family. It is now very ruined and covered in ivy. At the entrance to the main forest (on A47) is a giant stone fiddle, 5ft high, inscribed with an obituary poem to Denis McCabe, an inebriated fiddler who drowned when he fell off the Caldwells' barge in 1770. The Belleek Fiddle Festival at the end of June commemorates his demise.

To see the mysterious Bronze Age stone circle at **Drumskinny**, take the Castlederg road north from the fishing village of **Kesh** (population 670) for about 4½ miles. To add to the mystery some stones are lettered 'MOF'. This is unconnected with archaic forms of worship, merely the handiwork of conscientious Ministry of Finance officials anxious to distinguish new stones, imported to fill empty socket holes, from the ones already there.

Further west past Kesh, **Castle Archdale Country Park** is the departure point for the ferry to White Island. The exceedingly ruined old castle in the forest was built by John Archdale, an English planter from Norfolk, in 1615 and destroyed during the Williamite wars. 'New' Castle Archdale (1773) was used by the RAF and the Canadian Air Force from 1941 when this part of Lower Lough Erne was a base for flying boat squadrons. American Catalinas and British Sunderlands (developed and built in Belfast) took off from here to hunt for U-boats in the Atlantic. The stables of the eighteenth-century house contain a small exhibition featuring the Battle of the Atlantic. More concrete reminders of those days are the huge ramps at the yacht club at Goblusk Bay and, nearby, **Enniskillen Airport**, the former St Angelo airfield which was opened in 1941 and used by Dakotas.

Irvinestown (population 1,900) is enlivened in summer by a 10-day carnival and, since an international equestrian centre opened at nearby **Necarne Castle**, a steady stream of horsy people and their handsome steeds from springtime onwards. A clock tower with pinnacled battlements remains from the 1734 church of Dr Patrick Delany, then rector at Irvinestown, later dean of Down. His wife, Mrs Mary Delany (1700–88, née Granville), was a London literary and society hostess, confidante of Pope, Burke and Horace Walpole, and a favourite at court. Delany met her through his friend, Swift. After their marriage in 1743, Mrs Delany accompanied her husband all over Ireland, staying in all the great Anglo-Irish houses, and writing everything down. Her voluminous autobiography and correspondence, published in 1861–62, include spirited portraits of eighteenth-century Irish society.

ADDITIONAL INFORMATION

PLACES TO VISIT

AUGHER

Knockmany Hill
Access to the passage grave is difficult. Visitors are advised to telephone the DOE Environment Service (the monument's guardian) and express a scholarly interest.
☎ (01232) 235000

BALLYGAWLEY

President Grant Ancestral Home
☎ (016625) 57133 . Open April–September Monday–Saturday noon–5pm, Sunday 2–6pm.

BELLEEK

Belleek Pottery
☎ (013656) 58501. Tours all year from visitor centre Monday–Friday. China shop, museum and café open 7 days a week in summer.

Erne Gateway Centre
☎ (013656) 58866. Exhibitions. Open April–October daily, 10am–6pm.

BENBURB

Benburb Castle
For access to west tower exhibition ask at the priory — entrance in the village main street. ☎ (01861) 548170

Benburb Valley Heritage Centre
Milltown Road. ☎ (01861) 549752.
Open Easter–September Tuesday–
Saturday 10am–5pm, Sunday 2–7pm.

BROOKEBOROUGH

Vintage Cycle Museum
64 Main Street. ☎ (013655) 31206.
Open Monday–Saturday 2–8pm or
by arrangement.

ENNISKILLEN

Enniskillen Castle
☎ (01365) 325000. Open May–
September Tuesday–Friday 10am–
5pm, and Saturday and Monday
2–5pm. Also Sunday 2–5pm in high
summer. In winter open weekdays
only.

Castle Coole (NT)
☎ (01365) 322690. Open 1–6pm
April–September weekends, also
June–August daily. Always closed
Thursday.

FIVEMILETOWN

Fivemiletown Library
Main Street. ☎ (013655) 21409
Open Monday–Saturday except
Wednesday. (Hours rather limited.)

Blessingbourne Coach/Carriage Museum
☎ (013655) 21221. Open Easter–
September, telephone for times.

FLORENCECOURT

Florence Court House (NT)
8 miles south-west of Enniskillen
via A4/A32. ☎ (01365) 348249.
Open 1–6pm April–September
weekends, also June–August daily.
Always closed Tuesday.

Florencecourt Forest Park
Open daily until dusk.

Marble Arch Caves
☎ (01365) 348855. Open mid-March
to September from 10am; last tour
4.30pm. Heavy rain can affect water
levels and occasionally the caves are
closed. If in doubt check.

MONEA CASTLE

7 miles north-west of Enniskillen
on Derrygonnelly road (B81).
Always accessible.

LOUGH ERNE ISLANDS

Local boatmen take visitors out at
any time of the year. In summer
regular passenger cruises leave
from the Round 'O' jetty,
Enniskillen. Public ferries to
Devenish and White Island are
mentioned below. Hire craft range
from large cruisers to motor
launches and rowing boats hired
by the day or half-day. Public
moorings and jetties are free, and
so are most other jetties and
harbours. Visitors with their own
boat will find plenty of slipways. If
you want to land on an island but
cannot see a jetty, you are advised
to use a dinghy. The water may be
shallow. Some islands are privately
owned and visitors should respect
'private' notices by not landing
there. The Ordnance Survey (NI)
publishes outdoor pursuits maps
for the upper and the lower loughs
(see Fact File) which are useful for
navigating the waters.

Devenish Island
Ferry leaves from Trory April–
September 10am–7pm Tuesday–
Saturday and Sunday 2–7pm.
Signposted at A32/B82 junction
3 miles north of Enniskillen.

White Island
☎ (013656) 21333. Ferry from Castle
Archdale marina on Sunday
afternoons (2–6pm) April–
September, plus every day from
11am in high summer. Other
crossings on request.

EVENTS

Augher

Bilberry Sunday (late July)
Altnadaven, south of Favour
Royal.

Belleek

Fiddle Stone Festival (end June)
Irish traditional music.

Benburb

Fête (third Sunday in June)

Clogher

William Carleton Summer School
(early August)
Celebrates life and work of this
chronicler of Irish peasantry, plus
traditional fair.

Fermanagh Lakeland

Classic Fishing Festival (May)
Coarse fishing.

Irvinestown

Lady of the Lake Festival (mid-July)

International Horse Trials
(September)
Necarne Equestrian Park.

Garrison

*Lough Melvin Open Trout
Championship* (late August)
Fly fishing.

TOURIST INFORMATION CENTRES

Enniskillen

Fermanagh Tourist Information
Centre, Wellington Road. ☎ (01365)
323110. Open all year Mon–Fri 9am–
5.30pm, until 6.30pm in summer.
Easter–Sept Sat 10am–6pm, Sun
11am–5pm.

Tourist information is also available at:
Erne Gateway Centre, Belleek (see
above).

6

THE SPERRINS
& THE NORTH WEST

When the Four Citizens of London came to the north-west of Ulster in 1609, their guide was under instructions from the Lord Deputy of Ireland not to show them the **Sperrin mountains**. As agents for the City of London merchant companies, the visitors were looking at the region's investment potential, and the fear was that these rugged peaty hills would create a bad impression. Nowadays the Sperrins are the haunt of trout fishermen, turf-cutters and people panning for gold in the Foyle headwaters above the beautiful Owenkillew river. You may come across a hiker walking the Ulster Way, or small parties on archaeological tramps. There are thousands of standing stones and chambered graves across the moors, mysterious testaments to the prehistoric Irish who lived up here.

Threaded by streams and small roads, the main expanse of the Sperrins is bounded by the towns of Strabane, Dungiven, Draperstown and Newtownstewart. A section of the range spills south towards Omagh over the Owenkillew, and the north-east fringe is bisected by the **Glenshane pass** which has a friendly **roadhouse** at the highest point. There has been a pub at this lonesome place for over 200 years. It got mains electricity only in 1990. Water is still drawn from a well.

There are more hills further north, running along the east side of the fertile **Roe valley**, with craggy **Binevenagh** rearing 1,271ft over **Lough Foyle**. The highest peak, **Sawel**, is only 2,240ft but the range and its extensions are sprawling, and access to the landlocked settlements of Tyrone and County Londonderry was difficult until modern times. For the same reason, overland attacks on Derry — called Londonderry after 1613 because of its associations with London — were rarely successful. Built on a hill on the banks of the Foyle estuary, the city is close to the open sea, and enemies and allies alike found it easier to approach by water. The Vikings arrived this way, starting in 812 when they destroyed St Columba's monastery on the hill, and the Jacobite siege of 1688–89 was lifted after 105 days when English ships forced their way down the estuary to relieve the city.

Ireland's last Gaelic stronghold was the densely forested country of Tyrone. Here the Earls of Tyrone and Tyrconnell, O'Neill and O'Donnell, held out against the government in the later sixteenth century. The price of this defiance was confiscation of their lands and property, though some local Irish Catholic landowners managed to keep their estates following the Flight of the Earls in 1607. However, these too were forfeit after the 1641 rebellion. The beginning of this bloody and prolonged rebellion, which spread all over Ireland, was signalled by Sir Phelim O'Neill's seizure of Charlemont and Dungannon in Tyrone. The Irish wanted restitution of their lands. Their slaughter of Scots and English settlers was remembered 8 years later when Oliver Cromwell put the people of Drogheda to the sword.

South of the Sperrins the main centres of population are Dungannon, Cookstown and Omagh. The M1 from Belfast ends around **Dungannon** (population 9,400), a textile manufacturing town where visitor interest is focused on the glassware works of **Tyrone Crystal** (year-round tours) and, just south of the town, one of the most famous names in Irish linen history, **Moygashel Mills**. Dungannon was the chief seat of the O'Neills from the fourteenth century until the plantation, and the first bible in Gaelic was produced here on a printing press established by Shane O'Neill in about 1567. All trace of the O'Neill castle on the hill has gone. The **Royal School**, Northland Row, dates from the early seventeenth century. Its first headmaster died in the 1641 rebellion but the school reopened in 1662. The **bronze statue** in front of the present eighteenth-century building is ex-pupil **General John Nicholson**, killed storming Delhi during the Indian Mutiny (1857). The statue stood at the Kashmir Gate in Delhi until 1960. This same general pops up again in the market place in his home town of Lisburn, though the Dungannon bronze, by Thomas Brock, is nicer. **Northland Row** itself is a terrace of impressive Georgian houses. Just beyond the south end a Victorian church hall has been well converted into a restaurant.

The development of the Tyrone coalfields in the nineteenth century was not a success story. The coal is still there, waiting for someone to work out a way to extract it profitably. The countryside around **Coalisland** (population 3,800) where brick-making is a local industry, is disfigured by large-scale sand, gravel and clay extraction and the detritus of old coal mines. The town was briefly the inland port for

Engraving a large goblet at Tyrone Crystal, Dungannon

the coalfields. Industrial archaeologists enthuse about the beehive kilns, old brickworks chimneys and the derelict canal basin, and some of these features are being restored. A converted **cornmill** in the town centre is an exhibition and social centre, with the folk music club playing on the third floor. The wooden walls are lined with numerous pictures of Gaelic-football-playing Coalislanders and photographs of local boy Dennis Taylor, the amiable 1985 world snooker champion. Translucent Ulster pottery of an exquisite delicacy, made in 1890, stands out among displays on the mill's lower floors. Off the B161, not far from **Washing Bay**, **Mountjoy Castle** was built in 1605 to command the south-west corner of Lough Neagh. In this unfriendly O'Neill terrain, attack could come from any direction, and this ruined fort with four rectangular corner towers is remarkable for the number of gun loops ranged round the ground floor to give fire cover on all sides.

Parkanaur, west of Dungannon, is a pretty forest park with a Victorian garden and white fallow deer. Much history attaches to the fortified mansion and the church (of Donaghmore parish) at nearby **Castlecaulfield** (population 420). Sir Toby Caulfield, ancestor of the Earls of Charlemont, was an Oxfordshire knight who commanded Charlemont Fort during Mountjoy's 1602 campaign. He built the Castlecaulfield mansion in 1619 on the site of a Donnelly fort. The tolerant first Viscount Charlemont allowed the Catholic primate, Oliver Plunkett, to use the courtyard for ordinations in 1670, and John Wesley preached here on at least four occasions. Now in ruins, and incongruously surrounded by a housing estate, the mansion retains

Bronze Age stone circles at Beaghmore. *(Inset)* Ardboe Cross

a gatehouse with murder-holes, gunloops and the Caulfield arms over the top.

Outside the graveyard of the seventeenth-century **parish church**, a blue plaque commemorates the poet **Charles Wolfe** (1791–1823) who was curate of Donaghmore 1818–21. His famous lines on 'The burial of Sir John Moore after Corunna' were published in the *Newry Telegraph* in 1817:

> Not a drum was heard, not a funeral note,
> As his corse to the rampart we hurried.

Rector of Donaghmore from 1674 was the Rev. George Walker, better known as governor of Londonderry during the great siege. He was killed at the Boyne in 1690 and is buried in the south transept. The gabled porch is carved with cherubs holding a bible open at psalm 24. Various pieces inside the church, including the windows in the south nave, were brought from a vanished medieval church 2 miles north in **Donaghmore** (population 770), a village with a **tenth-century high cross** at the top of the main street. The cross, now rather worn, is 15ft tall and carved with biblical scenes. Close to the site of an early monastery associated with St Patrick, it was damaged in the seventeenth century. The obvious join midway up the shaft suggests that when it was reassembled in 1776, bits from two separate crosses were used. A pillar in the graveyard behind the cross is a modern memorial to Hugh O'Neill. A short distance down the Pomeroy road (B43) **Donaghmore Heritage Centre** in an old National School preserves townland maps and photographs and artefacts from vanished local industries. Donaghamore has a lively drama group, the Bardic Theatre.

The chief crowning place of the O'Neills, from the early twelfth to the seventeenth century, was 2 miles outside Cookstown at **Tullahoge**, headquarters of the O'Hagans, chief justices of Tyrone. There is a fine view of the old kingdom of Tyrone from the top of this tree-ringed hill. The circular graveyard nearby, with a wall round it, was the O'Hagan burial place. During the ceremony the king-elect sat on a stone inauguration chair, new sandals were placed on his feet, the assembled chiefs chanted his name in unison 'amid the clang of bucklers and the music of a hundred harps', and he was then anointed and crowned by the primate of Armagh. The last king to sit on the chair was the great Hugh O'Neill in 1593. The O'Hagan role as prominent law officers continued into modern times, and the first Lord O'Hagan (1812–85) was chancellor of Ireland.

The rebel leader, Phelim O'Neill, had himself inaugurated at Tullahoge in 1641. He had to manage without the chair — Lord Mountjoy smashed it in 1602. Sir Phelim epitomised the political turmoil and shaky allegiances of the day: he was simultaneously a knight of the realm, premier prince of Ulster (as recognised by the pope), member of parliament for Dungannon and executioner of many of his English and Scottish constituents. He remained at large until 1653 when he was captured near Newmills, north-east of Dungannon, hiding on the crannog in **Roughan Lough** (now popular with water-skiers), taken to Dublin and hanged for treason. Ruined **Roughan Castle**, a fortress with stubby round towers near the lake, was built by Sir Andrew Stewart in 1618.

The main street in **Cookstown** (population 10,500) is perfectly straight, 1¼ miles long with a hump in the middle, and 130ft wide. It was part of an ambitious town plan by William Stewart of Killymoon, an eighteenth-century Tyrone landlord. However, neither he nor his descendants ever got round to developing the town beyond this remarkable central avenue. Its great advantage, from the visitor's point of view, is convenient parking. The life and bustle of Cookstown, at the centre of good farming country, focuses wholly on the main street which, for some reason, changes its name no fewer than eight times. Although the shops and houses are rather ordinary, the broad avenue has a certain theatrical appeal, with the bleak outline of **Slieve Gallion** (1,737ft) looming up 8 miles directly north. Biggest building by far is **Holy Trinity**, a Catholic church halfway down the west side. Built in 1855 by J. J. McCarthy, it has a massive tower and spire, visible from far off.

The linen industry was important here. The father of the botanist Augustine Henry (born Cookstown 1857) was a Cookstown flax buyer, and there are old mills along the nearby Ballinderry river. The modern town is known for its sausages, made in the large bacon factory. There are livestock markets and a flourishing Saturday street market. A golf course occupies the parkland of **Killymoon Castle**, a Norman-revival castle designed for the Stewarts in 1802 by John Nash, the celebrated English architect (1752–1835). Its present owner lets visitors look round during 'reasonable hours'. South of the town is **Loughry Manor** (now an agricultural college), a plantation mansion which has associations with Dean Jonathan Swift. He stayed here as a guest of the Lindsay family while writing *Gulliver's Travels*, published in 1726. Portraits of 'Stella' (Esther Johnson, died 1728) and 'Vanessa' (Esther Vanhomrigh, died 1723) still hang in the Old Library. The Dean loved them both, and made them both miserable.

Ardboe high cross, over 18ft tall, stands inside a small railing on an early monastic site along a bleak stretch of Lough Neagh's western shore. Though much eroded, the tenth-century cross is impressive and has twenty-two carved panels. Old Testament scenes on the east side start at the bottom with Adam and Eve, with New Testament scenes up the west side. Nearby are the ruins of a seventeenth-century church and, in the corner of the graveyard, **Ardboe Pin Tree**, an old beech with its trunk hammered full of coins. A pin or, later, a coin, stuck into this special tree carried the believer's prayer for a cure. Prising a coin out will surely bring the disease with it. Poisoned by the metal inserted under its bark, the tree is quite dead. Lughnasa (Lammas) used to be celebrated at Ardboe, with praying at the cross and much washing in the lake. It is reckoned that eel fishing has gone on here for 5,000 years. The monks of the sixth-century monastery at Ardboe used eel oil in their lamps. The small farms around Ardboe are mostly owned by eel fishermen. From May onwards you can see them setting lines in sections up to 2 miles long. The catch is worth millions of pounds a year. The history of fishing on Lough Neagh is told at the nearby **Kinturk Cultural Centre**.

West of Cookstown, past **Drum Manor Forest Park** on the A505, a lane runs down to **Wellbrook Beetling Mill** in a lovely setting on the fast-flowing river. It started work in 1768 and was one of six beetling mills serving a local bleachworks. Beetling was the noisy process that gave sheen and smoothness to the linen cloth by pounding it with heavy wooden hammers, or beetles. The two-storey mill, big waterwheel and picturesque mill race have been restored by the National Trust. The seven large engines inside are in working order and there is an exhibition on linen-making. If your idea of how a mill race works is vague, a walk along the path at the back is instructive.

There are many ancient monuments around here. Be sceptical of signposting. As in other parts of Tyrone, direction signs are frequently vandalised, though local people will go out of their way to help if you ask. The impressive **Beaghmore Stone Circles** on the fringe of the Sperrins were discovered in the 1930s. Seven stone circles, three pairs and an odd one, and a dozen or so stone alignments and round cairns, have been cleared of peat. Most of the circle stones are small — no more than 2 or 3ft feet high. Many are barely a foot tall, and the tallest is only about 4ft. The site dates from the middle of the Bronze Age. Other similar sets of circles and alignments have

Wellbrook Beetling Mill, near Cookstown

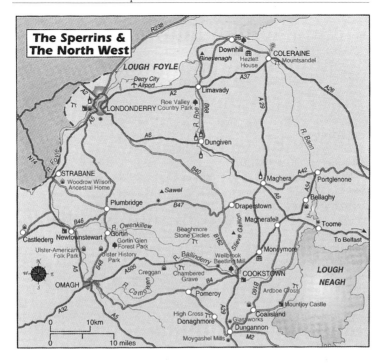

been found in the Sperrins, including Moymore near Lough Bracken, 2 miles from Pomeroy. The heathery windswept moors around Beaghmore are littered with the remains of other monuments which have been turned up by turf cutting.

Cregganconroe court grave, overlooking Cam Lough, is sign-posted off the main Cookstown–Omagh road (A505). It is typical of some 300 similar North Irish megalithic graves, where the narrow burial chamber is entered through a wider forecourt. A similar grave on the west side of Lough Mallon at **Creggandevesky**, was exca-vated a few years ago. To be up here at twilight is an eerie experi-ence, even on a summer day. The **Black Bog**, a very old, deep bog, north-west of the A505/B46 crossroads, supplies refined peat for the local craft industry of ornaments made from compressed peat, on sale at **Creggan Visitor Centre**, an interesting interpretive centre adjacent to the bog where visitors can hear the recorded voices of local storytellers, soft-toned, sad, sardonic, famous in their time.

A secondary road (B4) from Cookstown to Omagh runs through the upland village of **Pomeroy** (population 700), with a modern forestry school on the estate of the Rev. James Lowry, eighteenth-century planner of the village. The Anglican church (1841) in the neat market square later acquired a belfry and spire which, according to an inscription, were added by John and Armar Lowry as 'a tribute of attachment to their birthplace'.

American connections in the area are interesting. The grandfather of James B. Irwin, the Apollo 15 astronaut who drove round the moon in a buggy in 1971, was born in Pomeroy. Irwins still live in the house. James Shields, one of Lincoln's generals in the American Civil War, was born in 1806 near **Cappagh**, south of Pomeroy. The **Altmore Loan Fund building**, the Shields family bank, which flourished from 1852 to 1903, still stands in Cappagh's main street. James Shields, who emigrated at the age of twenty, defeated the great Confederate general, Stonewall Jackson, at Kernstown, Virginia. Jackson's own ancestral home, The Birches, is just across the Tyrone/Armagh border. President James Buchanan's father emigrated from Deroran, south-east of Omagh, to Pennsylvania where the future president was born in 1791. Buchanan, president from 1857 to 1861, was one of the only three first-generation Americans ever to occupy the White House. All three of them were sons of Ulster emigrants.

Eclectic snippets like this, and the broader picture of Ulster emigrations to the North American continent, can be discovered in the exhibition galleries of the **Ulster-American Folk Park** outside Omagh. It is a rewarding visit for anyone interested in the migration of Irish people over the centuries. Opened in 1976, the folk park developed round the cottage where **Judge Thomas Mellon**, founder of the fabulously rich Mellon dynasty, was born in 1813. His son, Andrew, built the steel town of Pittsburgh. Mellon money helped build the Waldorf Astoria, San Francisco's Golden Gate bridge and the gates of the Panama canal. Another Tyrone native, **John Joseph Hughes**, later archbishop of New York, left at the same time as the Mellons. His boyhood home, rebuilt stone by stone, has been moved into the park and so has the eighteenth-century home of **Robert Campbell**, the Rocky Mountains pioneer. The folk park also contains replicas of American log cabins and farmsteads and has a large databank on Irish emigration based on thousands of passenger lists from emigrant ships, including vessels bound for Australia, New Zealand and South Africa.

Omagh (population 17,300), a market town with a large agricultural hinterland, grew at the place where two rivers (Camowen and Drumragh) meet to form the wide, shallow Strule. The town centre is a hilly, architectural muddle of nineteenth-century and twentieth-century buildings away from the sparkling rivers down below. Despite this, and the frequent batterings which have made Omagh a security-conscious place, the town has character and a cheerfulness stemming, perhaps, from its 200 years as county town of Tyrone until local government reorganisation in 1973. The most prominent landmark is the **Sacred Heart Catholic church** (1893–99), with twin spires, unequal in height, dominating the somewhat earlier Anglican church, and the classical **courthouse** (1814, by John Hargrave) at the top of the steep main street. The Black Bell of Drumragh, said to be ninth-century, is preserved inside — to see it ask at the sacristy or call at 33 George's Street, right of the taller spire. A modern **youth hostel** is a little north-west of the town, up towards the waterworks. It is open all year.

Local trout and salmon fishing, and pike and roach in the Strule and Fairy Water, bring anglers into town for bait and tackle. Omagh is also a centre for wildfowling and for fishing the remote lakes to the west, beyond **Drumquin** (population 600). Playwright Brian Friel, author of *Philadelphia here I come* and *Translations*, was born in Omagh (1930), and Jimmy Kennedy (1903–84) who wrote 'The teddy bears' picnic' and 'South of the border'. Ulster poet John Montague (born 1929) grew up in nearby **Fintona** (population 1,350), an attractive little town well equipped with public houses, including the Poet's Pub, once owned by Montague's mother. Outside Fintona, **Seskinore Game Farm** rears pheasants and partridges, and woodcock and rough game attract field sportsmen to this part of the Sperrins.

Up towards the great gorge of **Gortin Glen Forest Park**, there are scenic drives around Mullaghcarn mountain (1,778ft) and Plumbridge on the Glenelly river. First, though, the B48 runs past the **Ulster History Park** where an outsize twentieth-century dolmen stands beside a futuristic visitor centre. For a one-stop lesson in nearly 9,000 years of 'human history', up to the end of the seventeenth century, this is the place to come. **Plumbridge** (population 250), hemmed in by crags at the bottom of a narrow valley, has a quaint cattle market. There has been periodic gold-rush fever hereabouts, and recent commercial prospecting in the area has revived the rumours. Locals tell you that it takes weeks of laborious panning in the headwaters of the Foyle to extract minuscule amounts of gold.

An attractive drive is east from Gortin, then north through the very scenic **Barnes Gap** to join up with the Plumbridge–Draperstown road (B47), running east along the **Glenelly valley** to **Sperrin hamlet** (at 570ft) at the foot of Sawel (2,240ft). If you have four hours or so to spare and the weather is clear, park at the nameless pub in Sperrin and stride out north. The pub is a landmark, by far the most substantial building hereabouts. Do not assume that it will be open. After 2 miles, leave the road and make for Sawel summit (1 hour) for superlative views of Lough Neagh, the Foyle estuary and the Mournes. Dart

Early settlements reconstructed at the Ulster History Park near Gortin

mountain (2,040ft) is half an hour's walk west along the ridge. Turn south to Cranagh hamlet (45 minutes) and regain the road conveniently close to the **Sperrin Heritage Centre** just below Dart. After refreshment at the café you will be in good shape to walk along the road back to your car at the pub with no name. Even at a lowly 570ft the B47 gives good views over the valley. Some people call Sperrin 'Mount Hamilton'. Ordnance Survey maps give both names.

From the Ulster-American Folk Park, the A5 passes between two small hills called Bessie Bell (west side) and Mary Gray (east) following the course of the Strule into **Newtownstewart** (population 1,500). James II spent the night here in 1689 on his way back from the unsuccessful assault on Londonderry. He got up next morning in a bad mood and ordered the Stewart castle, and the town, to be burnt down. In the main street a triple gable wall of the ruined castle still stands. The town's library is housed in the neat little **National School**,

Barnes Gap in the Sperrin Mountains

built from public funds in 1861 for £2,038.15s.9d.The Northern Bank building on the corner was the scene of a famous murder in 1871 when bank cashier William Glass was done to death and robbed of £1,600. District Inspector Montgomery, of the Royal Irish Constabulary, who was in charge of the case, turned out to be the murderer. The old police station, on the right as you enter the town from the Omagh direction, has been rebuilt as upmarket self-catering holiday accommodation and also contains the delightful **Dunbar Collection** — one man's thoroughly nostalgic collection of homely, domestic objects, toys and militaria — inside the **Gateway Centre**. Half a mile south-west, on a hill, is ruined **Harry Avery's Castle**, a fourteenth-century Gaelic stone castle — most unusual in Ulster. Only the massive D-shaped twin towers of the keep, built by Henry Aimhreidh O'Neill (died 1392), are left.

The great house of **Baronscourt**, country seat of the Hamilton family, the Dukes of Abercorn, is set in a landscaped park with terraced Italian-style gardens, and three lakes, one with a crannog in it. The mansion dates from about 1780. The park is private, although tourists staying in the holiday cottages near the golf course can arrange pike fishing and water-skiing on the lakes. Visitors to the estate garden centre, which has a café and craft shop, will notice the elegant **Agent's House**, built in 1741 by James Martin, architect of the cathedral at Clogher.

There is good angling in the Mourne around **Victoria Bridge** and **Douglas Bridge**. These are blink-and-miss hamlets on opposite banks of the river, but Douglas Bridge features in a ballad by the Irish-American poet, Francis Carlin:

> On Douglas Bridge I met a man
> Who lived adjacent to Strabane,
> Before the English hung him high
> For riding with O'Hanlon.

The outlawed 'Count' Redmond O'Hanlon, who was killed at Hilltown in 1681, was the political heir of Sir Phelim O'Neill. At one time a narrow gauge railway ran from Victoria Bridge to the lively little market town of **Castlederg** (population 2,600), full of little shops selling home-made cakes and jam, the remotest town in the province. Frontiersman Davy Crockett's people came from Castlederg. Democrat congressman, and a renowned hunter who could 'whip his weight in wildcats', Crockett (1786–1836) made his last stand at the Alamo fighting for Texan independence. A model of the fort is in **Castlederg Visitor Centre** on the Strabane road. Local crafts and products of the area are displayed there too. The 200 Alamo defenders, all killed, were avenged when Sam Houston — also of an Ulster family — finally routed the Mexicans in 1837. Castlederg's plantation **castle** built by Sir John Davies (1619) was besieged in 1641 by Sir Phelim O'Neill who, despite not being able to capture it, damaged it beyond repair. The **Anglican church**, with a good classical doorway, dates from 1731.

Sion Mills (population 2,000) was laid out as a model linen village by the god-fearing Herdman brothers, James, John and George. In 1835 they converted an old flour mill on the Mourne into a flax-spinning mill, and erected a bigger mill behind it in the 1850s. Their factory is still working. The village is an exotic mix of polychrome brick, black-and-white half-timbered buildings, and terraced millworkers' cottages, all set off by wide grassy verges, horse-chestnut trees and, on the Strabane road, some nice beeches. Nearly everything in Sion Mills except St Teresa's church was designed by

James Herdman's son-in-law, the English architect William Unsworth. **Sion House**, a half-timbered Elizabethan-style mansion with pepperpot chimneys, was planned by Unsworth at the same time as he was designing the first Shakespeare memorial theatre in Stratford-on-Avon (opened in 1879, destroyed by a fire in 1926).

More modest half-timbered buildings include the charming gatehouse, the recreation hall and **Old St Saviour's church**. Unsworth based his design for the polychrome Anglican church (1909) on a church in Pistoia in Tuscany. It has tall campanili and huge semicircular windows. By contrast the modern Catholic **church of St Teresa** (1963, by Patrick Haughey) is admirable for its severely plain lines — a long rectangle with a striking representation of the Last Supper on the slate façade. Oisin Kelly was the artist. The Sion Mills cricket team made headlines in 1969 when a West Indian touring team was defeated on the village ground.

The border town of **Strabane** (population 12,000) looks north-west across the Foyle to Lifford, a mile downstream in County Donegal. James II made his base here in 1688–89 for the attack on Londonderry. Unlikely though it seems now, Strabane was an important printing and book publishing centre in the eighteenth century. The only relic of that humanistic tradition is a little shop with a Georgian front in Main Street — **Gray's Printing Shop**, now a museum. Meetinghouse Street (blue plaque) was the birthplace of John Dunlap (1747–1812) who printed the broadsheets of the American Declaration of Independence which were sent round the world in July 1776. Dunlap published the Declaration a few days later on the front page of his little *Pennsylvania Packet* which grew into America's first daily newspaper (1784). James Wilson, grandfather of President Woodrow Wilson (1913–21), was also a printer, and editor of a Philadelphia newspaper. He served his apprenticeship in Strabane and emigrated in 1807. He married a girl from Sion Mills, Annie Adams, whom he met on the ship. The **Wilson ancestral home**, a thatched farmhouse at Dergalt, 2 miles down the Plumbridge road, is open all year. Some of the furniture is original. Wilsons live in the modern house next door and still work the farm.

Other notable emigrants from Strabane included William Knox who founded the Alabama Central Bank. He lost all his money in the American Civil War after loaning half a million pounds to the short-lived Confederate government. Alexander Porter, who became a supreme court judge in the state of Louisiana, was educated in the town. He was the eldest son of a United Irishman, the Rev. James Porter of Ballindrait, hanged after the 1798 rebellion. Alexander's brother, James, became attorney general of Louisiana. Even during the booming linen years there were plenty who had no stake in the town's prosperity — for example, the children of the Strabane workhouse, who were sent off to America in about 1840 — and there was a steady stream of emigrants from Strabane long before the great exodus at the time of the potato famine.

Londonderry & the Surrounding Area

Londonderry (population 72,300) is the province's second largest city. It stands on a hill on the Foyle estuary and, for most of its history, has been an important seaport. In World War II it was both naval base and airbase. Some 20,000 American sailors were stationed here, Al Jolson and Bob Hope came to entertain the troops, and the UK's largest convoy escorts across the Atlantic were centred on the port. Since the political tribulations of the 1970s and early 1980s a huge investment of cash, with more to come, has helped re-establish the city's credentials as the commercial and cultural centre of the northwest of Ireland. Textiles, shirt-making in particular, is a major industry. There can hardly be an Englishman, Scotsman, Welshman or Irishman without a few Derry-made shirts in the wardrobe.

St Columba founded the first monastery on the hill in AD546 which at that time was covered in trees and entirely surrounded by water. The city's popular name, Derry, derives from the Gaelic *doire* which means 'a place of oaks'. Columba went to Iona in 563 and began the conversion of Scotland and Northumbria by the Celtic Church. Meanwhile the Derry monastery thrived and, despite attacks of various kinds, successive communities of monks flourished here throughout the Middle Ages.

The royal charter of 1613, which gave Derry a mayor and corporation and added London to its name, envisaged it as both 'a town of war and a town of merchandise', and that is how it turned out. There are no visible remains of the pre-plantation town but the city has a wealth of eighteenth-century buildings, and there are vivid memorials to its long, tumultuous past. These, together with the soft-spoken, wry and friendly people, well aware of Londonderry's past reputation as a Northern Ireland trouble spot, give the place an interesting extra dimension which visitors will not encounter anywhere else in the province.

The English first came here in 1566 after a revolt by Shane O'Neill. They installed a garrison which was wiped out the following year after the arsenal — installed inside the medieval cathedral — exploded accidentally. There was another revolt in 1600, and in 1608 the fortifications were overrun by the O'Dohertys, chiefs of

An open-air market beneath the walls of Derry City,
with the Guildhall beyond

Inishowen. To prevent future rebellions, James I gave the City of
London responsibility for settling this whole region of Ulster. Accus-
tomed to stumping up vast sums for the crown, the City was on this
occasion cajoled and bullied into an intimate and permanent in-
volvement — the plantation of Londonderry, rebuilding and fortify-
ing the ruined medieval town, planning and building dozens of
smaller towns and villages, and supplying craftsmen to do the work.
The financial commitment was to last for hundreds of years.

A new county, called Londonderry, was created by combining
Derry town with the lands of the troublesome O'Cahans in the old
county of Coleraine and adding various tracts of Tyrone and Antrim.
The City of London set up a special body, The Honourable The Irish
Society, to manage their lands, keeping direct control over three
strategic main towns — Derry, Coleraine and Limavady — and

parcelling out the rest of County Londonderry between the twelve ancient London livery companies.

The great **seventeenth-century walls** which encircle the historic centre are 20–25ft high, 30ft wide in places and a mile round. Inside, four main streets radiate out from the Diamond, or square, to the four original gates, **Bishop Gate**, **Butcher Gate**, **Shipquay Gate** and **Ferryquay Gate**. Three more gates were let into the walls later. Completed by 1618 and still entire, with old cannon pointing over the ramparts, the walls are a most striking feature. Their first test came with a siege in 1641, and again in 1648, when supplies were brought in by sea, and lastly and most memorably, in the siege of 1688–89.

You can make a complete **circuit** along the top **of the walls** apart from a short section above St Columb's cathedral where you have to come down to go round Bishop Gate, which was rebuilt in 1789 in neo-classical style. One of the cannon over Shipquay Gate was a gift from Elizabeth I in 1590. Others were given to the city in 1642 by the Mercers, Grocers, Vintners and Merchant Taylors of London. The walls are punctuated at intervals with bastions and picturesque stone watch towers, and dozens of gunloops — small ones for muskets and large ones open at the top for cannon. Cast-iron peace-and-reconciliation moulded figures, rather like dummies used in transport impact research, have been installed at various points along the circuit.

The great siege began after thirteen apprentice boys seized the keys of the town and locked the gates against an approaching Jacobite regiment. Governor Robert Lundy had been prepared to admit the soldiers because, he said, the city was not adequately garrisoned and resistance would be futile. But there were an estimated 30,000 panic-stricken Protestants inside who feared they would be massacred. The citizens expelled the vacillating Lundy (who is still burnt in effigy every year in a sort of Guy Fawkes ritual) and civil administration was taken over by George Walker, a formidable Anglican clergyman from Donaghmore. The city thus declared for William of Orange and against King James II. James landed in Ireland in March 1689 and hurried north to restore his authority, arriving outside Bishop Gate on 18 April. Since his engineers were too few to scale the walls, he set up guns opposite Shipquay Gate and waited.

For the people inside, help was slow in coming. About 7,000 of them died of starvation and disease. Near the end cats and dogs were being sold in butchers' shops and even a rat cost a shilling. The besiegers built a wooden boom across the river (at the place where Boom Hall, a Georgian villa, now stands in lovely gardens) to stop supply ships reaching the town. On 28 July a ship commanded by

Captain Michael Browning, a native of Londonderry, sailed up the Foyle in the face of artillery fire, broke through the boom and relieved the city.

The siege had wide repercussions in Europe. It gave William a crucial breathing space to organise his army, paving the way to his decisive victory in 1690 at the Boyne — the battle which secured William as king of England and damaged the prestige of Louis XIV in Europe. This European dimension led Macaulay to call the siege 'the most memorable in the annals of the British Isles'. For Ireland it meant a Protestant ascendancy throughout the eighteenth century, and a long period of peace and stability that, so far, has not been experienced again.

There are two bridges over the Foyle that link the city with the county it administers. The very long modern road bridge across the widening estuary downstream virtually bypasses Derry. It came too late to save the city from a beltway that separates the historic centre from the river and from its south and west suburbs. The **Waterside district** on the east bank, where most of the city's Protestants now live, is linked to the old city by the double-deck Craigavon Bridge. On the west bank a couple of miles of 3ft narrow-gauge track is preserved as part of the **Foyle Valley Railway Centre**.

There is parking at the Guildhall in Foyle Street close to Shipquay Gate, convenient for getting up on to the walls. A plaque below the modern fountain in Foyle Street marks the quay where hundreds of thousands of emigrants embarked for America. The last sailing ship to carry Irish emigrants across the Atlantic was a copper-bottomed wooden clipper, *Minnehaha*, owned by William McCorkell & Co., a Londonderry shipping company. She could sail home in fifteen days, but the new steamships could do better and she made her final passenger run to New York in 1873. The bosomy figurehead from *Minnehaha*'s prow is preserved in the **Harbour Museum** behind the Guildhall. The **Guildhall** has dozens of stained glass windows illustrating almost every episode of note in the city's history. The story flows up the staircase and floods all the chambers with light. The building was burnt out in 1908 and bombed in 1972. The City of London finished restoring the glass in 1984 — the year the council, now with a nationalist majority, renamed itself Derry City Council.

A medieval-looking exhibition tower peering over the walls at Shipquay Gate is an agreeable fake on the site of Sir Cahir O'Doherty's long-vanished castle. Below the tower, the **Tower Museum** is a rewarding visit for anyone interested in the city's past. Sir Cahir's two-handed sword, very long and elegant, is on display and some fine silver includes two huge cups and a silver tankard made in 1709 to mark the centenary of the start of the Ulster plantation. A short video at the end of the museum tour, near the exit, is intended to bring visitors up to date on the political front.

From the river the main thoroughfare, Shipquay Street, rises steeply to the war memorial in the Diamond, passing basement pubs and shops and the entrance to a modern craft village. In the basement of **8 Shipquay Street** you can buy Irish linen, tweeds and woollens. Thomas Colby (1784–1852), who took charge of the Ordnance Survey's mapping of Ireland, lodged in this house. The survey was based on a triangulation system. The first triangle was at the Lough Foyle Base, a kind of huge spirit level established on the flat land of Magilligan strand. It was the first-ever mapping of a whole country on a large scale and produced the famous 6 inch-to-1 mile maps that showed 'every road and track, every stone wall and hedge, every river and stream, every house and barn'. It also preserved the identity of the rural neighbourhoods known as 'townlands' by recording the name of each one. The townland name is still part of any rural address in Northern Ireland, despite the post office's preference for postcodes. At the Diamond is the flamboyant Edwardian baroque frontage of **Austin's department store**, opened in 1906. 'First store in Ireland' says a notice. Many original fittings and the wooden staircase with broad polished balustrades are still there. An old-style fast-moving escalator whisks customers up to the third floor where there are good westerly views across the city from a 150-seater restaurant. In a corner of the room it is a surprise to come on a small **Met. Office** — and a chance for some pre-prandial study of weather maps and reports. Beyond Austin's, at 14 Bishop Street, is a heritage library and an excellent adjoining bookshop. The **Irish Society House** (1764) is well preserved and so is the classical **courthouse** (1813) across the road from the Regency-style former **bishop's palace**. Narrow side-streets and smaller roads in the shadow of the walls give some dramatic architectural perspectives.

The most interesting church inside the walls, and the chief repository of the city's turbulent seventeenth-century memories, is **St Columb's Anglican cathedral** built in 1633. The London link is proclaimed on the famous date stone preserved in the porch:

> If stones could speake then London's prayse should sound
> Who built this church and cittie from the grounde.

Among scores of plaques and memorials ranged round the walls is a marble monument shared by Colonel Henry Baker, a city governor who died on the seventy-fourth day of the siege, and Captain Browning, killed by a shot after his ship broke the boom a month later. One

Roe Valley Country Park, near Limavady

window depicts St Columba's sixth-century mission to Britain; another illustrates hymns written by Mrs C. F. Alexander (1818–95), wife of a bishop of Derry. Her *Hymns for Little Children*, published in 1848, went into sixty-nine editions during her life. The three represented here are 'There is a green hill far away', 'Once in royal David's city', and 'The golden gates are lifted up'. An organ case over the west door is by the celebrated wood carver, Grinling Gibbons, whose commissions included Hampton Court and the choir of St Paul's Cathedral in London. Two groynes near the organ are likenesses of George Walker, governor of Derry to the end of the siege, and George Berkeley (1685–1753), the metaphysical philosopher, who said that 'all reality is in the mind'. He held the lucrative post of Dean of Derry from 1724 until 1732, though he visited the city on only one occasion.

Among treasures in the **chapterhouse** are the seventeenth-century locks and keys of the city gates, Lord Macaulay's manuscript account of the siege, interesting paintings, and a pair of duelling pistols belonging to Frederick Hervey, fourth Earl of Bristol and Bishop of Derry (1730–1803). This Byronic nobleman, a flamboyant character whose name is preserved in all the Bristol Hotels in Europe, acquired the rich bishopric of Derry in 1768 and immediately began building churches and improving old ones. He spent £1,000 on putting an enormous stone spire on St Columb's but it was too heavy and had to be dismantled. Active in the Volunteer movement and a supporter of emancipation, the Earl Bishop is also remembered for his support for Roman Catholic and nonconformist church building, including Long Tower Church a few yards outside the walls. Go through Bishop Gate to see it.

Long Tower Church is the city's oldest Catholic church (1784–86). Its name recalls the great medieval cathedral, the Templemore, which was built by the Augustinian abbot O'Brolchain in 1164 when Derry was an important monastic centre. After the cathedral was flattened by the explosion of 1567, a twelfth-century round tower — the Long Tower — survived nearby for another 100 years or so. The present Long Tower Church has a most attractive interior, with steeply stepped galleries and double-gabled transepts.

Returning towards Bishop Gate, take the path to the left and walk along the outside of the western city wall. Down below are the acres of the 1960s Bogside housing estate, its **'Free Derry' monument** and graffiti rendered less strident by the creation of an urban park spread grassily over the hillside. The slogan dates from the troubled late 1960s. Civil rights demonstrations in the city in 1968 and riots in 1969 culminated in the 'Battle of the Bogside' in August that year. In common with other Catholic residential areas, the Bogsiders barricaded their neighbourhood, making it a 'no-go' (ie 'free') area for police and civil authorities. The words 'You are now entering Free Derry' were painted on the gable wall of a house which was subsequently demolished — except for the inscribed gable.

The large Catholic cathedral, **St Eugene's,** rising towards the north-west, was completed in 1873 to designs by J. J. McCarthy, though it had to wait thirty years more for the spire. The east window, a memorial to the cathedral's builder, Bishop Francis Kelly, depicts the crucifixion and seven Irish saints. St Eugene's is best reached from Strand Road (A2) which is also the route for the University of Ulster campus at Magee. The oldest pub in Derry, **Andy Cole's**, is at 135 Strand Road. Many pubs have regular Irish music sessions — check which nights with the tourist office, or just go to Waterloo Street which has at least four musical pubs vibrating with the insistent rhythms of reels and jigs. The music shop at 11 Bishop Street sells Irish musical instruments like *bodhráns* and tin whistles. Three miles beyond Magee College, at **Ballyarnet Field**, a cottage exhibition centre commemorates the transatlantic flight in 1932 by Amelia Earhart, the first woman to fly the Atlantic solo. She landed in this field. Check by telephone that the **Earhart Cottage** is open.

The 'polder' appearance of the coastal strip between Londonderry and the mouth of the **Roe** is an unusual landscape to find in Ireland. Drivers along the A2 east from the city will not see it except by turning down side roads, but it is most striking from the train. Reclaimed from the sea in the nineteenth century for flax growing, these fertile polders — called 'levels' locally — are actually below sea level and are drained by pumping stations. The crops now are grain and vegetables, mostly potatoes. In between the polders are mudflats and deserted runways of old wartime aerodromes. The lovely estuary of the Roe is a national nature reserve.

The aerodrome at **Eglinton** (population 2,200), 4 miles east of Londonderry, became the modern City of Derry Airport which has scheduled services linking north-west Ulster with Glasgow and Manchester. The village was created by the Grocers' Company in 1823–25 and has an elegant courthouse in the main street. At the same time the Fishmongers were developing their model farm at **Ballykelly** (population 2,300). The farmhouse has recently been turned into a retirement home, its green paddock destroyed. Appealing plantation buildings in Ballykelly include the Presbyterian church, a school, and a dispensary (now Bridge House). These north coast plantation villages still manage to retain their eye appeal despite the depredations of lax planning regulations in Northern Ireland, plus a general indifference to conservation.

Bishop Hervey built the Anglican parish church (1795), with three-stage tower, needle spire and interesting funerary monuments. North of Ballykelly bridge **Walworth House** is an eighteenth-century five-bay house with three intact flankers from the Fishmongers' earlier bawn. The ruins of the Company's church of 1629 are opposite the house. At the roadside (still A2) on the edge of Farlow Wood a mile before Limavady, **Sampson's Tower** was erected in memory of an early-nineteenth-century agent for the Fishmongers' estates. The large tree-fringed earthwork a few yards further on, on the other side of the road, is **Rough Fort rath**. At Broighter, north of here, a collection of prehistoric gold ornaments known as the Broighter Treasure (now in the National Museum, Dublin) was discovered by a ploughman in the 1890s. A hologram of the Broighter golden boat is in the Tower Museum, Londonderry.

Limavady (population 10,800) is a quiet market town on the Roe river, with some surviving Georgian features. It was created by an energetic Welshman, Sir Thomas Phillips, the City of London's chief agent in Ulster from 1609. W. M. Thackeray stopped for ale at the inn (demolished) in the main street in 1842 and wrote some verses about the barmaid, 'Sweet Peg of Limavady'. **No 51 Main Street** was the home of Jane Ross (1810–79) who noted down the famous 'Londonderry Air' ('Danny Boy') from an itinerant fiddler in 1851. She lived here with her three younger sisters, all unmarried, and a plaque commemorates her single great service in preserving the best known of all Irish melodies. The Ross sisters are buried across the road at the eighteenth-century parish church, which has a collection of several hundred tapestry kneelers, each one different. William Massey, prime minister of New Zealand (1912–25), was born in Irish Green Street in 1856 (plaque). The local hospital occupies a trim Victorian workhouse with all its 1841 buildings intact.

In the gorges of the **Roe Valley Country Park**, a mile south of Limavady, a hydro-electric plant, water mills and a weaving shed are among a tremendous collection of restored rural industrial buildings on the banks of the peaty red river. The park is popular for canoeing, camping and especially game fishing. Roe Park House, the early Georgian mansion built on the west bank by William Conolly, speaker of the Irish parliament, has been converted into a luxurious Radisson golf hotel.

The primeval forest of Glenconkeyne north-west of Lough Neagh was cut down early in the seventeenth century, a raw material for the plantation towns and villages in County Londonderry. The oaks and elms were floated down the Bann to build houses in Limavady and Coleraine, or used as firewood, in particular for smelting the iron ore deposits found around **Slieve Gallion**. By about 1640 most of the forest had gone. There are still reminders of the green gaiety of the ancient wood around **Springhill House**, a National Trust property a mile from Moneymore towards Coagh (B18). A thicket of old yews has survived in the grounds of this fortified seventeenth-century house, which is surely the prettiest house in Ulster.

Moneymore (population 1,250) is an unusually harmonious plantation town with many nice buildings along the wide main street. This was the Drapers' first settlement, and the first town in Ulster to have piped water (1615). Like so many such settlements, it was destroyed in 1641 and the present buildings, which include two market houses, two Presbyterian churches, a school and a dispensary, date from the Georgian period. The centre of interest shifted eventually from Moneymore to Draperstown which grew round a big livestock and linen market. The triangular green at

Mussenden Temple perched on the cliff edge above Downhill Strand

Draperstown (population 1,400) is a lively place on market days. A tour of the linen works at **Upperlands**, north-east of Draperstown, passes dams which once powered the old linen mill and an interpretive centre contains original weaving and bleaching machinery. The market town of **Magherafelt** (population 7,150) was part of the Salters' estates and has a large central square with wide roads leading off. **Castledawson** on the gravelly Moyola river which flows into Lough Neagh, retains a sturdy bridge and an unusually substantial, tall and handsome house called **The Gravel** in Main Street. The wooded estate of Moyola Park nearby was the home of James Chichester-Clark, Lord Moyola, briefly prime minister of Northern Ireland (1969–71).

Maghera (population 3,650) at the foot of the **Glenshane pass** was church property before the plantation and, quite unlike the settlers' towns, the streets are narrow. Its main interest is **Maghera Old**

Church on the site of a sixth-century monastery founded by St Lurach. In the Middle Ages Maghera was the seat of a bishop. The fine twelfth-century west door has sculpted sloping jambs, decorated with animal and floral motifs, and a massive lintel carved with a crucifixion scene. The door has a square head on the outside and a semicircular head on the inside. The seventeenth-century tower had a residence for the priest on the first floor. South of the church is an imposing **rectory** built in 1825.

Dungiven (population 2,800) was an O'Cahan stronghold until the plantation when it was granted to the Skinners' Company. The remains of their bawn are incorporated into a battlemented nineteenth-century mansion, Dungiven Castle, visible from the A6 on the east side of town. The ruined **Augustinian priory** of St Mary's, signposted on the same road, preserves the **tomb of Cooey na Gall O'Cahan** who died in 1385. The sculptured effigy, wearing Irish armour, lies under a traceried canopy in the thirteenth-century chancel. Six bare-legged warriors in kilts, standing in niches below the prone chieftain, were his foreign mercenaries, probably Scots, from whom he derived his nickname 'na Gall' meaning 'of foreigners'. It is the finest medieval tomb in Ulster. The priory church dates from about 1150 and was remodelled in the seventeenth century when a house and bawn were added. Park at the top of the lane and walk down to the ruins. A thicket of thorn bushes hung with rags, on the right, conceals a holy well — a bullaun, a stone with a hollow in it, filled with rainwater, guaranteed to cure warts and all sorts of other ailments too.

Ruined **Banagher** church, on a hill 2 miles south-west of Dungiven — take the minor Turmeel road from Dungiven town centre — was founded in about 1100 by St Muiredach O'Heney. The nave is the oldest part. It has an impressive square-headed lintelled west door, like Maghera but without the carvings. The nave window closely resembles the one at Dungiven Priory. On a sandhill close by is the saint's appealing little mortuary house (built about 1100) with a carved abbot on the gable end. 'Banagher sand' scraped from under the tomb is said to bring luck to all O'Heneys. A similar mortuary house, though more ruined, is at **Bovevagh** off the B192 6 miles north of Dungiven. It seems that the Dungiven, Maghera and Banagher churches all had the same twelfth-century architect.

The most famous bearer of the O'Heney name hereabouts is the poet Seamus Heaney, born in 1939 south of Bellaghy on the family farm, Mossbawn, at Tamniarin off the A6. Heaney, a Nobel prizewinner, has written incomparably of the places of his Ulster childhood and the flat landscape of Lough Neagh's western shore recurs many times in his poems. The imposing bawn at **Bellaghy**, which the Vintners' Company built in 1618, is the repository of many of his manuscripts and books and his radio and television broadcasts. The work of other living Northern poets is also on display. The Department of the Environment has restored the bawn walls and a large flanker tower.

The scenic Bishop's Road across Binevenagh mountain is joined from the A2 north of Limavady by taking the B201 for a mile and then turning left. The Earl Bishop built the road to improve access to Limavady from his palace at Downhill. After 5 miles stop at the **Bishop's View** for the panorama over the plain. A lovely 7-mile golden strand sweeps round to **Magilligan Point** where a martello tower, built in Napoleonic days, commands the approach to Lough Foyle. Swirling air currents around the point can waft gliders as high as 20,000ft and the Ulster Gliding Club is based at **Bellarena** nearby. A fish smokery in the big house at Bellarena (254 Seacoast Road) specialises in smoked salmon and sea trout. After the Bishop's View, the road swoops down to rejoin the A2 at **Downhill**. At the roadside a neoclassical gateway marks the entrance to Downhill demesne and the start of a lovely glen walk up to a windswept headland.

Downhill Palace, Bishop Hervey's huge uncomfortable mansion, was never much lived in. His favourite architect, Michael Shanahan, worked on the estate on and off from the early 1770s until about 1785, designing a magnificent library and a two-storey picture gallery to accommodate the art treasures which the bishop brought back from his European travels. Much of the collection was lost in a disastrous fire in 1851. During the 1939–45 war it was used as a military billet and partly dismantled afterwards. Now very ruined, it is a landmark for walkers on the Ulster Way. But the **Mussenden Temple**, a domed rotunda which the bishop used as his summer library, is maintained in perfect condition by the National Trust. Perched precariously on the cliff edge, it shudders a little whenever a train rushes past on the narrow ledge below the cliff. In the bishop's day, the vaulted basement was given over to Roman Catholic worship. A Lucretian inscription on the frieze round the dome translates, rather disconcertingly: 'It is agreeable to watch, from land, some one else involved in a great struggle while winds whip up the waves out at sea.' Inspired by the Temple of Vesta at Tivoli, the temple was built in honour of Mrs Frideswide Mussenden, the bishop's young cousin, though she died before it was completed in 1785. He bequeathed the Downhill estate to her brother.

Downhill strand, where the bishop held horseback races between his clergy, is popular for surf fishing, especially bass. The view east from the Mussenden Temple embraces the fine beach and sandhills at the resort of **Castlerock** (population 1,000) and the first of a string of fine golf links that stretch eastwards along the coast. On the A2 at Liffock crossroads a mile south of Castlerock, **Hezlett House** is a long, low, thatched rectory of 'cruck' construction dating from 1690 — an exceptionally old house in Irish terms. The building method involved standing curved timbers, or crucks, in pairs to form a series of uprights and arches and then building the house round this frame. There are no foundations — the frame stands on the bare rock.

Coleraine (population 20,700), a sedate market town and boating centre above the Bann estuary, is linked to Belfast and Londonderry by rail and has a modern university campus on the outskirts. It was an important place in the early days of the London plantation and held out against the Irish in 1641, though the fortifications never amounted to much more than earthen ramparts. A number of functional office blocks and factories are evidence of the town's administrative and manufacturing interests. Apart from a handsome town hall, the centre is unexceptional. However, the river aspect is lively. It has a picturesque weir and locks upstream at **The Cutts**, an old town bridge, a quay where coasters load potatoes in exchange for coal, trains swooping across the river on a railway viaduct, a large boating marina downstream and, out at the estuary, waders and wildfowl busy in the reed beds.

At the **Guy L. Wilson memorial garden** at the University of Ulster, hundreds of daffodil varieties are in bloom in spring. They perpetuate the name of a celebrated Ulster daffodil breeder who died in 1961. Bulbs directly descended from Wilson's stock can be bought in his home town of Broughshane, County Antrim, from late August.

Mountsandel, on the east bank of the river a mile south of Coleraine, is said to be the earliest inhabited place in Ireland. It is an oval mound 200ft high, and according to the scientists, post holes of a wooden dwelling found here are 9,000 years old. More interesting than these ancient holes, however, is the commanding position of the mound overlooking the Bann, particularly striking seen from the river. The site is signposted from the road. St Comgall of Bangor founded a monastery at **Camus** 2 miles upstream from Mountsandel on the west bank of the river, separated from it now by the A54. The only trace of this foundation is a small graveyard with part of the shaft of a red sandstone high cross and a bullaun, a large stone with a deep hole in the centre, of the kind found all over Ireland. These stones probably started as mortars, used with a pestle to grind things up, but they are often found near a church and were commonly used as fonts and for cures. The climate ensures that there is always water in an Irish bullaun.

ADDITIONAL INFORMATION

PLACES TO VISIT

ARDBOE

High Cross and 'Pin Tree'
Access from Cookstown: B73 east, 9 miles, signposted.

Kinturk Cultural Centre
10 miles east of Cookstown off B73, follow signs for Ardboe.
☎ (016487) 36512. Open daily 9am–5pm and 7.30–11.30pm.

BELLAGHY

Bawn
Castle Street. ☎ (01648) 386812. Open Monday–Saturday 10am–5pm (until 6pm in summer) and on Sunday afternoon.

CASTLEDERG

Visitor Centre
On Strabane road. ☎ (016626) 70795. Open April–October Tuesday–Saturday 11am–4pm and Sunday afternoon.

CASTLEROCK

Hezlett House (NT)
☎ (01265) 848567. Open April–September weekends noon–5pm, also weekdays except Tuesday in July and August.

COALISLAND

Cornmill Heritage Centre
Lineside. ☎ (01868) 748532. Open Monday–Friday 10am–5pm, also weekends by arrangement.

COOKSTOWN

Wellbrook Beetling Mill (NT)
Off A505 4 miles west of town. ☎ (016487) 51735. Open April–September weekends 2–6pm, also weekdays except Tuesday in July and August.

CREGGAN

An Creagán Visitor Centre
On A505 midway between Omagh and Cookstown. ☎ (016627) 61112. Open daily 11am–6.30pm, closes 4.30pm in winter. Restaurant, shop.

DONAGHMORE

Heritage Centre
☎ (01868) 767039. Open Monday–Friday 9am–5pm, other times by arrangement.

DOWNHILL

Mussenden Temple (NT)
☎ (01265) 848728. Access to grounds all year. Temple open weekends April–September noon–6pm and daily in July and August. To visit crypt ask at Bishop's Gate lodge.

DRAPERSTOWN

Plantation of Ulster Centre
50 High Street. ☎ (01648) 27800. Explains the context of the famous 1607 episode of the Flight of the Earls. Open Monday–Saturday 11am–5pm and Sunday afternoon in summer.

DUNGANNON

Heritage World Family Centre
26 Market Square.
☎ (01868) 724187. Exhibition on the great famine. Open Monday–Friday 9am–5pm.

The Linen Green, Moygashel
Main Road, Moygashel.
☎ (01868) 753761. Linen from the adjacent Moygashel Mills is sold through two factory shops. One stocks household linens and furnishing fabrics, the other is the Paul Costelloe Factory Store — high fashion clothing for men and women, open Monday–Saturday 9.30am–5.30pm. Enquire about other new visitor attractions.

Tyrone Crystal
Killybrackey, Coalisland Road.
☎ (01868) 725335. Tours Monday–Friday, plus Saturday in summer. Telephone for times. Factory shop, café.

DUNGIVEN

Priory
☎ (01232) 235000. Ruins always accessible. To inspect O'Cahan tomb telephone in advance or ask at last house in approach lane.

LIMAVADY

Roe Valley Country Park
☎ (015047) 22074 (warden). Always open. Visitor centre open daily September–May 10am–5pm, June–August 10am–8pm.

LONDONDERRY CITY

Earhart Cottage
Ballyarnet, 3 miles north of city. Take A2/B194. ☎ (01504) 354040. Open Monday–Thursday 9am–4.30pm and Friday morning.

Foyle Valley Railway Centre
Near Craigavon Bridge (west bank). ☎ (01504) 265234. Open Tuesday–Saturday 10am–5pm.

Guildhall
☎ (01504) 377335. For guided tour Monday–Friday 9am–5.30pm telephone superintendent.

Harbour Museum
☎ (01504) 377331. Open Monday–Friday 10am–5pm (closed 1–2pm).

Long Tower Church
Open 9am–9pm.

St Columb's Cathedral
☎ (01504) 267313. Chapterhouse open Monday–Saturday 9am–5pm. (4pm in winter). Closed 1–2pm.

St Eugene's Cathedral
Always open.

Tower Museum
☎ (01504) 372411. Open Tuesday–Saturday 10am–5pm, plus Monday and Sunday afternoon in July and August.

Walls of Derry
Always accessible. Guided tours in summer start from tourist office, 44 Foyle Street.

MONEYMORE

Springhill House (NT)
☎ (016487) 48210. Open April–September weekends 2–6pm, also weekdays except Thursday in July and August.

NEWTOWNSTEWART

Gateway Centre
Grange Court, 21 Moyle Road.
☎ (016626) 62414. Dunbar mini-museum open daily from Easter to September.

OMAGH

Ulster-American Folk Park
☎ (01662) 243292. On A5 3 miles north of Omagh. Open April–September Monday–Saturday from 11am (last admission 5pm), Sunday from 11.30am. In winter Monday–Friday from 10.30am.

Ulster History Park
On B48 7 miles north of Omagh.
☎ (016626) 48188. Open April–September Monday–Saturday from 10.30am (last admission 5pm), Sunday from 11.30am. In winter Monday–Friday only.

PLUMBRIDGE

Sperrin Heritage Centre
274 Glenelly Road, Cranagh.
☎ (016626) 48142. On B47 9 miles east of Plumbridge. Open Easter–October from 11am daily, except for Sunday morning.

STRABANE

Gray's Printer Museum & Art Gallery
49 Main Street. For opening times telephone: ☎ (01504) 382204.

President Wilson Ancestral Home
☎ (01504) 883735. Dergalt, 2 miles south-east of Strabane, signposted off Plumbridge road. Telephone for hours.

UPPERLANDS

Wm Clark & Sons
☎ (01648) 42214. Factory tours by arrangement Monday–Thursday 9am–5pm and Friday morning.

EVENTS

Cookstown

100 Road Race (April).
Motorcycling

Limavady

Jane Ross Festival (end April–early May)
Drama, music, lectures, sports.

Londonderry City

North West Storytelling Festival (April)

International Jazz & Blues Festival (May)

Air Show (end May–early June)

Banks of the Foyle Hallowe'en Carnival (October)
Theatre, poetry, film, music.

Omagh

Appalachian & Blue Grass Music Festival (September)

TOURIST INFORMATION CENTRES

Coleraine

Railway Road. ☎ (01265) 44723. Open all year Monday–Saturday 9am–5pm (6pm in high summer).

Cookstown

48 Molesworth Street.
☎ (016487) 66727. Open Easter–September Monday–Friday 9am–5pm, Saturday 10am–4pm. Closes later in high summer.

Killymaddy

Killymaddy Tourist Amenity Centre, Ballygawley Road, Dungannon. On A4 2 miles west of Parkanaur Forest Park. ☎ (01868) 767259. Open daily all year 10am–4pm. Longer hours in summer.

Limavady

Council Offices, 7 Connell Street.
☎ (015047) 22226. Open all year Monday–Friday 9am–5pm, plus Easter–September Saturday 9.30am–5.30pm.

Londonderry

44 Foyle Street. ☎ (01504) 267284. Open all year Monday–Friday 9am–5pm, plus Saturday from Easter, and Sunday July–September. Closes later in summer.

Omagh

1 Market Street. ☎ (01662) 247831. Open all year Monday–Friday 9am–5pm, plus Saturday Easter–September.

Strabane

Abercorn Square. ☎ (01504) 883735. Open April–October Monday–Saturday 9am–4.30pm. Closed in winter.

Tourist information is also available from:

Castlederg Visitor Centre, 26 Lower Strabane Road (see Castlederg above).

Cookstown Council Offices, Burn Road, Cookstown. ☎ (016487) 62205.

The Bridewell, Church Lane, Magherafelt. ☎ (01648) 31510.

7

THE CAUSEWAY COAST
& THE GLENS OF ANTRIM

The north Antrim coast became an instant tourist attraction after a description of the **Giant's Causeway** was published in 1693 by the Royal Society. Ever since, people have flocked to look at and sit on and clamber over this amazing geological phenomenon, and have their photograph taken against its tall colonnades. The dramatic beauty of this whole stretch of coast, where craggy headlands give way to sandy bays and small harbours, is much more than a bonus for visitors to the Causeway. The **coastal drive** from Portrush round to Larne is 60 miles of exceptionally magnificent scenery.

The artist Susanna Drury, who was painting from about 1733 to 1770, helped make the Causeway famous in Europe. Her work may be seen in the Ulster Museum, Belfast. A pair of her pictures, one showing the east, and the other the west prospect, painted on vellum in about 1740, were engraved and circulated widely on the continent. The origins of the columnar structures excited great speculation, particularly among two rival groups of eighteenth-century British and French scientists. The Neptunists said the columns were sedimentary rocks, formed by chemical precipitation in the water. The Vulcanists said they were igneous — the result of volcanic action. By the nineteenth century everyone acknowledged that the Vulcanists were right. The cliffs all the way along the north Antrim coast are still of interest to scientists and geologists. Flows of molten lava buried a whole series of older rocks and protected them from atmospheric destruction. These old rocks now jut out as many-coloured cliffs along the edge of the plateau — red sandstone, chalk, coal, blue clay, iron ore, black basalt. **Fair Head**, a 626ft cliff at the extreme east end, has sixteen different strata.

The Causeway proper is a mass of basalt columns packed tightly together, formed by volcanic rock contracting as it cooled. The tops of the columns form stepping stones leading from the cliff foot and disappearing under the sea. Altogether there are about 40,000 of these strangely symmetrical columns, mostly hexagonal but some with four or five, and others with seven or eight sides. The tallest are 40ft high, and the solidified lava in the cliffs is 90ft thick in places.

The ancient Irish must have wondered at the Causeway and inevitably there are many fables. Basically, though, this was giants' work and, more particularly, the work of the giant Finn McCool, the Ulster warrior and commander of the king of Ireland's armies. When he fell in love with a female giant on Staffa, the island of Fingal's cave off the Scottish coast, Finn built this commodious highway to bring her across to Ulster. Fingal is Finn, of course, and there are similar rock formations on Staffa. Like Mrs Drury's paintings, the celebrated description by W. M. Thackeray in his *Irish Sketch Book* (1842) conveys a sense of the fantastic, a fabulous lunar landscape: 'When the world was moulded and fashioned out of formless chaos, this must have been the bit over — a remnant of chaos … '. In 1930 H. V. Morton described it as resembling 'an over-photographed actress' and by 1986 it was time for Unesco to bestow the ultimate accolade by adding the Giant's Causeway to its World Heritage List of top monuments and sites.

It is easy to linger long in the visitor centre where the Causeway's geology, flora and fauna, social history and so on, are very well presented. Early visitors got here on horseback or by boat. Then the train from Belfast brought people to Portrush where they transferred to jaunting car or horse charabanc. In 1883 the Giant's Causeway Tramway opened — the first hydro-electric tram in Europe. It ran on a narrow gauge railway from Portrush to the Causeway until 1949. One of its 'toast-rack' carriages is on display. But do not allow the visitor centre to detain you. Hurry on down to see the real thing.

A short circular walk starting from the centre goes down to the **Grand Causeway** and past majestic stone amphitheatres and rock formations with fanciful names like the Honeycomb, the Giant's Boot and the King and his Nobles, and up the **Shepherd's Steps** to the cliff top and then back along the high level path to the visitor centre. Beyond **Port Reostan viewpoint**, the low level path which continues east to Benbane Head, past Port na Spaniagh and Lacada Point where gold treasure from the wrecked Spanish Armada galleass, *Girona*, was recovered by divers in 1968, has been closed for several years because of serious erosion. In summer a minibus shuttles between the visitor centre and the Grand Causeway.

Returning to the carpark, you may notice an incongruous white-washed Austrian Tyrolean church — a 1915 conceit by Clough Williams-Ellis, architect of Portmeirion in Wales. It is a schoolhouse,

The Giant's Causeway

now a **museum**. A bronze relief of a girl asleep by a pitcher, at the entrance, is by Rosamund Praeger. The louvred bell tower is not the only eccentric rooftop round here: the profile of the visitor centre mimics the malt-house roofs of the whiskey distillery at Bushmills 2 miles south of the Causeway.

Golf at Royal Portrush, with the White Rocks a magnificent backdrop

The resort of **Portstewart** (population 6,500), with its small sheltered harbour, substantial houses along the promenade, and 3-mile strand stretching to the Bann mouth, always had more pretensions than neighbouring Portrush. A railway station, for example, was not permitted in Portstewart for fear of bringing vulgar people to the town. The railway company had to build the station a decent but inconvenient distance away, and visitors came the last mile by steam tram. The big motorcycle race now held here every May, with bikes roaring along the roads around Portstewart, would surely have appalled that genteel nineteenth-century society. The motorcar, on the other hand, was tolerated, and drivers — far too many of them sometimes — still enjoy the traditional practice of taking their cars down to the sea and driving along the firm sands of **Portstewart Strand**. The seafront buildings are unexceptional. Dominican nuns have built a large convent round **O'Hara's Castle**, an early-nineteenth-century stucco building on a cliff at the west end of the town. A squat house with two drum towers near the beach was the birthplace of Sir George White VC (born 1834) who led the relief of

Ladysmith in the Boer War. Cruises to the Causeway operate in summer from both Portstewart and Portrush. A 12ft high bronze boat sculpture near the boating pool is a reminder that Jimmy Kennedy's famous song 'Red sails in the sunset' was inspired by a Portstewart sunset.

Portrush (population 5,700) has a beautiful position on **Ramore Head** peninsula jutting out into the Atlantic, with sandy beaches running east and west, and picture-postcard seaside terraces above the harbour. The grassy clifftop at the end of the promontory is haunted by ornithologists, especially in autumn when the wind blows from the north-west, who have humped their tripods and telescopes up here to watch a ceaseless flypast of geese and gulls. The resort has the usual seaside amenities, including a large 'virtual reality' entertainment complex, indoor water slides, a hilarious raft race across the harbour in May, and summer theatre shows in the redbrick town hall, a bulbous and jolly Victorian pile. Spiral patterns of fossil ammonites have been preserved on flat rocks on the shore below Lansdowne Crescent, and the geological significance of these tiny sea creatures is explained in a small **exhibition centre** nearby.

Two-mile-long East Strand is backed by the sand dunes of the celebrated Royal Portrush Golf Club, scene of many Irish golf championships. The British Open has also been held here. The strand ends at the **White Rocks**, limestone cliffs weirdly weathered into caves and arches, most notably the Cathedral Cave which is reached by a steep path from the road. This cave is 180ft deep with two enormous limestone columns supporting the roof at the seaward entrance. The picnic site at the carpark nearby is a good place to stop for lunch. The view is splendid. **The Skerries**, a chain of small grassy islands a couple of miles offshore, can be inspected at close quarters by excursion boats from Portrush.

The romantic ruin of **Dunluce Castle** teeters on the edge of an isolated crag. Some of it actually fell off during a storm in 1639, carrying away the kitchens, the cooks and all the pots. In the thirteenth century Richard de Burgh built a Norman castle on this desirable site. Defenders could come and go through the large sea cave that slopes up into the castle precincts, and a drawbridge lay across the deep chasm now spanned by a wooden footbridge. In the late sixteenth century the MacDonnells, Lords of the Isles, ruled all this north-east corner of Ulster from their stronghold at Dunluce. Sir John Perrott came up from Dublin in 1584 and ejected Sorley Boy MacDonnell after pounding the castle with artillery. As soon as Perrott returned south, having left an English garrison in charge, Sorley Boy regained possession after one of his men, employed in the castle, hauled various MacDonnells up the crag in a basket. The garrison was wiped out and the constable hanged over the wall.

Sorley's antecedents are clear from his name: *somhairle* is from the Norse for 'summer soldier' or Viking, *buí* is 'yellow' in Gaelic. The Scots were in the habit of leading raiding parties against both the Irish and English and many, like the MacDonnells, stayed on. This yellow-haired summer soldier was soon able to repair the damaged castle with proceeds from the wreck of the Spanish treasure ship *Girona* which sank off the Causeway in October 1588. The pitifully few survivors — only five out of 1,300 men — were put up at Dunluce and sent home via Scotland.

The castle fell into decay after Sorley's descendants, the Earls of Antrim, moved to more comfortable accommodation at Glenarm, in the Glens of Antrim, in the mid-seventeenth century. The extensive ruins include two thirteenth-century towers, a Scottish-style gate-house (about 1600), and the remains of a great hall, part of a seventeenth-century house built inside the defences. From the windows there is a fine view through the limestone arches of the White Rocks. The cave underneath Dunluce can, with care, be visited by boat or dinghy in calm weather. It is one of many narrow sea caves along this coast.

The little port and beach resort of **Portballintrae** (population 760) is reached by a loop road off the A2. It has nice hotels and a half-moon bay. Beyond is Bushfoot Strand and the western end of the Causeway cliffs. The Bush is a great salmon and trout river, with good stretches from Bushmills village up to Stranocum. **Bushmills** (population 1,400) was traditionally the last stop from Belfast before the final push to the Causeway when travellers restored themselves with a few glasses of whiskey from the **Old Bushmills Distillery**, in business since 1608. It is the world's oldest legal whiskey distillery. The village has an attractive square with solidly built houses and a Victorian clock tower vaguely resembling an Irish round tower. Many tourists make a beeline for the distinctive malt-houses of the distillery where the product can be sampled, in moderation, during a tour of the works.

The pear-shaped crag of **Dunseverick**, where the coastal path and the B146 almost converge, is crowned with the very fragmentary ruin of a small sixteenth-century castle, a poor thing to look at. But never mind the castle, listen to the legends: the human history of this impressive crag is long and interesting. Dunseverick, the capital of the ancient kingdom of Dalriada, was the terminal of one of Ireland's five great highways from Tara, near Drogheda, and a main jumping-off point for Scotland. Irishmen from Dalriada had established a

Above: Dunluce Castle occupies an impregnable, if precarious, cliff-top position

Opposite: Bushmills is the world's oldest legal whiskey distillery

colony on the Argyll coast by the fifth century — the colony which St Columba joined and from which he established Iona. Dunseverick is also featured in Ireland's oldest love story, the ninth-century *Longas mac n-Usnig* ('The exile of the children of Usna'), as the legendary landing place of Deirdre of the Sorrows and the sons of Usna. Deirdre, the intended bride of King Conor, falls in love with his bodyguard, Naisi. To escape the king's wrath they flee to Scotland, together with Naisi's two brothers. Fergus, another of Conor's warriors, in good faith persuades them that the king has forgiven them and that it is safe to return. They land at Dunseverick (some accounts say east of Ballycastle) and take the road south to Conor's court at *Emain Macha* (Navan Fort) at Armagh. But the vengeful king kills the brothers and takes Deirdre for himself, whereupon she dashes her head against a stone and dies. Outraged by Conor's treachery, the noble Fergus destroys the palace.

Another ruined gatehouse with a spectacular position is **Kinbane Castle**, built by Colla Dubh, Sorley Boy MacDonnell's brother, on a long white promontory which is signposted off the B15 2 miles east of Carrick-a-rede. There are fine views of Fair Head and Rathlin Island from the path leading down to the castle from the cliff-top carpark. Watch out for erosion and steep drops. A profusion of wild flowers, including orchids, grows beside the path in early summer. The cave that goes right through the promontory is only accessible by boat.

Crescent-shaped **Whitepark Bay** is in National Trust care. It has a youth hostel and a mile of golden sand backed by grassy dunes, and is flanked at the west end by the picturesque hamlet of **Portbraddan**. An odd slate-roofed church (privately owned) squeezed in next to a house measures only 12ft by 6½ft, the smallest church in Ireland. There are caves at the raised beach at the other end of the bay, and Neolithic flints have been found here. A footpath leads round to **Ballintoy** harbour, a sturdy limestone harbour set among rocks, lively with small boats and dinghies, and people having tea in the café. The local boatmen will readily take visitors fishing or for trips along the coast. **Sheep Island**, a perpendicular stack with a flat grassy top half a mile offshore, has an enormous cormorant colony. The rats that killed off the island's colony of puffins have themselves been routed and the puffins have come back.

The switchback road down to the harbour passes a charming

white church in a meadow. Its tapered square tower has little pinnacles at the corners and very small windows. In 1641 the Earl of Antrim came to the rescue of local Protestants who had taken refuge inside the original church on the site and were being besieged. An eighteenth-century landlord of the village was Downing Fullerton, whose family name is perpetuated in Downing Street, London, and Downing College, Cambridge. When the castle at Ballintoy was dismantled in 1795, the staircase and oak panelling was taken to Cambridge and installed in the college.

The rope bridge at **Carrick-a-rede** is a great tourist attraction and quite scary. Swinging 80ft above the sea and made of planks strung between wires, it starts bouncing up and down as soon as you step on it. There is no safety netting on the sides and a large notice warns of the risks of crossing. Despite this, or perhaps because of it, there is a steady stream of visitors keen to cross the perilous 60ft-wide chasm to the small rocky island on the other side. The bridge gives access to the commercial salmon fishery on the south-east side of the island. It is removed in September at the end of the fishing season and put up again in April.

Carrick-a-rede means 'rock in the road' — the road taken by Atlantic salmon returning to spawn in the rivers. The tidal conditions and the deep water are ideal for salmon netting and the fishery has been here for at least 350 years. An engraving of 1790 shows a rope bridge at the rock. A cunning system of nets intercepts the fish as they move westwards, keeping close to the shore searching for their ancestral waters. Until recently a steep path from the main road ran down to the bridge across a field. Now the approach is via a made-up path along half a mile of cliff top from Larrybane carpark where there is a National Trust **information centre**, aquarium and tea shop; campers can pitch a tent for the night here. A lime kiln on chalky **Larrybane Head** is a remnant of past quarrying operations.

Between the Causeway and the Glens of Antrim, **Ballycastle** (population 4,000) is a lively little resort with a variety of diversions and things to see. In late August the town hosts the Ould Lammas Fair, Ireland's oldest popular fair, held here since the MacDonnells obtained a charter in 1606. In its heyday the fair lasted a week. Now a two-day event, it has sheep and pony sales and several hundred street stalls crammed into the Diamond and down Fairhill Street. The Diamond is lined with some agreeable houses, with **Holy Trinity church** on one side. An attractive classical parish church with an octagonal spire, it was built in 1756. The very big clock face, big enough to read from a long way off, is out of all proportion to the square tower. Inside is a star-spangled blue ceiling and memorials to the Boyd family who built up the town in the eighteenth century. The red sandstone memorial with pink marble columns in front of the church was erected to a local nineteenth-century benefactor. A plaque over a newsagent's shop at **21 Ann Street** recalls that here John McAuley, a Ballycastle woodcarver, wrote the ever-popular song which asks:

> Did you treat your Mary Ann
> To dulse and yellow man
> At the Ould Lammas Fair in Ballycastle-O?

Dulse is an edible seaweed. Yellow man is a rock-like bright yellow toffee so hard that it has to be broken with a hammer. It is best to suck a small piece, slowly. Across the street, the butcher's shop at No 18, Wysner's, is celebrated for its sausages.

On steep Castle Street **Ballycastle Museum** now occupies the town's eighteenth-century courthouse, with a view of Fair Head from the door. Lower down the street **MacDonnell's pub** (established 1744) invites any visiting singer or instrumentalist to step inside — a reminder that this is one of the best places in Northern Ireland to hear traditional Irish music, particularly in June when there is a three-day music and dance festival (Fleadh Amhrán agus Rince). At the bottom is the **Antrim Arms**, the hostelry where Marconi stayed in 1898.

An early-seventeenth-century MacDonnell castle at the Diamond has vanished completely but the bones of Sorley Boy, who died in 1590 aged 85, are preserved in a vault at the ruined friary of **Bonamargy**, half a mile outside Ballycastle on the A2 to Cushendall. Sorley's descendants, the first Earls of Antrim, are also buried here. Inscriptions on the tomb of Randal MacDonnell, second earl (died 1682), are in Gaelic as well as the more usual Latin and English. The Gaelic translates with typical Celtic gloom: 'Every seventh year a calamity befalls the Irish. Now that the Marquis has departed, it will occur every year.' The tombs are not accessible to the public. Founded for the Franciscans by Rory MacQuillan in about 1500, the friary's survival for 150 years after the dissolution of the monasteries (1537) is something of a puzzle. A flat stone incised with a cross just inside the main entrance to the church marks the **grave of Julia MacQuillan**, a seventeenth-century recluse known as the Black Nun. Her choice of burial place ensured that worshippers would walk on her when entering the church, thus perpetuating her perfect humility. Sailors lost at sea in the two World Wars and washed on to this treacherous coast are buried in a plot with a large cross in the graveyard corner. They include crewmen from HMS *Drake*

Carrick-a-rede rope bridge

torpedoed off Rathlin in 1915. A bit of Ballycastle golf course seems to have jumped across the A2 and comes right up against the grave-yard. The rounded mountain of **Knocklayd**, rising 1,695ft to the south-west, featured in an elaborate geologists' hoax in 1788 when, according to Dublin newspapers, it erupted and engulfed the neigh-bourhood in boiling lava.

A modernistic memorial near Ballycastle harbour recalls the ex-perimental wireless link which Marconi and his assistant, George Kemp, established in 1898 between Ballycastle and Rathlin Island. Signals were transmitted over a distance of 6 miles between a mast erected near the island's east lighthouse and a house on top of the cliff at Ballycastle. Other transmissions to Rathlin were made from the

Ould Lammas Fair, Ballycastle

spire of the Catholic church in Moyle Street.

Rathlin Island (population 100) is a 40-minute boat trip across the sound from Ballycastle, and only a dozen or so miles from the Mull of Kintyre in Scotland. Shaped like a boomerang with one arm about 4 miles long and the other about 2½, the island has **three lighthouses** and high white cliffs round most of the coast. The tip of the shorter arm is just 3 miles from Fair Head, the mighty headland that marks off Ulster's north-east corner. In the angle of the boomerang, the sheltered modern harbour at Church Bay is a staging post for yachts heading for the Hebrides. Birdwatchers, botanists and divers (scoobies) wait around the quay at Ballycastle for a boat to transport them and their gear across the sound. Rathlin boatmen like to direct your attention to *Slough-na-Morra*, 'the swallow of the sea', a whirlpool at the southern tip of Rathlin where St Columba is said to have narrowly escaped drowning on a voyage from Ireland to Iona in the sixth century. The first recorded shipping disaster in Rathlin Sound was in about AD440 when Brecain, son of Niall of the Nine Hostages, and his fleet of fifty curraghs were lost in a great tide rip. However, scoobie interest tends to focus on more recent wrecks, like *Drake* and *Loch Garry*, sitting upright 100ft down near Rue Point since 1942. The long, very deep underwater cliffs on the north-west side of the island are also popular scoobie haunts.

A passenger ferry to the island leaves from Ballycastle twice a day all year, more frequently in summer. You can also make your own arrangements with local boatmen. Bear in mind that crossings are dependent on weather conditions. For the visitor, the island's delightful primitiveness is more apparent than real. A guesthouse, a licensed restaurant, a pub, a hostel and two shops remove any imperative to do the round trip in a day. You can however visit every corner of the island on foot in two days. In fact walking is the best way to get around. The most distant place, the **nature reserve** at the west end, is less than 5 miles from the harbour. In summer there is an unofficial, somewhat unpredictable, minibus service.

The ownership of Rathlin, definitely Irish since a famous seventeenth-century court case, was disputed between Ireland and Scotland on a number of occasions, and the island's history has been regularly punctuated by battles and massacres. Sir Francis Drake landed guns on Rathlin in 1575 when his commander, the Earl of Essex, massacred the MacDonnell population while Sorley Boy MacDonnell looked on helplessly from the mainland. The MacDonnells were again massacred in 1642, this time on the orders of Archibald Campbell, eighth Earl of Argyll. It should be said that the MacDonnells did their own massacring when the need arose.

Fishing, farming and tourism are the islanders' chief sources of income. The islanders' efforts to promote activity holidays were helped after they rescued Richard Branson, the Virgin tycoon, when his transatlantic hot-air balloon fell into the sea off Rathlin. The grateful billionaire underwrote an activity centre at Church Bay. Herring, mackerel and flatfish are plentiful around the shore. Lobster fishing is one of the more profitable occupations. Boats from Ballycastle, Portrush and Portstewart take cod, haddock, skate and other large fish. Electricity is generated by three giant wind turbines on Kilpatrick Hill, the highest point, with a central diesel/battery facility at the harbour, ready to cut in when the wind drops. The turbines and overhead cables are not particularly aesthetic but Rathliners consider it a small price to pay for modern comforts — until the 'mains' came in 1992, they relied on bottled gas and diesel.

Salty winds rake the island all year round and stop trees from growing more than a few feet; the landscape is virtually treeless. There are many dry-stone walls and scattered ruined cottages with pairs of big gate pillars, inhabited when the population was much larger. The patterns of small arable fields criss-crossed with lazy beds are clearly visible on the sloping land at the east end behind the harbour. The water supply is still pumped along miles of plastic tubing that lies around on the surface of the ground. The first car on the island arrived in 1955 for the district nurse's use. Now there are a number of cars, vans, motorbikes and tractors jolting over the rough tracks. Islanders are exempted from paying road fund tax which, since there is only one bit of road to speak of, is only fair.

The cliffs of Rathlin are home to vast numbers of seabirds. The 350ft cliff towering 100ft over the west lighthouse above **Bull Point** is the best place from which to see them, guillemots, kittiwakes, razorbills, crowded in tens of thousands on ledges and rock stacks, and puffins standing on grassy mounds outside their burrows. The lighthouse light is actually at the foot of a square four-storey tower which has chimney pots and sash windows. It was completed in 1919, the year the south lighthouse was built at Rue Point. Most Rathlin caves can be visited only by boat in a flat calm. The high caves before Bull Point are jammed to the roof with iron girders, steel plates and chunks of engines from ancient wrecks, wrenched from the seabed by Atlantic storms — an awesome reminder, on a sunny day, of the ferocious winter storms that lash these parts.

The most famous cave is **Bruce's Cave**, below the **east lighthouse** at the other end of the island, where some of the cliff formations have similarities with the Giant's Causeway. Robert the Bruce hid here in 1306 after his defeat by the English at Perth, and it was a Rathlin spider whose arachnoid energies gave the despondent warrior new heart and sent him back to Scotland to win the Battle of Bannockburn. The **east lighthouse**, looking, one feels, as a lighthouse ought to look — a tall confident black-and-white cylinder — was erected in 1856. The track from the harbour passes **Knocknascreedin** or 'hill of screaming', the Gaelic soubriquet being acquired after the 1642 massacre. Concrete slabs lying in grass east of the lighthouse enclosure and marked with the name 'Lloyds' are the remains of the Marconi wireless mast of 1898. The lighthouse keeper does not live here any more. Like all Northern Ireland's lighthouses, the Rathlin ones are now controlled automatically.

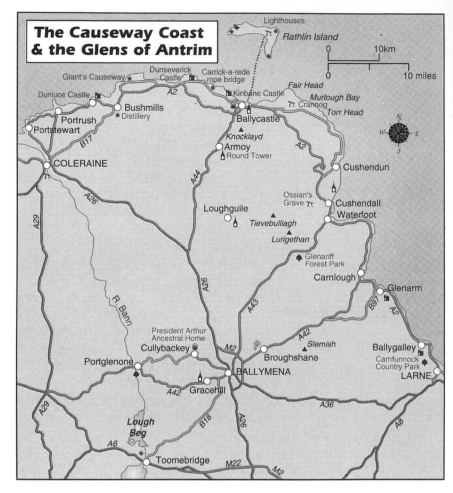

The Causeway Coast & the Glens of Antrim

Lighthouses

Rathlin Island

0   10km

0   10 miles

Giant's Causeway

Dunseverick Castle

Carrick-a-rede rope bridge

Kinbane Castle

Fair Head

Murlough Bay

Crannog

Torr Head

Dunluce Castle

A2

Bushmills
Distillery

Ballycastle

Knocklayd

Armoy
Round Tower

A2

Portrush

Portstewart

B17

COLERAINE

A26

Cushendun

Ossian's
Grave

Cushendall
Waterfoot

Loughguile

Tievebulliagh

Lurigethan

A29

A44

Glenariff
Forest Park

Carnlough

Glenarm

R. Bann

A26

A43

B97

A2

President Arthur
Ancestral Home

Cullybackey

M2

A42

Slemish

Ballygalley

Carnfunnock
Country Park

LARNE

Portglenone

Broughshane

A29

BALLYMENA

A42   Gracehill

A36

A8

Lough
Beg

B18

A26

A6

Toomebridge   M22

M2

Some 6,000 years ago a Neolithic axe factory on Rathlin was producing distinctive axe heads of porcellanite which have been found all over Ireland and in parts of England. It was one of three main axe factories in the British Isles. The others were at Tievebulliagh near Cushendall, County Antrim, and at Langdale in Cumbria. Stone Age men discovered a small outcrop of this rare, very hard, fine-grained blue stone in **Brockley** townland on the west side of the island. North of Brockley at **Doonmore** is an ancient rath with some extremely thick stone walls on the top. At **Knockans**, south-east of Brockley, a stone sweat house, a kind of early sauna, is close to the scant remains of a monastic settlement.

The island's main monastic site, where St Comgall of Bangor established a foundation in the sixth century, is in the Church Quarter near Rathlin's two churches. The small **Anglican parish church**,

Glenariff

which was rebuilt in 1815, has a lovely position close to the water, backed by whin-covered slopes. Inside is a memorial to the Rev. John Martin, rector here in 1723–40, and monuments to the Gage family, resident landlords of Rathlin from the eighteenth century. Mrs Catherine Gage, who died in 1862, is commemorated by two shapely maidens in diaphanous gowns of gleaming white marble. The Gages have gone now but they built the long low manor house (now converted, with hostel accommodation) that extends along the water-front at Church Bay. A short distance back up the track is a modest little Catholic church of 1865, Rathlin's main place of worship, next to the priest's house.

From Ballycastle, tourists will in general stay with the coast road but, if time permits, a short detour inland is worthwhile. This whole area — the coast, the glens and the bleak peaty Antrim plateau — is designated an area of outstanding natural beauty (AONB). Outside the AONB, beween the A44 and the western edge of the plateau, is an interesting area of small trout streams and quiet country lanes rarely seen by visitors. Leave Ballycastle by the A44 and, just before **Armoy** — a sleepy village recently in the news for having a remarkable number of twins — take the Loughguile road, so straight you would think the Romans built it, passing after half a mile the stump of **Armoy round tower** with a neat plain parish church a few feet away, and on to **Magherahoney** to visit **St MacNissi's Catholic church** with its unusual stations of the cross, some made by the Ulster artist Cherith McKinstry. MacNissi, who made a pilgrimage to Jerusalem in the late fifth century and returned with his bag full of holy relics, is much associated with this part of Antrim; on again to **Loughguile** (2½ miles) where you may be able to see inside **All Saints'**, an Anglican church which has a beautiful triptych window with glass by Mayer & Co. from the original Munich factory. You can drive along the south shore of Loughguile lake for a glimpse of a very large and exotic cottage beyond the lake on the fringe of a wooded estate (private). The estate was the seat of the first and last Earl Macartney (1737–1806) but he was away governing the colonies so long that he never finished building his castle.

US president William McKinley's ancestor, James McKinley, emigrated to America from this area in the 1740s. The McKinley family home was west of Armoy near **Dervock** where, on summer afternoons, **Benvarden Gardens** may be visited. James's nephew, Francis McKinley, was hanged as a United Irishman and the family house was burned down as a reprisal by the local yeomanry. A painting in the Giant's Causeway visitor centre shows the house in flames.

After Loughguile lake, you soon reach the A44 again, very close to the impressive castle mound (motte) of **Knockaholet** built inside a ring fort. Returning now to Ballycastle, rejoin the A2 which runs east across the Antrim plateau, past Ballypatrick forest, past Watertop Farm which opens to visitors and has pony-trekking facilities, across one end of the 'vanishing lake' of **Loughareema**, and down to Cushendall. After heavy rain the lake can flood the road and then it suddenly runs dry. This is no puddle. When full, it is 25ft deep in places, with some large black trout shimmying about. Then the water drains away rapidly through porous chalk under the mud and the lake, and the trout, vanish completely. Last century, when this inland road was just a track, it was not unknown for coach horses to gallop into a watery grave at Loughareema, taking the passengers with them.

If you are not to miss the exhilarating heights of **Fair Head**, you must turn left off the A2 3 miles from Ballycastle and follow the lane up to a small National Trust carpark. The cliff top is about a mile on foot from here north across heathery boggy scrub. You can follow the Trust's yellow circle markings for a bit but after half a mile their route swerves round to the east, away from the cliff edge. Buzzards, sparrowhawks and ravens frequent the desolate tableland and you may see small flocks of red-legged choughs. Walking north you pass, on the left, **Lough na Cranagh**, the largest of three lakes in the vicinity. The exquisite oval-shaped island in the middle is an artificial lake dwelling, a crannog, with a stone revetment 6ft above the water level. It is believed to have been a royal residence of the Dalriada kingdom, and connected with Dunseverick. (The crannog can also be viewed from the road — without getting out of the car! — before you reach the carpark.) From the headland is a superlative view of Rathlin and the hills and islands of Scotland, very close indeed across the narrow North Channel. **Grey Man's Path**, a convenient short cut for wild goats foraging on the cliffs, plunges dramatically down a steep gully. It is actually less difficult to negotiate than it looks, though inexperienced walkers should avoid it.

Murlough Bay, the loveliest of all the bays along the Antrim coast, is in the lee of this great headland. Unless you want to walk to it, you should return to the carpark and drive round via Ballylucan where the turning is well signposted. The contrast between the scrubby top of Fair Head and this lush green place is most striking. Below the chalk escarpment, buttercup meadows and trees run down nearly to the water's edge, with sheep and a few cows grazing the slopes. The main carpark is up above the bay but there is a smaller one on a hairpin bend further down, past the **stone cross memorial** to Sir Roger Casement, who was executed for treason in 1916.

Regarded by Irish nationalists as a martyr, Casement had a brilliant career in the British colonial civil service; in particular, he reported on labour conditions in the Belgian Congo and Peru. In 1911 he accepted a knighthood. However, he believed that the war with Germany offered a genuine opportunity for a successful Irish rebellion, and he went to Berlin to negotiate for military aid against Britain. At the height of the war he came back to Ireland with a shipload of armaments and landed from a German submarine on the Kerry coast. The plan did not go well. He was arrested and hanged at Pentonville. In 1965 his remains were taken to Dublin after representations by the Irish government and buried alongside O'Connell and Parnell at

Glasnevin (despite persistent rumours about his unsavoury sexual life). The Murlough Bay memorial was erected by his cousin, Mrs Parry of Cushendun.

A scenic road, very steep and winding, runs from Murlough Bay past **Torr Head**, where a modern **Celtic cross** commemorates Shane 'The Proud' O'Neill, killed by the MacDonnells in 1567 shortly after they defeated him at Farsetmore, County Donegal. Like other Ulster clans at that time, the MacDonnells had tired of his bullying. The road wriggling from here down to the National Trust village of Cushendun is hedged with wild fuchsia and honeysuckle.

Two of the 'Nine Glens' of Antrim, Glentaisie and Glenshesk, cut north to the bay at Ballycastle. Better known, however, are the Glens running west to east, bisecting the mountainous region all the way from Cushendun down to Larne. The physical isolation of the small communities of farmers and fishermen, which has left the Glens with a wealth of myth and legend, was alleviated in 1834 when a Scottish engineer, William Bald, blasted a road out of the chalky cliffs for a distance of 28 miles up the eastern seaboard, passing by the foot of each of the Glens. The road was later extended to Ballycastle. Names of the traditional nine Glens with their popular translations are, from north to south: **Glentaisie**, Taisie's glen — Princess Taisie, daughter of the king of Rathlin, who escaped being kidnapped by a Norwegian king when her fiancé, 'Long Nails' Congal, beat off the invader's boats in 200BC; **Glenshesk**, sedgy glen; **Glendun**, brown glen; **Glencorp**, glen of the slaughter; **Glenaan**, glen of rush lights; **Glenballyeamon**, Eamonn's townland glen; **Glenariff**, ploughman's glen; **Glencloy**, glen of hedges; and **Glenarm**, glen of the army.

Cushendun (population 350), once a highly fashionable watering place, is admired for the quaint Cornish architecture which Ronald McNeill, first (and last) Lord Cushendun, and his Cornish wife, Maud, commissioned from Clough Williams-Ellis (1883–1977). The square with small white-washed terraces is approached through large gate pillars. It was built in 1912. A row of cottages with hanging slates on the upper storey, facing the sea, was erected in memory of Maud in 1925. Williams-Ellis, remembered for Portmeirion in North Wales, also designed Lord Cushendun's large neo-Georgian house, Glenmona Lodge, set among trees in the middle of the bay. Now a home for the elderly, it has an eccentric five-arch arcade at the front. The white Georgian house at the north end of the beach, Rockport Lodge, was the home of a local poetaster, Moira O'Neill, whose real name, Nesta Higginson, suited her verses much better than the romantic alias she adopted. The ivy-covered ruins of a MacDonnell castle above Rockport House off the Torr Head road

Glenarm

was where Shane 'The Proud' was killed by Sorley Boy MacDonnell and his head sent to be spiked at Dublin Castle. Cave House, yet another substantial Cushendun mansion, occupies a secluded position in an amphitheatre of cliffs at the end of a red sandstone cave 60ft long. The only approach is through this cave. The poet John Masefield (1878–1967) knew the house well. He married a daughter of the Crommelin family who built the house in 1820. It is now a religious retreat.

Beautiful **Craigagh Wood**, west of the village, conceals a rock where mass was said in the eighteenth century. It is carved with a crucifixion scene and is said to have been brought here from Iona. The Gloonan Stone nearby, opposite the Catholic church, has two hollows made, they say, by St Patrick's knees. The name is from the Gaelic *glúine*, meaning 'knees'. An immense red stone **viaduct** with three arches, built by Charles Lanyon in 1839, carries the A2 over the tawny-coloured Glendun river. Glendun has the wildest scenery of all the Antrim Glens, and the walk up to the waterfalls is memorable. The B92 from Cushendun rejoins the A2 to Cushendall south of the viaduct.

Ossian's Grave, on the north-east slopes of the pointed mountain of **Tievebulliagh** (1,320ft) is signposted to the right (west) a mile before Cushendall. There is a carpark behind a house about half a mile up the lane from where a short walk brings you to an atmospheric little meadow with Ossian's Grave — actually a Neolithic court grave — in the middle and a **memorial** cairn to the Antrim Glens poet **John Hewitt** (1907–87). The site of Tievebulliagh's ancient porcellanite axe factory is near the summit. From Ossian's Grave there are lovely views to Glendun, Glenaan and Scotland, and to the south-west is **Trostan** (1,817ft), highest mountain on the plateau. The warrior–bard who gave his name to what is known as the Ossianic Cycle was the son of Finn McCool. The legends about Finn and his warrior band, the Fianna, originate from the third century. James Macpherson (1736–96), who translated and popularised them in the 1760s, added quite a few elements of his own but the tales are none the worse for that. Ossian is said to have returned from the fabulous kingdom of *Tír na nÓg*, the land of the ever-young, to find St Patrick preaching Christianity to the Celts. Despite the saint's best efforts, Ossian preferred the old gods and died unconverted.

Three glens converge at **Cushendall** (population 1,400) where the river meanders past a golf course into the bay. The red sandstone **curfew tower** on the corner of Mill Street was built in 1809 by Francis Turnly, an East India Company nabob, as 'a place of confinement for idlers and rioters'. North of the village, **Tieveragh Hill** is a small curiously rounded volcanic plug which is one of the best-known supernatural places in the Glens, a haunt of the 'wee folk'. A cliff path north from the beach leads after a mile to the delightful ruins of thirteenth-century **Layde Old Church**, an important burial place of the MacDonnells. It was rebuilt at least three times and served as a parish church until 1790. Fine stones in the graveyard include a cross to Dr James MacDonnell, a pioneer in the use of chloroform for surgical operations. He was also an organiser of the famous Belfast festival of Irish harpers in 1792.

Going south, flat-topped **Lurigethan** (1,153ft) looms on the right. Straight ahead are the fragmentary walls of a sixteenth-century castle on the cliff just before you pass under Red Arch. **Red Bay** boatyard, which builds wooden boats, has fishing boats and tackle for hire.

Iron ore was mined in upper Glenariff until the end of last century and was loaded at Red Bay. The shell-strewn sand on the beach here has a noticeable red tinge to it. Between Red Bay pier and Waterfoot village are several interesting caves. The biggest one, Nanny's Cave, is 40ft long and was inhabited by Ann Murray who was aged 100 when she died in 1847. She supported herself by spinning and knitting and was known to the revenue men for selling 'poteen' (illicit whiskey). In the eighteenth century the children of Red Bay learned reading and writing at a hedge school inside another of these caves. Hedge schools were unlicensed Irish schools run by unlicensed schoolmasters or itinerant priests, in the open air if nowhere else could be found, from the late seventeenth century. They were replaced by the National School system after Catholic emancipation (1829). The **school cave** can be entered just beyond Red Arch. **Waterfoot**, also called **Glenariff** (population 370), hosts the *Feis na nGleann*, one of the liveliest of the *feiseanna*, competitive festivals of Irish sport and culture, which are held in summer in various parts of Northern Ireland. The waterfalls and woodlands of **Glenariff Forest Park**, best known of all the Antrim Glens, should not be missed. In spring and early summer the upper glen is luxuriant with wild flowers, and there is a superb view from the café in the visitor centre.

The A2 now follows every indentation of the coast round **Garron Point**, where there is a marked change in the rock from red sandstone to limestone. After the chalky White Lady formation, watch out at a bend in the road for a large limestone rock with a bronze inscription, a rather dreadful poem, by Frances Anne Vane Tempest, Marchioness of Londonderry (1800–65). Immediately round the point a lane winds up to **Garron Tower**, a castellated blackstone mansion overlooking the sea, where she entertained on a grand scale. An inscription at the front door was written by, and about, the marchioness. The house is now a secondary school. In July it fills up with literary folk attending an annual summer school started in memory of the poet John Hewitt.

The quarries above **Carnlough** (population 1,500) are worked out now but until the 1960s the sturdy white bridge over the main road carried a railway which brought limestone down to the harbour. The bridge, an adjacent clock tower and old courthouse, all made of large squared blocks of limestone, were built by the Londonderrys in 1854. The marchioness was not able to resist having a few words about herself inscribed on a plaque which was set into the bridge on the south side, to be seen and read from the carriages passing underneath. The **Londonderry Arms** hotel, built about the same time, was briefly owned by Winston Churchill who came on a visit while he was Chancellor of the Exchequer. The harbour is a port of call for yachtsmen visiting the Glens. Lobster and crab are caught here and flatfish spearing is advertised on the main road. Carnlough has a nice sandy beach, a tourist office at 14 Harbour Road, an **art nouveau pub** of 1912 (McAuley's) and, like most of the villages down this coast, camping and caravan sites.

Glenarm (population 600), which exports limestone and powdered chalk from the harbour, developed after Randal MacDonnell built a hunting lodge in the glen in 1603. When Dunluce on the north coast was abandoned, the lodge was enlarged and Glenarm became the principal seat of the Earls of Antrim. To view **Glenarm Castle**, a theatrical pile of turrets and cupolas, go into the glen through a stone arch at the top of the village street, with parking beyond. The castle is clearly visible across the river. There was a major rebuilding around 1750, and the Tudor parts are nineteenth-century. The main entrance to the private demesne is a barbican archway with fake portcullis slits and boiling oil holes. A stone crest dated 1636, from the original castle, is set in the front. The lower glen is planted with Forest Service conifers but the woodlands of the upper glen, covenanted to the National Trust by the fourteenth earl in 1980, are pleasant enough. Very rarely, the castle gardens are open to the public. At the shop on the pier you can buy superior farmed **salmon**, reared in a natural way in the strong tides in Glenarm bay. Entirely chemical free, it is said to be the best farmed salmon available to the London market. The village itself has a self-possessed air, a nice place to explore on foot.

South of Glenarm, the road hugs the shore past a tumbled heap of limestone known as the Madman's Window, and on down through Ballygalley, passing **Ballygally Castle**, an engaging plantation castle which is now a hotel. Apart from sash windows, the original building is little changed since it was built in 1625. After **Carnfunnock Country Park** and then **Drain's Bay** — the name is a corruption of *draighean*, Gaelic for 'blackthorn' — with a view of **the Maidens'** lighthouses out to sea, the road snakes through Blackcave Tunnel, towards the ro-ro traffic rumbling off the ferries at Larne.

At Glenarm you have the option of turning inland to see something of the mid-Antrim region. The road joins up with the A42 which runs across the shallow valley of the Braid river, through Broughshane and into Ballymena, biggest town in County Antrim.

The flat landscape around Broughshane is relieved by **Slemish**, a small extinct volcano (1,437ft) which can be seen from a great distance. Evidence from St Patrick's writings suggests that this solitary hill is where Ireland's patron saint herded swine as a boy slave. Captured on the coast of Britain by pirates, Patrick was brought to the north of Ireland where he worked for 6 years for Miluic, chieftain at

Slemish, where St Patrick worked as a boy slave

Slemish, before making his escape. He returned in 432, a grown man, to convert the Irish to Christianity. Slemish is a place of pilgrimage on St Patrick's Day (17 March) though not particularly well signposted. An easy way to get to it is to go into Broughshane, passing the Carncairn daffodil nursery on the right, and then turn left on to the Ballyclare road (B94). After a mile turn left, right after 3 miles, right after 700yd, and a lane runs up between dry-stone walls to a carpark. From the top, a scramble of less than 700ft, look north to the ruins of old **Skerry church** on a hill where Miluic's fort once stood .

Several well-known daffodil breeders have lived at **Broughshane** (population 1,900), and the village gardens in spring are bright with drifts of daffodils and narcissi. Rare bulbs directly descended from daffodils created by Guy Wilson, a distinguished Broughshane hybridist, can be obtained from **Carncairn daffodil nursery** on the Carnlough road (A36) outside the town. Linen merchant Alexander Brown, who became famous as the banker of Baltimore, Maryland, was born (1764) in the big house beside the nursery. The parish church graveyard contains a copy of the famous tenth-century high cross at Monasterboice (County Louth). It marks the grave of the naturalist and collector John Grainger, whose private collection of 60,000 objects started the Ulster Museum's collection. As rector of Broughshane (1869–91) he had a roomy rectory. He needed every inch of space to put his things in.

The seventeenth-century settlers of **Ballymena** (population 29,000) came mostly from south-west Scotland. The Bard of Dunclug, David Herbison (1800–80), who was born in Mill Street, captured the lowland accent and intonation in his ballads and songs. That distinctive voice, only slightly modified, still predominates. The town's prosperity was based on the linen industry which, with other textiles and some engineering, continues in a small way. Now this whole area, including Ballymoney to the north, is overwhelmingly agricultural. Crowds up to 3,000 attend Ballymena's four weekly livestock markets, and the Saturday variety market has been going strong since 1626 when the Adair family obtained patents from Charles I. Local blackstone, the basalt which covers most of the Antrim plateau, is characteristic of the town's solidly built banks and sober churches. The **People's Park** was given to the town by the Adairs whose best-known member must be Dr Robert Adair. He was the 'Robin' of the love song 'Robin Adair' written by the spirited Lady Caroline Keppel whose parents tried, unsuccessfully, to end her romance with the young Ballymena doctor. Eaton Park is named after the family of Timothy Eaton (1834–1907) founder of the Canadian chainstore. Timothy is well remembered hereabouts. His birthplace, a farmhouse at **30 Killyfleugh Road** (blue plaque), is signposted off the A43 north of Ballymena. Ballymena Academy (emblem: the industrious ant) has produced judges, doctors, and outstanding athletes such as Mary Peters, pentathlon gold medallist in the 1972 Olympics in Munich, and Willie John McBride, Irish international and captain of the British Lions rugby team. The school's best-known pupil, historically speaking, was Roger Casement, but his name does not appear on the school roll.

A well-run crafts exhibition centre on Main Street attracts visitors to **Ballymoney** (population 8,250) where a modest courthouse (1838), some Georgian townhouses and a handful of churches are among the understated charms of this self-possessed little town. A mile to the west, the parkland and interesting eighteenth-century walled garden at **Leslie Hill** are open to the public.

The centre of **Gracehill** (population 680), just west of Ballymena, is much as it was in the eighteenth century when a small band of Moravians (United Brethren) settled here. The village is built round a green, with separate houses for the brothers and sisters who lived by making clocks and lace. The **church** (1765) contains interesting stained glass windows and a central pulpit. A long path down the middle of the grassy **cemetery** separates the graves of men from those of women, a Moravian burial custom which is still observed.

A signpost at **Cullybackey** on the Portglenone road (B96) indicates that the **ancestral home of Chester Alan Arthur**, US president 1881–85, is up a lane through potato fields, an awkward sharp turn. His father, who later became a Baptist clergyman, emigrated from here in 1816 and settled in Vermont. Arthur himself, a physically huge man, enjoyed good living and fine suits and was an excellent salmon fisherman. Baking and traditional crafts, such as crochet and quilt-making, are demonstrated in the thatched cottage during the summer months.

Until the mid-eighteenth century, **Portglenone** (population 1,250) had the only bridge across the 35-mile-long Lower Bann, apart from Coleraine near the estuary. In the seventeenth century a drawbridge was pulled up at night to protect the settlement from 'tories', or outlaws, lurking in the forests on the opposite bank. At **48 Main Street**, facing a pleasant elongated market place, a plaque records that Timothy Eaton, who later emigrated to Toronto and made a fortune from retailing, learned the drapery business in this shop 1847–52. He worked 16 hours a day and slept under the counter.

Portglenone Forest is an appropriate place to find a memorial to the Tyrone-born botanist Augustine Henry (1857–1930) who introduced fast-growing American conifers like the sitka spruce and Douglas fir to the British Isles. It is a commercial forest with a big chunk of sitka spruce but it also preserves the old woods along the Bann and there are plenty of beech, oak and other deciduous trees.

South of Portglenone, at **Toomebridge** (population 700) where the Bann flows out of Lough Neagh, is a **wild eel fishery**, the largest in Ireland, where visitors can call in. Demand in Europe for Lough Neagh eels is insatiable. At the height of the fishing season every day tons of brown eels are taken to Holland by vivers truck or flown out from Belfast International. Elvers, baby eels that look like little silver matchsticks, are a sought-after delicacy there; but they are not appreciated in Ireland, and most of them are allowed to grow to maturity in the lough. Large quantities are collected at Coleraine and brought to Lough Neagh by lorry. Left to their own devices, elvers take a year to make their way up the Bann. Salmon, on the other hand, swim up in a month. If you take a trip along the Bann after 1 May, there are dramatic piscatorial scenes of anglers tussling with these beautiful fish at every lock and weir.

ADDITIONAL INFORMATION

PLACES TO VISIT

BALLYCASTLE

Ballycastle Museum
59 Castle Street. ☎ (012657) 62942.
Open July and August noon–6pm.
To visit at other times telephone.

Bonamargy Friary
Ruins always accessible.
Unfortunately, the vault containing
the MacDonnell tombs has been
closed.

Watertop Open Farm
☎ (012657) 62576. Open daily
July–August. Pony trekking,
tours, boating etc.

BALLYGALLEY

Carnfunnock Country Park
On A2 1 mile south of Ballygalley.
☎ (01574) 270541. Park always
open. Telephone to check café/
visitor centre hours.

BALLYMONEY

Museum/Heritage Centre
33 Charlotte Street. ☎ (012656)
62280. Open April–September
Tuesday–Saturday 10am–12.30pm,
2–4pm.

Orchard Arts & Crafts Centre
Main Street. ☎ (012656) 67784.
Open Monday–Saturday 10am–
5.30pm. Works by local artists,
paintings, ceramics, jewellery.
Occasional wood turning
demonstrations. Crafts for sale.

Leslie Hill
Macfin Road, signposted from A26
roundabout 1 mile west of
Ballymoney. ☎ (012656) 66803.
Estate open every Sunday
afternoon from Easter to
September, plus Saturday in June
and daily July–August.

BUSHMILLS

Old Bushmills Distillery
☎ (012657) 31521. Tours all year
round Monday–Friday, also
Saturday in summer. Telephone for
details.

CARRICK-A-REDE

Rope Bridge
In position from late April to
September only. Access along a
cliff path (15-min walk) from
Larrybane off A2 5 miles west of
Ballycastle. Carpark charge.

CULLYBACKEY

President Arthur's Ancestral Home
Open mid-April–September except
Sunday. For details of craft
demonstrations telephone the
council offices in Ballymena.
☎ (01266) 660300.

DERVOCK

Benvarden Garden
On B67, 7 miles east of Coleraine.
☎ (012657) 41331. Open June–
August every day 2–6pm except
Monday.

DUNLUCE CASTLE

☎ (012657) 31938. Open Monday–
Saturday 10am–7pm, Sunday
2–7pm (4pm in winter). Closed
Sunday morning October–March.

GIANT'S CAUSEWAY

Permanent access. To identify
geological features buy the NT
leaflet (includes a good map) at the
Giant's Causeway Centre, open daily
10am–5pm with extended evening
hours July and August. Café.
☎ (012657) 31855

Causeway School Museum
☎ (012657) 31777.
Open July–August.

The open-top Bushmills Bus
between Coleraine and the
Causeway operates from end June
to end August. ☎ (01265) 43334

GLENARIFF

Glenariff Forest Park
On A43 Ballymena–Waterfoot
road. ☎ (012667) 58232 (head
forester). Open daily from 10am.

GLENARM

Glenarm Castle and Gardens
Opening is usually confined to
mid-July holiday. For information
contact the Estate Office
☎ (01574) 841203

Glenarm Salmon Farm
☎ (01574) 841691

PORTRUSH

Dunluce Centre
☎ (01265) 824111. 'Virtual reality'
entertainment, interactive nature
trail. Open every afternoon April–
September plus mornings in high
summer. Winter: weekend
afternoons only.

RATHLIN ISLAND

Crossings twice daily in each
direction year round (weather
permitting) between Ballycastle
harbour and the island. Extra
sailings in summer. ☎ (012657)
69299 (Caledonian MacBrayne).
For access to the west lighthouse
platform to view the bird colonies
contact the RSPB warden:
☎ (012657) 63948

TOOMEBRIDGE

Toome Eel Fishery
Lough Neagh Fishermen's
Co-operative Society Ltd.
☎ (01648) 50618

EVENTS

Ballycastle

Horse Ploughing Match (mid-March)

Fleadh Amhrán agus Rince (mid-June)
Traditional Irish song and dance.

Ould Lammas Fair (end August)
Oldest traditional fair in Ireland.

Ballymena

Ulster Traction Engine Rally (mid-July)

County Antrim Agricultural Show (June)

Broughshane

Belfast–mid-Antrim Motor Run
(end July)
Vintage cars.

Slemish Mountain Pilgrimage (17 March)

Carnlough

John Hewitt Summer School (late July)

Sheepdog Trials (September)

Causeway Coast

Black Bush Amateur Golf Tournament
(early June)
Played over four links courses.

Glenariff

Feis na nGleann (late June)
Gaelic games   hurling, camogie,
etc.

Portrush

Raft Race (late May)

Portstewart

North West 200 (mid-May)
Motorcycling.

Rathlin

Festival Week (second week July)
Model yacht races, céilís, sports,
theatre.

Regatta (end August)
Yacht and boat races.

TOURIST INFORMATION CENTRES

Ballycastle

7 Mary Street. ☎ (012657) 62024.
Open all year Monday–Friday
9.30am–5pm, plus Saturday 10am–
4pm from Easter to September.
Longer hours plus Sunday 2–6pm
in high summer.

Giant's Causeway

Giant's Causeway Centre,
44 Causeway Road. ☎ (012657)
31855. Open all year Monday–
Sunday 10am–4.30pm. In summer
open until 7pm.

Portrush

Dunluce Centre, Sandhill Drive.
☎ (01265) 823333. Open April–
September Monday–Friday 9am–
5pm, longer hours in high summer,
plus weekend afternoons in spring/
autumn. Closed in winter.

24 Haymarket
London SW1Y 4DG
☎ (0541) 555 250/0171-766 9920
fax 0171-766 9929

135 Buchanan Street
Glasgow G1 2JA
☎ 0141-204 4454
fax 0141-204 4033

USA
551 Fifth Avenue, Suite 701
New York NY10176
☎ (212) 922 0101
or (800) 326 0036
fax (212) 922 0099
e-mail: info@northern-ireland.com

CANADA
111 Avenue Road, Suite 450
Toronto M5R 3J8
☎ (416) 925 6368
fax (416) 925 6033

GERMANY
Taunusstrasse 52-60
60329 Frankfurt/Main
☎ (069) 23 45 04
fax (069) 23 34 80

For more information about accommodation and activity and special
interest holidays in Northern Ireland contact these addresses in:

AUSTRALIA
All Ireland Tourism
Level 5, 36 Carrington Street
Sydney NSW 2000
☎ (02) 9299 6177
fax (02) 9299 6323

FRANCE
Mailing Express
189 rue d'Aubervilliers
75886 Paris Cedex 18
Minitel 3615 Nord Irlande
☎ (01) 40 05 10 29
fax (01) 40 34 38 96

NEW ZEALAND
Walshe's World Ltd.
Dingwall Building
87 Queen Street
Auckland 1, DX 69051
☎ (09) 379 3708
fax (09) 309 0725

In addition, prospective visitors can get information about Northern
Ireland from British Tourist Authority offices worldwide. Consult your
telephone directory in:

Amsterdam, Auckland, Bangkok, Brussels, Buenos Aires, Chicago,
Copenhagen, Helsinki, Hong Kong, Johannesburg, Lisbon, Madrid, Milan,
Osaka, Oslo, Prague, Rio de Janeiro, Rome, Seoul, Singapore, Stockholm,
Taipei, Tokyo, Zurich.

INDEX